The Development of Education in Serbia and Emergence of Its Intelligentsia (1838-1858)

Milenko Karanovich

EAST EUROPEAN MONOGRAPHS, BOULDER
DISTRIBUTED BY COLUMBIA UNIVERSITY PRESS, NEW YORK
1995

To Snežana and Melanie

CONTENTS

ABBREVIATIONS

AS	***Arhiv Srbije*** (The Archives of Serbia)
DSS	***Družstvo Srbske Slovesnosti*** (The Serbian Literary Society)
IIB	***Istorijski institut u Beogradu*** (The Institute of History in Belgrade)
JAZU	***Jugoslavenska akademija znanosti i umjetnosti*** (The Yugoslav Academy of Sciences and Arts)
JPD	***Jugoslovensko profesorsko društvo*** (The Association of Yugoslav Professors)
KK	***Knjažeska kancelarija*** (The Prince's Office or Chancery)
L	***Licej*** (Lyceum)
MPs	***Ministarstvo prosvete*** (The Ministry of Education)
NS	**New Style**
OS	**Old Style**
SAN	***Srpska akademija nauka*** (The Serbian Academy of Sciences)
SUD	***Srpsko Učeno Društvo*** (The Serbian Learned Society)

PREFACE

The education of the first intellectuals in modern Serbia and the Constitutionalists' contribution to their creation is a subject which has not yet been sufficiently illuminated. True, numerous works have been written in Yugoslavia and abroad, but they only partially and indirectly touch upon it. I took up this work with the desire to cast more light on the subject and to deal with it in its entirety on the basis of heretofore unused materials, in addition to those used previously, because knowledge of it is indispensable to an understanding of the creation and modernization of the Serbian state. I limited myself to the Constitutionalist period (1838-1858) because this was the period of Serbian history in which the process of modernization and creation of the first group of native educated people began. I do not claim that this work completely illuminates this question, and even less that it is the final word. I tried to present a great deal of new materials, to view and analyze this question as part of the entire Serbian history of that time, and I hope that this work will be a solid base for those historians to whom new and yet undiscovered sources will be available.

My intention was to give more consideration to such questions as to what extent did Serbia's schools prepare the first educated people for the positions which were entrusted to them, how much education altered their way of life, how they behaved toward the uneducated and backward circle in which they had been brought up, whether the majority or a small minority of them accepted and propagated liberal ideas, and so on. Unfortunately, because of the lack of sources, especially memoirs of the people who received their higher education in Serbia, I could not answer some of these and similar questions, and for some of them I found only partial answers. The authors of a few existing memoirs deal mainly with political struggles and with dynastic intrigues, which were among the chief characteristics of the Constitutionalist period, whereas they devoted little space to the period of their education and to their professional, social, and cultural life. Even this little was often general information written in several paragraphs or on a few pages.

The main part of my research was done in Yugoslavia. The bulk of information was gathered in the following institutions: the Archives of Serbia, the Archives of the City of Belgrade, the Archives of the Serbian Academy of Sciences and Arts, the Archives of the Institute of History, the University Library "Svetozar Marković," the People's Library of the Socialist Republic of Serbia, and the Library of the St. Sava Seminary, all in Belgrade, and the University Library in Zagreb.

Since almost all of the documents used in this work are dated according to Old Style (Julian calendar), which in the nineteenth century was twelve days behind New Style (Gregorian calendar), I used both, one after the other (e.g., January 1/13, 1844 or October 30/November 11, 1844). The geographic and personal names are written in their original forms corresponding to the Library of Congress system of transliteration. Names of Western derivation are written in their proper Latin form. In translating direct quotations, I tried to preserve the style of the original.

The research for this work was assisted by a travel grant from the University of Wisconsin-Madison and the Vilas Fellowship (William F. Vilas Trust Estate), both of which I appreciate very much.

This work has been made possible by the assistance of numerous persons and institutions to whom I am most grateful. I am particularly indebted to Professor Michael B. Petrovich for his valuable advice, suggestions and criticism, and to my friend, Mr. Milan M. Radovich, of the Memorial Library, University of Wisconsin-Madison, who read the first draft of this work and gave me many useful suggestions.

I would also like to express my special gratitude to Mr. Robert Gakovich, Memorial Library, University of Wisconsin-Madison; Mr. Richard C. West and Mr. Thomas S. Sermak, University of Wisconsin-Madison. In Belgrade: Mrs. Anastasija Papahristu-Milojević and Mr. Stevan Knežević, the Archives of Serbia; Mrs. Marija Ševković and Mr. Nebojša Lazarević, University Library "Svetozar Marković"; Dr. Milorad Radević, the Institute of History; Dr. Dušan Kašić, Rector of the St. Sava Seminary; Dr. Mihailo Bjelica, the Yugoslav Institute of Journalism; Mr. Tanasije Ilić; and Dr. Vladimir Grujić. In addition, I am grateful for their assistance and understanding to: Mr. Michael Djordjevich, President of the Studenica Foundation; Mr. Dragoslav Georgevich; Dr. Mateja Matejić, Mr. and Mrs. Slavko Stokovich; and Dr. Alex N. Dragnich.

My appreciation for the typing of this work from my not easily legible manuscript goes to Mrs. Clifford Kamin.

With special respect and gratitude I will remember Mr. and Mrs. Risto Stanić from Belgrade, without whose devoted care and moral support I would not have been able to complete my research in Yugoslavia.

INTRODUCTION

Serbia, which was under Turkish rule for several centuries, began the struggle for her liberation in 1804. Although she achieved considerable success and liberated a large part of her territories, she was forced to lay down her arms. The chief causes for her defeat were disagreements among the leaders of the insurrection and the peace treaty between Russia and Turkey concluded in Bucharest in 1812.

After returning Serbia to their rule, the Turks carried out mass executions of her inhabitants, plundered them, and required from them large tributes. Such treatment caused great discontent which in the spring of 1815 grew into a new insurrection. This time, after fifteen years of armed struggle and negotiations, the Serbs achieved a great, although not complete, success. In 1830, Serbia was granted autonomy with hereditary Prince Miloš Obrenović , the leader of the insurrection of 1815, as ruler. But, she was obliged to pay an annual tribute to the sultan, Turkish military troops remained in her cities, and the sultan had great influence over her internal and foreign policy.

Autonomy and the rise of capitalism which replaced the outlived Ottoman feudal system, enabled Serbia to go the way of progress. Prince Miloš obstructed that development a great deal, especially in the economic field. His rule was indeed autocratic because his word was law. He appropriated the great part of the state wealth for himself, required the peasants to work on his estates without pay, did not respect private property, brutally punished opponents of his rule, and opposed the establishment of effective social institutions. Such a reign caused dissatisfaction in all strata of Serbian society and very often armed conflict resulted.

Popular leaders, bureaucrats, and wealthy merchants, who can be considered the first bourgeoisie of the young Serbian state, took advantage of the general dissatisfaction in the country and created a coalition with the aim of limiting the Prince's power, removing all obstacles to the development of capitalism, and securing the leading role for themselves in the creation and implementation of state policy. In order to realize that aim, they began to champion a constitution which they considered the best weapon for limiting the Prince's power. For that reason they are known in the historiography under the name *"Ustavobranitelji"* (the Constitutionalists).

The dissatisfaction of the people, the occasional armed conflicts, and the extensive political activity of the Constitutionalists forced Prince Miloš to accept the first constitution in Serbia in the beginning of 1835. But due to pressure from the Ottoman Empire, Russia, and Austria, which considered it too liberal, it was abolished before it went into effect.

The suppression of this first constitution did not cause the Constitutionalists to cease their political activity. The constitutional question became even more prominent and this time the Great Powers who had sharply protested the first Serbian constitution, worked openly to insure that a moderate constitution would be introduced in Serbia, a constitution which would make it possible for them to strengthen their influence over her internal and foreign policy. Serbia received the constitution from Sultan Mahmud II at the end of 1838 and, therefore, it is known under the name of the "Turkish Constitution." Under this constitution, Prince Miloš's power was indeed limited. A council of senators, or the *Soviet* as it was called officially, was created with legislative, executive, and judicial powers. It was composed of seventeen members who were selected "among the people's chiefs and the most notable Serbs." They were responsible to the sultan and only he could replace them. The *Soviet* had more power than the prince because no decree, law, order, or resolution could be issued or promulgated without its approval. By this constitution, the Prince became more or less a marionette in the hands of the oligarchy of seventeen people who decided the destiny of Serbia for the next twenty years. Because the members of the *Soviet* were for the constitution, this period of Serbian history, from 1838 to 1858, is known as "the regime of the Constitutionalists."

The proud and once powerful Prince Miloš could not endure this humiliation for long, so he abdicated in favor of his elder son, Milan, in June of 1839. Milan, who was seriously ill, died twenty-six days after accession to the throne. He was succeeded by Miloš's younger son, Michael. From the very beginning of Michael's reign, tense relations existed between himself, trying to preserve the ruler's power, and the *Soviet*, which tried to increase its existing power and make the Prince only a figurehead. That tension reached its culmination in August of 1842 when a leading Constitutionalist, Toma Vučić - Perišić, organized a revolt against Prince Michael. The revolt ended at the end of the same month in favor of the Constitutionalists. Prince Michael escaped from Serbia, and the Popular Assembly, under the influence of the Constitutionalists' leaders, elected as their new Prince Alexander Karadjordjević, the son of Djordje Petrović -Karadjordje, the leader of the First Serbian Insurrection of 1804.

Alexander Karadjordjević's confirmation by the Sultan did not permanently settle the question of the ruler, and the stability of the

Constitutionalists' regime was not consolidated. Russia and Austria expressed their dissatisfaction and required a new election for a prince. Turkey granted this requirement and new elections were held in the middle of 1843. Alexander Karadjordjević was again elected, thanks mostly to the active support of the Constitutionalists who were interested in the re-election of their candidate.

With the new Prince, who was indeed a marionette, at the head of the state, the Constitutionalists worked through the *Soviet* to completely dominate the political life of Serbia until their downfall in 1858. From the very beginning of their domination, the Constitutionalists altered the course of Serbian foreign policy.

One of the principal tasks in their foreign policy was to liberate themselves from Russian and Austrian influence, especially after 1844 when a new plan for Serbian foreign policy, the so-called *Načertanije*, was made. They tried to direct Serbian foreign policy toward France and England, which were the main opponents to the spread of Russian and Austrian influence in the Balkans. Then, too, England and France were geographically rather far from Serbia to be able to directly interfere in her internal policy. It should be noted that the Revolution of 1848-49 and the Crimean War (1853-56), which were the most important political events during the Constitutionalists' period, did not have any noteworthy effect on the course of their internal and foreign policy.

The creation of various institutions as grounds for the organization and modernization of the state was their chief preoccupation in internal policy. During their reign significant progress was made in the economic development of Serbia, the first judicial and administrative mechanism was established, numerous reforms were carried out, the first liberal ideas were brought in, a solid foundation for the educational and cultural institutions was laid, and the first group of native intellectuals who were educated in the country and abroad emerged.

It is important to point out that during the entire period of the Constitutionalists' regime, a tension dominated Serbian political life which interfered a great deal with the normal development of the state. Besides the discord between the regime and the followers of the Obrenović dynasty, there was no harmony among the Constitutionalists themselves. This political tension reached its culmination at the end of 1858 when the opposition, with the help of the young liberals, dethroned Prince Alexander and returned the throne to old Miloš Obrenović . With the return of Prince Miloš to Serbia, the reign of the Constitutionalists' oligarchy came to an end and the autocracy, with certain limitations, was re-established.

Educated Serbs from Vojvodina, in the Austrian Empire, had a leading role in the internal development of Serbia in the first half of the nineteenth century. They were not only the initiators of numerous actions and reform but most often they also carried them out. Their contribution was especially noticeable in educational and cultural matters as will be seen throughout the pages of this work.

The Serbs from Vojvodina, who lived within the framework of the Austrian Empire, had much more opportunity for economic and cultural development than the Serbs in Serbia, which was under the rule of the backwards Ottoman Empire. Under the influence of the enlightened absolutism of Maria Theresa and Joseph II, Vojvodina showed significant progress in her economic and cultural-educational development at the end of the eighteenth and the beginning of the nineteenth centuries. For example, the first Serbian gymnasium was opened in Sremski Karlovci in 1791, a cultural-literary society called the *Matica Srbska* was founded in 1826, the Serbs from Vojvodina began to publish their first newspaper in Vienna in 1791, and so on. In addition, their young men had an opportunity to be educated in the fine Austrian and Hungarian schools and universities.

In the beginning of the nineteenth century, especially after the Serbian Insurrection of 1804, educated Serbs from Vojvodina moved to Serbia and took upon themselves virtually all the responsible administrative and diplomatic functions because at that time Serbia had only a few men of her own who were even literate, let alone educated. After 1830, when Serbia received her autonomy, the migration of educated Serbs from Vojvodina to Serbia increased, and they began to dominate her entire life. Thanks to their diligent work, Serbia overcame numerous obstacles on the road of progress, and by the 1860s, she had almost all the prerequisites for the development of a modern state.

CHAPTER I

THE FIRST STEPS IN EDUCATION

*True zeal for race fortified and forced me to shut
my eyes and to plunge headlong through this
thorny thicket, though I might emerge all torn
and bloodied on the other side, just so a path
might be made to make it easier for someone else
to venture across.*

Vuk Stefanović Karadžić

1.

There is no doubt that culture in the medieval Serbian state had a significant place and was rather highly developed. This is shown by numerous cultural monuments that managed to survive the many wars which were fought on Serbian territory. But, after Serbia was defeated by the Turks on the Kosovo field in 1389, black clouds covered the cultural life of the Serbian people for several centuries.

From the end of the fourteenth to the beginning of the nineteenth century, there is not any information which would indicate the existence of a regular Serbian school in the territory of Serbia. The only focus of literacy, but a focus which smoldered with an almost invisible flame, was in the churches and monasteries. Priests and monks were the only literate men during this period. This is confirmed by the significant words that Aleksa Nenadović, the father of the well-known Archpriest Mateja, directed to Mihailo Mihaljević after the Peace Treaty of Svishtov in 1791.

> ...I am going back [he said] across the Sava River. Since I have neither a scribe nor any other educated men, I will go from monastery to monastery and I will ask every monk and every priest in every monastery to write down that never again should anyone who is a Serb believe the Germans.[1]

Monks and priests did very little to educate Serbian youth. There were several reasons for that: the indifference of the children's parents, the semi-literacy and limited knowledge of most clergymen, the primitive methods of education, and poverty.

Only those young men who wanted to be monks or priests learned how to read and write. Everyone who had decided to devote his life to the ecclesiastical profession looked for a teacher either among the monks in the monasteries or among the priests in the villages. Usually every monastery had a few pupils but their main occupation was to perform daily household chores; to learn how to read and write was secondary. For this reason, these future ecclesiastics could be rightly called the house-servants of monks and priests, not the pupils. Since the age of these young men varied, their daily work was divided according to their ages and physical abilities. The younger ones "during the summer tended goats, sheep and hogs; they planted and weeded onions, followed the oxen during the plowing, and harvested hay, plums, etc." The older ones "went to the villages with the monks to beg for charity." Since there was much work to be done during the summer, the pupils studied very little or next to nothing. The regular tutoring and learning were conducted during the winter months. "In the morning all the pupils brought fire wood. Besides, the older one watered the monks' horses and the younger ones cleaned the rooms. After that, they gathered in a room where they were taught by a monk or a deacon how to read, or every pupil studied with his ecclesiastic."[2] Usually, during the summer these young men forgot the greater part of the material they had learned in the winter and it was not rare that "some of them after four and even five years did not yet know how to read."[3]

In these schools very little was taught. It was considered most important to prepare the pupils to be able to read while little if any attention was paid to writing or mathematics. The main reason for that was because the clergymen could perform their duties without being completely literate. It often happened that the pupils who wanted to learn how to write well had difficulty achieving their goal because a great number of the priests and monks who worked as tutors did not know themselves how to write well - some of them did not know how to write at all.

The pupils in the monasteries and with village priests began to learn from manuscripts, because textbooks did not exist. True, some of the ecclesiastical teachers began to use "a Moscow elementary reading book, which was too difficult" and which "usage was to discontinue after a long time of torment during which the pupils did not achieve any success."[4] Since suitable textbooks did not exist and manuscripts were too hard for the beginners, those teachers who knew how to write wrote for each pupil what he had to learn every day. When the pupils learned how to read, they usually read the prayer book and the Psalter and that was the end of their education. Everybody who could read those two books was considered an educated man and enjoyed special position and respect in a backward Serbian society that knew no higher education. Thus, for instance, Vuk Stefanović Karadžić, well known Serbian linguist, writer, and educator during the first half of the nineteenth century, learned only in Sremski Karlovci in 1806 that a much higher education existed than the prayer book and the Psalter which he had studied in Serbia.[5]

Although the knowledge which a small number of Serbian pupils received in the monasteries or from the village priests was more than limited, they could attain a high position on the ladder of the ecclesiastical hierarchy. Every such pupil "could be if he wanted," wrote V.S. Karadžić, "a priest, monk, teacher, archpriest, archimandrite, and if he had enough money, he could even be a bishop."[6]

Despite the fact that the method of teaching and education in general was on a very low level and only partly prepared an insignificant number of people to serve the enslaved country, the role of the monasteries and the ecclesiastics should not be underestimated; they were the only torch which lighted the way and instilled hope in the backward masses. In addition, these ecclesiastical institutions, no matter how primitive, helped the Serbs to preserve their language, religion, and ethnic identity. Also, they were the cradle of Serbian national liberation movements at the beginning of the nineteenth century. Even later, when the secular schools were opened, numerous monasteries continued their function in making people literate and in general education. It is sufficient to mention only some of the many monasteries, for example, Trnava near Čačak, St. Nicholas near Kablar, Bagoveštenje (Annunciation) on Rudnik Mountain, Žiča, Bogorodja, and many others.

In the beginning of the nineteenth century, the teaching of youth was not conducted only in the monasteries and in the village priests' homes, as other sources of education existed. One of these sources was private teachers. They were hired usually be a district (*nahija*)[7] or a group of parents. But such a form of teaching was not widespread and there is only evidence of it at the end of the eighteenth and the beginning of the nineteenth century. These private tutors usually came from Austria (Vojvodina) and Serbia. They only knew how to read and write a little so that it was not reasonable to expect too much from them. Mostly they were tradesmen or artisans. When no other opportunities for making money occurred, they opened schools, or rather a classroom in private houses, but they would frequently close them in order to take completely different jobs where they could earn more money.[8]

The method of these businessmen teachers was almost identical to the method used by the ecclesiastics. The prayer book and the Psalter were the main texts the pupils were obliged to learn. The major difference between the ecclesiastics and the hired teachers was that the pupils taught by the latter studied all day with only a short break for lunch; they were not burdened by housework. In spite of that, the results of the pupils' efforts were poor not only because the teachers had limited knowledge, but they also usually had no experience in teaching. Lessons were often discontinued after several months, and sometimes even sooner.[9]

In these "schools," where the difference in ages among the students was often large, the teachers tried to establish discipline and force the pupils to work diligently by threat and use of physical punishments: "your skin, my bones," or "your meat, my bones," the parents used to tell the teacher when they brought their children for the first time to school.[10] Recalling his school days which had been spent in such a school in Loznica in 1796, V.S. Karadžić later wrote:

> When I went to school in Loznica it was the custom that the teacher physically punished his pupils every Saturday afternoon without any reason other than because it was Saturday. If someone had already been punished for some reason in the morning or even in the early afternoon of the same day it was not counted.[11]

It should be mentioned that some youth, although only a small number, had learned how to read at home and later went to the monasteries in order to improve their skill. Naturally, only the children whose parents were literate and could help them, could use that method of education. It happened sometimes that some artisans who were literate or semi-literate gratuitously tutored some children to read. There were cases where some children tried to learn to read and write on their own, but only an insignificant number of them succeeded in that attempt.

Among the many obstacles which worked against the rapid and effective education of youth, the shortage of the educational materials was especially noticeable. Suitable textbooks, as already mentioned, did not exist; moreover, books in general were rare and extremely hard to get. Likewise, the shortage of writing materials was such that they were almost impossible to acquire. It was not rare that pupils wrote on small boards of lime-tree, sand, leaves, or the like, or they wrote on paper using dissolved gunpowder in water instead of ink.[12]

Although it could be concluded from the foregoing that Serbia had a rather great number of literate people before her First Insurrection in 1804, it was not so. Their number was so small that they could have been counted on the fingers. "During the Insurrection," wrote B. Cunibert, the personal physician of Prince Miloš, "except for several priests, nobody knew how to read and write."[13] The main reason for this was that the greater number of the pupils in the existing so-called "schools" never actually learned how to read and write, and a substantial number of those who did learn how usually forgot, because they had neither the opportunity nor the time to read anything. Only an insignificant number of them managed to preserve and enrich their knowledge. Yet, their role before, during, and after the First Insurrection was of great value because they were the only ones who could have performed diplomatic and administrative duties in the newly developing state.

2.

Thanks to the reforms of Sultan Selim II (1789-1807), the conditions of the Serbs in the Pashalik of Belgrade were improved a few years before the First Serbian Insurrection: the economic policy became more free, the general attitude of the Turks toward the Serbs was more lenient, and the possibility for improvement of the local administration became greater. All these changes, although modest, brought positive results in the development of Serbian society. For example, production and commerce were increased which accelerated the process of stratification within Serbian society. A stratum of the village well-to-do was gradually formed, made up mostly of cattle and hog merchants. As their economic strength grew, their political influence as peasant leaders also became stronger. They led the masses, not only in order to liberate Serbia from the foreign yoke, but also to abolish the outlived Ottoman feudalism which was a big obstacle to the economic development of the country. Since the First Serbian Insurrection destroyed this system, it was both a war of liberation and a revolution. With the destruction of the Ottoman feudal system, capitalism began gradually to penetrate into Serbia and alter her society. The traditional communal joint families (*zadruge*)[14] began to dissolve, a money economy replaced the original barter system, a strong central state apparatus began to form, local administration was reorganized, and so on. All of these changes increased demand for literate people. Not only the leaders of the Insurrection but also some individuals among the people were aware of this.

Even before the First Insurrection, some individuals, especially the local village leaders, used to bring private teachers to their homes in order to teach their children how to read and write. Sometimes some of the other village children were taught along with them. This method of education became more frequent during the Insurrection. For instance, it was conducted in the home of Vojvoda Luka Lazarević from Šabac, Hajduk Veljko Petrović from Brza Palanka, Nikola Milićević from Lunjevci, Milutin Savić Garašanin from Garaši, and many others.

> Milutin (Garašanin) [writes M.Dj. Milićević] did not know how to read and write, but he had a school in his home in where his children and the children of his village studied. He brought the teachers from the area north of the Sava River [today's Vojvodina]. There is some information about Mijailo Borisavljević and Avram Gašparović. Later, Prince Miloš hired Avram Gašparović to be a teacher to his sons.[15]

Some of these privately taught children later occupied high positions in the political life of Serbia. Notably, Ilija Garašanin, the son of Milutin Savić, became one of the most well-known Serbian statesmen of the nineteenth century.

At the time of the First Insurrection, a great need for literate men arose, therefore many elementary schools were opened. "During the reign of Black George [Djordje Petrović-Karadjordje (1804-1813)] in Serbia," wrote V.S. Karadžić, "schools were opened in almost all the towns and cities, and also in some villages."[16] Initiative for the opening of elementary or "small" schools, as they were called at the time, was taken by Karadjordje and by other leaders of the Insurrection, although it was not rare for such an initiative to come from the people. Thus, for example, the priests and mayors of the villages of Orašac and Ušće sent a letter to Archpriest Mateja Nenadović, one of the leaders of the Insurrection and the most literate Serb in Serbia at that time, asking him for his assistance in concluding a contract with a teacher, Andrej, who had started to teach two classes in their villages but had discontinued both of them before the end of the school year. They concluded the letter with the following words:

> We ask you especially to arrange for us by your command a school, that we might build a school with your help, because not every man knows what either a school or an education is.[17]

Archpriest M. Nenadović wrote later of that letter: "You can see that people already in that time wanted to build their schools fast, and that villages expressed their desire in regard to this in writing."[18] Such initiative on the part of the village populations was welcomed by Karadjordje, who often expressed his praises and satisfaction in order to stimulate the people to persist in their intention.[19]

In the draft of the *Praviteljstvujušći soviet* (State Council), the highest organ of the government of 1805, special attention was paid to education. Among six planned ministries there was the Ministry of Education, whose principal task was to recruit the best ecclesiastics and to spread education in the villages. It had under its control churches, schools, teachers, and all who worked on the spread of education. In early 1811, the *Praviteljstvujušći soviet* was expanded into a real government with the creation of the ministries as planned in the draft of 1805. When the Ministry of Education was established, it was the first such ministry in Serbia. On this occasion, that is, on January 18/30, 1811, Dositej Obradović (1742-1811), well-known Serbian philosopher, writer, and educator from Vojvodina, became a member of the *Soviet* and was appointed the first Minister of Education. Djordje Petrović-Karadjordje informed him about his appointment by a letter in which he said:

> As a sign of our recognition of your reputation, excellence, and awards we unanimously elect, nominate, and appoint you a member of the *Soviet* and the Minister of Public Education. I do hope that you will work diligently at your new job, that you will increase the countless contributions that you made to your country, and that your name will indeed remain immortal in the eternal records of our country.[20]

At the same time, the local administrations were informed about Obradović's appointment, his functions, and his competence. In this communiqué it was pointed out that if they needed teachers, they were to consult with the Ministry of Education.[21]

Unfortunately, Dositej Obradović kept this office for only a very short time because he died on March 28/April 9 of the same year. Ivan Jugović,[22] one of the most educated Serbs of that time and also from Vojvodina, was appointed his successor.

Although D. Obradović was the Minister of Education for a very short time, his influence on the cultural and educational fields was great because he had played an important role in the shaping of the Serbian educational policy since 1807, when he came to Serbia. If it is taken into consideration that Obradović was "a receptive spirit who stood on the level of the European education of his time and at the same time was a real polyglot,"[23] then it is easy to imagine how much his cultural work had to mean to backward Serbian society and the *Praviteljstvujušći soviet*. Of the twelve members of that group in 1807, for example, only four were literate, two of them hardly knew "how to write their names," while one knew how to write a little better than the first two, and only one "knew how to write and read better than all priests and monks, and many leaders' clerks throughout Serbia."[24] It should be emphasized that D. Obradović, in only a few months as the Minister of Education, succeeded in giving a new direction to schools in Serbia.

> Although his spiritual structure [wrote Dušan Jovanić, the Yugoslav historian of pedagogy] was built under the very different influences of religious mystique, Russian dogmatic literature, Greek church reformers, German Protestantism, French and English nationalism, Obradović still completely assimilated the progressive ideas of the European middle-class education of the eighteenth century. His critical attitude toward the church prepared Serbian society, not only for the autonomy of schools in relation to the church, but also meant an end to clerical domination in the spiritual leadership of the Serbian people.[25]

A few years after the Insurrection broke out, some influential people, though almost illiterate, realized that the elementary schools could not prepare the personnel needed for the more and more complicated state jobs which had been performed until that time mostly by Serbs from Vojvodina. Suggestions were made by some members of the *Soviet* for the opening of a higher school in which some general and special subjects would be taught. According to V.S. Karadžić, who was one of the first students in the high school (*Velika škola*), the suggestion for its opening was made by Mladen Milovanović, a member of the *Soviet*; the suggestion was then accepted by Karadjordje and the whole *Soviet*.[26]

After a short preparation, the High School was opened officially on September 1/12, 1808, in Belgrade. On that occasion Karadjordje said in his speech:

> Look, we have enough arms for the defense of Serbia, but we do not have enough skillful men to govern her. If we knew how to lead the state as well as how to lead the army, we would be now in a different position. Please study, therefore, so you will be able to continue our work so fortunately begun. All our hopes for that are in you.[27]

The curriculum for the High School was developed by Ivan Jugović (Jovan Savić) who was its first teacher. For Serbia at that time, Jugović was a very educated man; he had a degree in Hungarian law from Budapest and had been the professor in the Second Latin School in Sremski Karlovci before he came to Serbia. He taught for only a short time because as early as the beginning of 1809 he was appointed the head secretary in the *Praviteljstvujušći soviet*, and after D. Obradović's death in 1811, as has been indicated, he was appointed Minister of Education. Besides Jugović, the professors of the High School during its existence were: Miljko Radonić, Lazar Vojnović, Mihalio Popović, Gliša Živanović, and the well-known poet Sima Milutinović, as well as Jovan Miljković who taught church singing, and Captain Petar Djurković who taught military training.[28]

The requirements for enrollment in the High School were a knowledge of reading, writing, and some mathematics because they were the only subjects which were studied in the elementary schools. According to Ivan Jugović's plan, the education in the High School was to last for three years and the following subjects were to be studied: general history, general geography with drawing (*krokiranje*), statistics, mathematics, composition, German language, common prayers, state and criminal law, moral instruction, church singing, fencing, and training with rifles.[29]

Usually young men who had graduated from the elementary school attended the High School in order to prepare themselves for a future as administrators, teachers, and judges.[30] The first students of this school were the sons and relatives of the distinguished leaders (Karadjordje's, Milenko Stojković's, Mladen Milanović's, Vaso Čarapić's, Jakov Nenadović's, and others), but there were also several talented youths who were the sons of ordinary people.[31]

V.S. Karadžić left a picturesque description of the classroom and the method of teaching in the first days of the High School's existence. He wrote:

> Benches did not exist in the schools, so the students sat by the walls on straw chairs. In the beginning Jugović did not teach anything but history and mathematics. He dictated history from his own manuscript and the students wrote it down. Afterwards, he explained it to them. While teaching history he often also talked about geography and for that he required several maps, which were hung on the wall. He taught mathematics from memory and was surprisingly skillful, especially in fractions (*Brüche*); as our people say: "He could pout it [knowledge of mathematics] even into a wooden head."[32]

After the end of the school year 1808-1809, the High School had to discontinue its work because of changes in the war which had been going on since 1804. The High School was resumed in 1810-11, at which time the second grade (class) was opened; in 1811-12 the third grade was begun. That year the first class of seven students graduated from the school. The next school year, that is 1812-13, the second class of students graduated. The High School was again closed in 1813, when the Ottoman Empire reestablished its rule over all of Serbia, and that was the end of the High School's existence. Although the High School operated for only a short time, forty students desperately needed by the newly resurrected Serbian state graduated from it.[33]

It cannot be said that the High School in Belgrade was a real gymnasium or secondary school. It was "to fill a special need, a specially combined mixture of a gymnasium and a vocational school."[34]

It is important to mention that during the First Insurrection a seminary or *Klirikalna škola* (Clerical School), as it was officially called, was also opened in Belgrade. Unfortunately, there is very little information about this school. The only known description of the seminary was left by its contemporary, Lazar Arsenijević-Batalaka. He says that in early 1810, Karadjordje, in an agreement with the *Soviet*, assigned to Dositej Obradović one of the Turkish houses "with a large courtyard and a large garden containing every kind of fruit tree and vine." By July of the same year, D. Obradović had renovated the house and applied to the *Soviet* for permission to open a seminary in it, a seminary "in which Serbian sons would be prepared as future ecclesiastics and elementary school teachers." The permit was granted to Obradović and he continued preparation for the opening of the new school. He asked his friend Vikentije Rakić, monk and writer from Trieste, to come to Belgrade in order to establish the seminary and be its first teacher. V. Rakić accepted the offer and came to Belgrade in 1810. The school began operation in the fall of the same year. Rakić was its only teacher, with an annual salary of 150 talers and a lodging which was in the same house as the school. Besides teaching in the school, he was obliged to preach in the Belgrade church.[35]

According to L. Arsenijević, the seminary existed until 1812 and "theology and church singing" were taught in it.[36] It is not known exactly how many students graduated from this school. In some documents seven are mentioned, but Arsenijević says that only four students graduated from the Clerical School, while Dušan Petrović found five names: Matija Popović, Milovan Popadić, Simeun Sekulić, Milosav Radojčić, and someone by the name of Tomo, whom Sima Milutinović, a Serbian poet of that times, calls *zvonkopjevac mladi* (Young Chanticleer).[37]

In addition to a resolution of the question concerning future ecclesiastics, Karadjordje wanted to liberate the Serbian church from the Greek bishops (*Phanariots*). In agreement with the *Soviet*, he decided to replace the Belgrade metropolitan Leontius with Hadži-Melentije Stefanović, archimandrite of Rača Monastery, metropolitan's vicar and former chief of the Zvornik district (*nahija*), but he did not succeed in this effort.[38]

During the First Insurrection, when a big part of Serbia was liberated, schools began to proliferate and the number of literate persons grew rapidly. From the beginning of the Insurrection in 1804 until it was crushed in 1813, about 1,500 pupils went through the Serbian schools with most attending only the elementary schools.[39] This was no small number if we keep in mind that Serbia at that time was continually at war with the Turks and that she had neither enough means nor opportunities for a normal system of education.

During this period female children were completely illiterate because not a single one went to school. It is strange that Dositej Obradović, who had advocated the education of female children in his books, did not issue any decree about it.

Although education during the First Insurrection was on a very low level without even a uniform curriculum, and although students did not have needed books and writing material, this time marked the first serious step toward education of a relatively large portion of the population. This period can rightly be called the beginning of organized education in Serbia and the period in which education of youth was no longer left completely to individuals; now for the first time, the government took a leading role upon itself.

3.

After 1813, when Serbia again came under Turkish rule, many schools were closed and education died almost completely for the next two years. The result was very similar to the period before the Insurrection. But, after the outbreak of the Second Insurrection in 1815 under the leadership of Miloš Obrenović, the schools in Serbia began to be opened again. During the Insurrection they did not show any noticeable results because their work was often interrupted by war operations. Although illiterate, Prince Miloš was aware of the importance of schools for the liberation of the country and the development of the state. Therefore, from the beginning of his leadership he paid considerable attention to education and to the improvement of the entire cultural life of the country. However, Serbian historiography, with some exceptions, has a negative opinion of Prince Miloš's cultural policy. The view has been widespread that Prince Miloš had a hostile attitude toward educational institutions because, once established, they could become strongholds of opposition to his unlimited power in the political and economic life of the state. Such an opinion is, however, completely wrong and without any real support. Archival documents, newspaper articles, and notes of contemporaries give us a completely opposite picture. We learn from them that, especially after 1830 when Serbia received her autonomy, Prince Miloš implemented an active policy "in order to establish in Serbia a solid ground for educational and cultural progress which had to come immediately after political and economic liberation from the Turks."[40]

From 1815 to 1830 new schools in Serbia were opened very slowly; as a result, elementary schools did not reach the number that existed during Karadjordje's reign and the creation of higher schools was no more than a desire on the part of isolated individuals. The schools of that time could be divided into the categories: ecclesiastical, communal or village, and private.[41] State schools did not exist because the central state administration, burdened with numerous problems concerning the war with the Turks, was not able to engage itself in opening schools and spreading literacy. That function was left to individuals, communes, and churches. Usually each group hired teachers and paid them separately, but there were some cases in which teachers were paid collectively by communes, churches, and children's parents. In some places, for example in Belgrade, the church took all burdens upon itself and paid teachers for all children whether some parents were or were not able to bear the expense for their children. Prince Miloš did not approve of such an educational policy and informed church tutors "that he did not find it fair for churches to pay teachers from their budgets for those children whose parents are able to pay themselves. Therefore, it was ordered that in the future churches would pay from their budgets only for the poor children, whereas the wealthy parents would be obliged to bear expenses for their own."[42]

Teachers were paid very poorly and often could not even be sure they would receive their small salaries. Therefore, poor men who had no other way to support themselves went into the teaching profession. They were so poor they had to be exempted of all taxes and surtaxes. The very low salaries and the insecurity of the teaching profession were the principal reasons that the quality and structure of teachers were at a low level; that is also why it was not possible to expect much from them. Many of them were not qualified to teach. They were mostly ecclesiastics, former shopkeepers, craftsmen, and merchants. A certain number were semi-literate, and most of them had only "a certain primitively worked out routine of teaching."[43]

During the Second Insurrection the teachers were mostly Serbs from Vojvodina and only a few were Serbs from Serbia. Later, the number of native teachers was increased but the teachers from Vojvodina continued to hold a majority for a long time. Despite the fact that many Serbs from Vojvodina worked as teachers in Serbia, their number was not sufficient, and there were schools which could not find teachers. That situation was aggravated by the practice of having the teacher-ecclesiastics ordained into the priesthood "only if they had the qualifications for it and if they were of good character."[44]

During this period no written law concerning education or curriculum existed. Teachers taught what they wanted, or rather what they knew. Most often, teaching consisted of reading and a little bit of writing, while not even in this period did mathematics receive any particular attention.

From August 26/September 7, 1830, when Sultan Mahmud granted the *Hatt-i Şerif*[45] to Serbia, a new period in her history began. Because of this document Serbia, after those many years of fighting, received her autonomy; the territory was given the status of an independent Ottoman vassal state. The new state was guaranteed internal self-government, free of Turkish interference, and Miloš Obrenović was recognized as the hereditary prince. Articles 11 and 18 of the *Hatt-i Şerif* were extremely important for normal educational and cultural development of the state. Article 11 stated: "The Serbs will be free to establish hospitals, printing shops, and schools for public education of her youth," while Article 18 stated: "The metropolitan and bishops elected by the people will have to receive their appointments from the Greek patriarch in Constantinople, but in spite of that, they will not be obliged to come to this capital."[46]

Now, free to establish schools and presses, and free to elect her own high ecclesiastical dignitaries, who until that time had been appointed by the Greeks, Serbia could systematically plan and develop and education program and prepare her youth to be leaders in the political, economic, and cultural life of the state. The government, with Prince Miloš at the head, immediately took important steps in that direction. There is no doubt that the year 1830 marks a turning point in the history of the Serbian people because after a few centuries of servitude the Serbian state resurrected itself. Although not completely free, she still could, as a vassal state with her own prince, determine the direction of her future development and thus control the destiny of her people.

What Dositej Obradović was to Serbia during the period of Karadjordje, V.S. Karadžić was during the period of Prince Miloš's first regime (1815-1839) - advocate of rapid expansion of education and cultural progress of the state. As early as 1820, when Serbia did not yet have her autonomy, Karadžić suggested to Prince Miloš that he open a high school for select young men "from fifteen to twenty years of age, who are somewhat able to read and write ... in which three intelligent and capable teachers would teach for three years: **a general history of this world, geography, statistics, Serbian grammar, a little bit of mathematics, a little bit of rhetoric, a little bit of logic, a little bit of natural history, a little bit of physics**, etc."[47] If we analyze this suggestion we shall see that it was unrealistic and almost unfeasible. It appears that V.S. Karadžić badly overestimated the ability of Serbian young men when he thought that those who were "somewhat able to read and write" would be able to understand such difficult subjects as physics, logic or statistics. This suggestion quite properly was not accepted at that time; it was to be another ten years before Karadžić's goal would be achieved.

Even out of Serbia, for he spent a large part of his mature life in Austria, Karadžić did not give up the struggle for a rapid educational and cultural progress for his people. One his best known and most courageous actions in that field was the letter which he sent to Prince Miloš on April 12/24, 1832. In that letter he sharply criticized the Prince's internal policy and devoted a great deal of the letter to Miloš's attitude toward schools and the educated people.

> Just because educated people raise rebellions against the government [writes Karadžić] you should not be afraid of education and therefore despise schools and delay their decree. I think that educated people (who have to be **good**) most willingly obey wise and just government, because they know that human society cannot be without government and that all people cannot be either emperors, or kings, or officials, or rich. Even the most common people rebel against unjust government.... So, if Your Highness wishes that your people do not rebel, I think that to be afraid of schools and education can hardly help. I think **first** that everybody in our country should enjoy full justice, so that an intelligent and honest man,

> judging with his own common sense, can wish
> nothing better....[48]

At this time, there was much to be criticized in Prince Miloš's policy, including his educational and cultural policy, and in his manner of ruling. Yet, it should be pointed out that while V.S. Karadžić blamed Prince Miloš almost exclusively for the slow progress made in education prior to 1830, he overlooked the "external difficulties which pushed into the background this important element in the national life of the Serbian people."[49] Among those difficulties were the war against the Turks, Miloš's political involvement in the effort to gain autonomy for Serbia, financial difficulties, lack of qualified teachers, and the impossibility of erecting public institutions until 1830, according to the definitive plan.

In the last decade of his first reign, Prince Miloš paid special attention to educational and cultural development using many educated Serbs from Vojvodina as teachers because they knew the Serbian language and were therefore able to help their brothers across the Sava River to establish a solid base for education and other activities. Significant decrees regarding the erection of schools and organization of curriculum were issued. Numerous state elementary schools were opened, secondary, vocational, and higher schools began to work, the first printing house in Serbia was opened, the first newspaper, books, journals, and textbooks were published, a bookstore was opened, amateur theaters started, and so on.

One of the most significant activities in the 1830s was the issuing of the first decrees concerning the organization of schools and teaching; these new decrees were the basis for educational and cultural development. Since the Serbian people were without a group of educated men, the organization and opening of schools in liberated Serbia were entrusted to the Serbs from Vojvodina. And since Serbia did not have any educational tradition, these newcomers issued the first directives and organized school life modeled after the schools from which they graduated in Hungary because they did not know any other. From the 1830s until the later half of the nineteenth century, the school system was not altered very much; its makers and the administrators of educational policy, with small changes and adaptations, followed the school system of the Serbian neighbor to the north.

The first of the more significant school laws in newly liberated Serbia was completed in 1833. It was *"Ustav narodni škola"* (The Constitution of Public Schools), which was approved by Prince Miloš. It is not known whether that long manuscript of forty-two pages was written by one person or a "legislative commission" which was mentioned around 1830.[50] There is speculation that its author was Dimitrije Tirol, one of the better educated Serbs from Vojvodina, who worked actively in the educational and cultural fields in Serbia, but at this time the theory remains only a hypothesis.

It is a demonstrable fact that the Hungarian schools were models for the author or authors of this constitution.[51] Its introduction points out strongly that education is important and useful for every man, and "that it is very necessary that benevolent and capable teachers sow seeds of necessary and useful education and knowledge into young children's hearts beginning from early youth, in order that they might grow up educated and as adult men give the fruit of their education to their country, thereby also making themselves happy."[52] The Constitution also emphasizes that all school institutions would be called public schools and that they would be divided into elementary, intermediate, and high.[53] Even today it is unknown whether that first major law concerning the schools was ever printed and whether it ever went into effect. It is only known for certain that the manuscript was prepared for publication and that it was sent to the printing-house because on the back of the manuscript there is a note:" ad No. 682 year [to the press]."[54]

On March 21/April 2, 1836, the first office of the directorship of all schools in Serbia with an annual salary of 400 talers plus 200 talers for travel expenses was established.[55] Petar Radovanović, gymnasium professor, was appointed the first director. On the day of his appointment, another important document concerning the educational progress was issued. It was entitled "Instructions for the Director of all Schools in the Principality of Serbia" and was issued in Kragujevac. These instructions list twenty articles which define in detail the director's functions. He was obliged to visit all the schools in the country twice a year, once in March and once in August. Since the makers of this document were in doubt themselves whether the director would be able to visit all schools twice, they added in Article 2: "if he is not able to visit the schools exactly twice, at least he should do it once for sure." In order to lighten the director's work and strengthen control over the schools, the director was required by the same Instructions to appoint school superintendents in every place where schools existed and to define their duties. For example, if a priest were to teach religion in a school he should also be, according to the Instructions, the superintendent of that school. The superintendent's position was honorary and was not paid, yet he was obliged to concern himself with all questions concerning education and to make improvements with the help of the *Soviet*. His duty was also to report to the *Soviet* twice a year about work in the schools.[56]

It should be noted that the Instructions of 1836 were not the first directive to a school director, but it was the first one which went into effect. The first instructions to a school director were included in the previously-mentioned "Constitution of Public Schools" of 1833, but as far as we know, at that time the office had not yet been established so those first instructions could not have been used.[57]

In the report of the Ministry of Education concerning the condition of the Serbian schools which was given in 1841 to Gerasim V. Vashchenko, Russian Consul General in Belgrade, it can be seen that prior to 1838, Serbia did not have a set of required subjects for the elementary schools.

> The teachers in them [the elementary schools] [it was stated in the report] taught in whatever way they knew.... The subjects which had to be taught were not defined, but the pupils studied here to read and write the Serbian language, mathematics, a little bit of Serbian grammar, and Slavic grammar here and there.[58]

Petar Radovanović's report to the *Soviet* of July 28/August 9, 1836, contains similar information.[59]

It is necessary to point out that the official documents of representatives of educational policy in Serbia at that time are not quite accurate and it would be mistake to rely entirely upon them. For example, in the report of the Ministry of Education quoted above, it was stated that in the 1830s in the elementary schools "the subjects which had to be taught were not defined." Such a statement cannot be completely accepted, although at the time it was accepted by many and many still accept it, because documents in the archives show, not only that the subjects were defined for every grade, but also that specific textbooks were prescribed.[60] Our opinion is that it would be better, on the basis of sources available today, to conclude that the law of 1833 defined the subjects which should have been taught, but that it probably never went into effect. Therefore, and because of their limited knowledge, "all teachers ... taught subjects in their classes according to their knowledge and to their desire and in such a way as they knew and wanted."[61]

The lack of a uniform curriculum for the elementary schools was one of the most important causes for poor knowledge among the pupils. Besides, there was a large differentiation in knowledge among pupils of different teachers. Therefore, after 1836, when Petar Radovanović submitted his report, the Serbian educational policy-makers began to think seriously about a uniform curriculum for the elementary schools. This curriculum, which was the most significant educational decree during Prince Miloš's first regime, was issued on August 11/23, 1838, under the title "Specification of Subjects which are to be Taught in the First and Second Grades of Elementary Schools." At the same time, one other important document was issued with the aim of improving elementary education. It was the first instruction to the elementary school teachers entitled "The Instructions to the Teachers of State and Communal Schools in the Principality of Serbia," which was written by the Minister of Education, Stefan Stefanović-Tenka.[62]

In this first curriculum for the elementary schools in Serbia the name "normal school" was introduced and soon accepted throughout the country. According to the same curriculum, the elementary (normal) school was divided into two grades, and instruction in each of them lasted for two years.[63]

It is not necessary to list all subjects which were specified by the first curriculum of 1838 because this work does not deal with the development of pedagogy in Serbia. It is sufficient to mention that by this document the content of some subjects was enlarged and some new subjects were introduced. For example, more attention was paid to the Serbian language: its grammar had to be studied in detail and more time had to be spent on composition. Mathematics was enlarged by adding fractions and square roots. National history and the German language were introduced as new subjects.[64] This curriculum also shows how much attention was paid to the German language. "This year," the document reads, "both grades [higher classes] should begin teaching the German language - reading and writing, and if the necessary books are lacking, the teacher will try to get them, namely a German elementary reading book and a reader."[65] This language was taught as early as the elementary schools because a knowledge of it, regardless how limited, was necessary and often indispensable for anybody who had any connections with Austria. Commercial ties were especially common because Austria was the principal market for Serbia. From 1838 to 1844, German was taught in all four grades. Yet, in 1844 German was not mentioned among the subjects taught. Later, on February 24, 1845 (O.S.), it was introduced again, but this time only in the fourth grade of the elementary school in Belgrade.[66]

The elementary school teachers received for the first time detailed directions concerning teaching, behavior, relations towards pupils, priests, secular persons, and the like by the already mentioned "Instructions" of 1838. Among the most important articles of this document are Articles 4, 7, and 8. In them it was pointed out that "teachers are to work with children three hours in the morning, and three hours in the afternoon," that "it is not necessary that teachers teach subjects mechanically ... but on the contrary, every teacher is obliged to explain everything, including the smallest things, well to his pupils so that they can understand everything perfectly..." and teachers were advised to prepare themselves for classes, because "it would be indeed a shame," it was emphasized, "if a teacher could not first of all understand well and perfectly those subjects which he teaches in school...."[67]

Specification and *Instructions* of 1838, as has been indicated, were the most important educational documents issued during Prince Miloš's first regime; they could have been very useful if there had been a capable teaching staff to carry them out. However, Serbia did not have capable teachers, and so a complete implementation of the decrees "exceeded the ability of the existing teaching staff."[68]

Because of the dissatisfaction in the country which had been caused by his unlimited and cruel rule, Prince Miloš was forced to consider some changes in his internal policy and to give up some of his absolute power. He promised the Popular Assembly (*Skupština*) in 1834 to grant a constitution to the nation and to introduce legal reforms. A little later, Prince Miloš appointed five ministers among whom was a Minister of Justice and Education. Lazar Teodorović was appointed the first Minister of Justice and Education, but he was replaced after only a few days by Djordje Protić. During the same year the Department of Education was separated from the Department of Justice and transferred to the Ministry of Foreign Affairs which was headed by a well-known cultural figure from Vojvodina, Dimitrije Davidović. However, nothing important was achieved by this transfer because the appointed ministers acted not as the ministers, but as relatively powerless subordinates of Prince Miloš. The ministers' position was not essentially changed until December 10/22, 1838, when the so-called Turkish Constitution was granted to Serbia by the Sultan. The new constitution limited Prince Miloš's authority and the function of the ministers was protected.

According to the Constitution of 1838, the Minister of Justice was at the same time also the Minister of Education. His function in the field of education was defined by Articles 21 and 22 of the Constitution and consisted mainly of spreading education and opening new schools.[69] Oddly, as early as February 2/14, 1835, when Serbia got her first constitution, the functions of the Minister of Education were defined, but the minister (Stefan Stefanović-Tenka) was not actually appointed until May 10/22, 1838. Thus, the Ministry only began to work officially on May 29/June 10, 1839.[70]

After 1830, Prince Miloš's legislative program for education called for the erection of new buildings, besides churches which were to be exclusively used as elementary schools. Those buildings usually had a room or two where the teachers could live. Until that time, buildings for school needs were not erected but ordinary houses, with some adaptations or without them, were used for that purpose.[71]

Prior to 1830, when she received her autonomy, Serbia had sixteen town schools and several village schools with a combined enrollment of around 800 pupils and twenty-two teachers.[72] The schools were mostly communal and were financed from local resources with a great deal of help from the pupils' parents. The government, at that time a still semi-autonomous Serbia, did not allocate large funds for the spread of education, but it also did not obstruct its development since every commune which had the material means for the opening of a school was permitted to do so. But after receiving autonomy in 1830, the passive educational and cultural policy of Prince Miloš and his associates was replaced by a more active one. Thus, for instance, during 1835 and 1836 by the order of the Prince, twenty-six elementary schools were opened (two in every district) at the state's expense. The state also paid the teachers' salaries, and every teacher received from 100 to 150 talers annually.[73] The number of schools was gradually increased so that, according to Petar Radovanović's report of 1836, Serbia had seventy-two elementary schools with the same number of teachers and an enrollment of 2, 514 pupils in the 1835-36 school year. On the basis of their source of support, these schools can be divided into three groups - state, communal, and private. There were twenty-six state schools, twenty-seven communal schools, and nineteen private schools.[74] If this number of schools is compared with the population, it comes out that there was one school for every 9, 419 inhabitants since, according to the census of 1834, Serbia had a population of 678,132.[75] After 1836, the number of elementary schools was further increased so that at the end of Prince Miloš's rule in 1839, there were eighty-four schools attended by 2,916 pupils.[76]

On the basis of the statistical data presented it may be concluded that in autonomous Serbia up to 1839, the number of elementary schools and pupils rapidly increased; in that eight-year period more than sixty new schools were opened and were attended by around 2,000 pupils.

According to "The Constitution of Public Schools" of 1833, the elementary schools should have been divided into "small" and "regular" schools. The small schools would have to be opened "in every larger village and small town in the Principality of Serbia" with one teacher who would teach in the Serbian language the following subjects: the alphabet, reading from the primer and reader, the short catechism, world history, writing, and basic rules of mathematics.[77] The regular schools, on the other hand, had to be opened "in every larger town of every district in which the district administration existed." It was intended that these schools offer more than the small ones; they had to have three grades with one teacher for every grade, and in them the pupils had to study the following subjects: knowledge of letters from the alphabetical table, phonetics and reading from the primer and reader, writing, common prayers, short catechism of Serbian Orthodoxy, world history, elementary rules of mathematics, and orthography.[78] Since this Constitution probably never went into effect, it may be assumed that these schools with their clearly defined subjects were not opened.

Because of the lack of a uniform curriculum until 1838, the teachers taught in their schools what they knew and used what books they could get. According to Milovan Spasić, general director of the elementary schools in Serbia in the 1850s, the following subjects were most often taught: "Primer, prayer book, Psalter, the four operations of mathematics, writing, prayers, world history, and in some places catechism and Slavic grammar."[79] "The way," writes Spasić, "the subjects were taught was generally mechanical, because there were no prescribed rules which the teachers could follow, and hardly any of them had any knowledge of teaching methods."[80]

Until 1836, it was usual for representatives of communes to look for teachers and conclude contracts with them. Customarily these individuals were men who enjoyed special trust among the people. After the position of director of all schools was established, the director "found and presented new teachers, especially for the state schools, and after they were approved by the *Soviet* he oriented them to their job."[81] The greater number of teachers were Serbs from Vojvodina, a certain number were teachers from other provinces outside of Serbia (Slavonia, Croatia, and some provinces in the framework of the Ottoman Empire), and only an insignificant number were native Serbs. For example, in 1836, of seventy-two existing teachers only twenty-one, or 39 percent, were from Serbia, and the other fifty-one, or 61 percent, came from provinces outside of Serbia. Of the latter, forty-four, or 53 percent of the total number, came from Vojvodina, while seven, or 8 percent, came from the other provinces outside of Serbia.[82]

During this period, a great number of teachers had been engaged in different occupations before they became teachers. Thus, for example, Petar Radosavčić, a teacher from Belgrade, was a butcher before he became a teacher.[83] Not only did such men not have any training for the teaching profession, they also lacked the moral quality needed for the education of youth. It is sufficient to mention that, for example, Tsintsar Kosta Zaka, a teacher in Belgrade in 1832, was a "debauched person and vagabond," that the Greek, Toma Solar, was "in prison for his crimes," and Kosta Ignjatijević, a teacher from Ćuprija in 1836, was "a swindler and liar about whose adventures much could be said."[84] Therefore, it is not surprising that on July 20/August 1, 1836, Petar Radovanović informed Prince Miloš and the *Soviet* that of sixty-eight teachers only sixteen were completely capable of teaching higher grades. Of the rest he writes, "But among the other fifty-two there are several who could improve themselves."[85] Naturally, from such teachers a miracle could not be expected, but since Serbia did not have better, those dilettantes had to be kept until the new state could educate a native teaching staff to gradually replace them.

The elementary school pupils came from all strata of the Serbian society, but they were chiefly peasant children because Serbia at that time was almost completely an agrarian country. The pupils were of different ages. Most often, especially in the villages, elementary school students were grown up young men. There were even pupils who had deserted from the army. In such cases they were not forced to return to the army and to resume their military obligation, but were allowed to attend schools regularly.[86] In the villages a small number of younger children did attend the schools, but such younger students were more common in the towns and cities.

In Serbia during the 1830s, the need to educate female children was not felt; in the villages there could not be found one woman who was literate, while in the cities and towns only a very few of them knew how to read and write. When Otto D. Pirch, a Prussian army officer, asked about the education of female children during his journey through Serbia in 1829, he was told: "They will neither be engaged in trade nor have a profession, therefore why do they need the skill of reading and writing, except to be able to understand love letters and to answer them?"[87] However, some educated people did suggest the education of female children. As early as 1821, Dimitrije Davidović in his patriotic appeal of August 3/15 pointed out the need for their education. He even suggested that a school could be opened in his house where girls could learn how to read, write, cook, sew, embroider, knit, and so on. His wife and sisters-in-law would teach them and the teaching would be free.[88] This suggestion was not accepted and Serbia had to wait more than twenty years for her first separate girls' school. Yet, though a girls' school did not exist, a certain number of female children, especially in the cities, were educated. They attended schools together with male children. For instance, in 1832 among 211 Belgrade pupils there were sixteen girls.[89] The girls who attended schools together with boys received only the most elementary knowledge. It is not known how many girls learned how to write and read before 1839.

In the 1830s, as has been shown, elementary education faced many problems. One of them continued to be the lack of writing material. It was not rare to have pupils write with goose quills. Usually the pupils were obliged to bring feathers from home to school where the teacher cut them. It became an unwritten law that the teacher kept every third feather for himself.[90] Merchant Mihailo Drvenjak brought the first writing slate in the 1830s but until the 1840s only a small number of the wealthier pupils had them.[91]

The lack of suitable textbooks also caused a major problem and seriously hampered the rapid and effective spread of education. It was partly solved by the first publication of textbooks in Serbia at the end of Prince Miloš's rule.

Publishing began in Serbia after 1830 when the first printing press was purchased. Besides books, newspapers and journals, textbooks were also published. In the beginning they were translations of foreign textbooks, but later textbooks were written by the teachers who taught in the higher schools of Serbia. With the opening of new schools, the need for textbooks was considerably increased and the educational policy-makers informed the Prince of it. "It is indispensably necessary," wrote Stefan

Stefanović-Tenka, to Prince Miloš on June 14/26, 1838, "to have needed school books written and published immediately and without any delay."[92] It seems that Stefanović's letter to the Prince had positive consequences because after 1838, school textbooks were published more often. It should be added that the curriculum of the same year contributed greatly to the writing and publication of textbooks; without them it would have been impossible to implement that curriculum and carry out uniform teaching in the elementary schools.

Among the first textbooks for elementary schools published in the Principality of Serbia, the two elementary reading books published in 1838 deserve mention. The first was *Srbski bukvar, ili nova azbučna knjižica za prvo nastavlenije mladeži u narodnim normalnim školama Knjažestva Serbije* (Serbian Primer, or a New Alphabet Booklet for the Elementary Teaching of Youth in Normal Public Schools for the Principality of Serbia),[93] which was written as an official duty by Petar Radovanović. It was reviewed and approved for publication by a committee composed by the Belgrade gymnasium professors. The second book was published under the title *Mali učitelj ili srbski bukvar sadržavajući u sebi pravila cerkovnog i graždanskog čitanja, nuždne molitve i mnoge polezne predmete za srbsku decu* (A Small Teacher or Serbian Primer which Contains the Rules of the Ecclesiastical and Secular Readings, Necessary prayers, and Many Useful Subjects for Serbian Children). It was written by Gligorije Zorić, a director of all elementary schools in Serbia after November, 1838.[94]

The next year, 1839, the first reader was published in Serbia. Its author was Dimitrije Isailović, chief of personnel in the Ministry of Education and it was published under the title *Mala čitaonica za načalno upražnenije mladeži u nižim normalnim školama Knjaževstva Serbije* (A Small Reader for the Elementary Education of Youth in Lower Normal Schools of the Principality of Serbia).[95] This reader was divided into six chapters and treated numerous subjects, especially natural science. It was not only the first reader, but remained for a number of years the only one actually suited to the needs of Serbian youth.[96] In this period D. Isailović wrote one more textbook. It was *Nemački bukvar s prevodom srbskim* (A German Primer with Serbian Translation)[97] which was written in 1838 probably because of the introduction of the German language in elementary schools by the first curriculum. It should also be noted that there was a textbook for religious subjects. In contrast to the previously mentioned textbooks, this one was a simple translation from the Russian language under the title *Kratko hristijansko poučenije za serbsku decu* (A Short

Christian Instruction for Serbian Children.)[98] It was translated by Gligorije Zorić and was published in 1837. Other books which were published before 1839 were not of any great significance for elementary school pupils.

Although the publishing activity of this time was not very fruitful, it was significant because Serbia had finally begun to publish her own textbooks, which were written by her teachers or educational administrators and printed in the state printing house in Belgrade.

The financing of schools was a problem which would plague Serbia for a long time. As has been seen, only a certain number of the so-called *praviteljstvujušće* (state) schools were supported by the state while all the rest of them were financed by communes and individuals. In spite of that, Prince Miloš was dissatisfied with the state school financial policy and was of the opinion that only higher schools, the schools which prepared state officials, had to be subsidized by the state. He wanted to make the communes completely responsible for the financial support of the elementary schools. In a letter of June 25/July 7, 1836, to the *Soviet* he wrote:

> Small [elementary] schools in which our youth
> would only learn reading, writing, and a bit of
> mathematics, should be left to communes and
> those which are willing could keep them; our goal
> is the benefit of the entire state, not the benefit of
> some individuals.[99]

In order to enable communes to pay their teachers on time and increase their salaries, which were very low, some revenues which until then went into the state treasury were ceded to the communes. But since these additional incomes were insufficient some teachers had to be paid by special local surtaxes and some by other state funds. Such methods of supporting elementary schools lasted until May, 1841. Then on the basis of a government decision of September 14/26, 1840, these forms of subsidy were abolished and communes became obliged to finance all elementary schools, whereas the state took upon itself to finance all other schools.[100]

Because of financial difficulty, some attempts were already made in 1836 and 1837 to establish a central school fund from which teachers could be paid, but without any success. Not until 1841 was such as fund finally officially established.[101]

Prior to 1830, only a small number of Serbs lived in the cities and towns of Serbia. But after the country won autonomy, the Serbian urban structure gradually changed. The emigration of Turks and other nationalities and the economic development of the state precipitated a rapid influx of the population into cities. As an example, the number of Belgrade inhabitants in 1834 was 7,033 but by 1846, the population had more than doubled to 14,371.[102]

A great number of foreigners, especially Greeks, Jews, and Tsintsars (Vlachs), remained in Serbia after her liberation and their role in the economic and cultural development of the young Serbian state was large. Therefore, it is not surprising that in addition to Serbian schools there also existed schools of other nationalities. Undoubtedly, the Greek schools were the most important; for a long time they were considered to be the best elementary schools in Serbia. For that reason, and because of the importance of the Greek language in Serbia at that time, many Serbian parents sent their children to the Greek schools after they had graduated from the Serbian elementary schools. The best known Greek school was not in Belgrade but across the river in Zemun (Vojvodina) "which was a higher educational institution of some kind to the young Greeks from Belgrade and to some young distinguished Serbs."[103] Besides Belgrade, there were also Greek schools in other Serbian cities. It is known that they were in Negotin, Šabac, and Smederevo. Information about their work is not preserved but it may be assumed that they did not operate uninterruptedly; undoubtedly they operated only when the means for their support existed or when competent teachers could be found.[104]

There is also very little information about the schools of Serbia's Jews in the first half of the nineteenth century. It is only known that they existed, that instruction was not conducted in the Serbian language, and that they were supported by the Jewish religious communities. The tax register (*harački defter*) for 1827 is the oldest known document which proves that Belgrade had a Jewish school during the first reign of Prince Miloš. It shows that among 239 registered tax-payers, twenty-two persons were teachers, pupils, and rabbis.[105] Since instruction in the Jewish schools was not conducted in the Serbian language, their role in the educational and cultural development of Serbia was insignificant.

Tihomir Djordjević, a well-known Serbian cultural historian, writes that in Prince Miloš's time, Serbia also had several Turkish schools and one German school.[106] There is some evidence of Turkish schools, which were probably private,[107] but there is no evidence that a German school existed.

It is true that in 1829 Pavle Verner (Paul Werner) was given permission to open a German school, but he probably never did so.

Despite the fact that as early as 1820 V.S. Karadžić had pointed out a need for opening a high school because existing elementary schools could not give needed knowledge to the future officials of the political, cultural, and economic life of Serbia, Prince Miloš did not show any interest in the opening of such a school until Serbia's liberation. However, after the liberation the Prince himself realized that such a school was indispensable to Serbia. With Karadžić's cooperation, in the fall of 1830 Miloš brought to Serbia Dimitrije Isailović, a professor of the Teacher Preparatory school in Sombor. The intention was for him to establish a high school. Indeed, in the same year Isailović opened a school in Belgrade which closely resembled the high school which Ivan Jugović had opened in 1808. Besides Prince Miloš's sons, Milan and Michael, thirteen other students attended Isailović's school, which was officially called *Viša škola*, in the first year of existence. Since a curriculum for this school did not exist and Dimitrije Isailović was its only professor, he prescribed which subjects would be taught and how he would teach them. In the first year the following subjects were taught: Serbian syntax, Serbian grammar, anthropology, world history, German reading and writing, nature study, general geography, and arithmetic.[108]

In the first year of operation the *Viša škola* showed poor results because Prince Miloš required that Isailović teach his sons French and German "which immediately became his chief task, and teaching in the *Viša škola* remained an incidental one."[109] The next year, that is 1831, the examination was held, but nobody passed it. Therefore, students remained in the same grade studying the same subjects.[110] During 1831 Isailović was transferred to another duty, and his professor position was given to Atanasije Teodorović, also from Vojvodina, who taught in the *Viša škola* for the next two years. But he also did not achieve any significant results.[111] His report of 1833 shows that the number of subjects taught was enlarged and the *Viša škola*, although with only one teacher, began to look more like a gymnasium. The same report also shows that the following subjects were taught: Serbian syntax, German grammar, anthropology, empirical psychology, ethics, nature study, physics, geography, arithmetic, and composition.[112] Some sources indicate that in 1833 "Latin reading" was also taught in the *Viša škola* and that great attention was paid to it.[113] It is difficult to establish whether Latin reading was indeed a subject, and if it was, whether it was actually the Latin language that was taught or only the Latin alphabet, the knowledge of which would help students in under-standing Western languages, especially German. We think that Latin reading was not taught as a separate subject because Atanasije Teodorović had no reason not to mention it in his report. Even without Latin reading, the list of subjects which were taught is impressive if it is borne in mind that those were the first years of higher education in Serbia, that the students' knowledge was limited, and that only one man taught all those subjects.

The *Viša škola* operated in Belgrade until the fall of 1833 when, by Prince Miloš's order, it was transferred to Kragujevac. It is not known for sure why Miloš transferred this school but presumably he wanted to have stronger control over its work; this could be accomplished by the transfer because Kragujevac was then the capital of Serbia.

The transfer to Kragujevac partly stabilized the *Viša škola* both materially and with regard to personnel. Already in the school year 1834-35, it had three professors, one for each grade, and a prescribed curriculum which had to be taught. The professors were: Dimitrije Isailović, Isidor Stojanović, and Grigorije Novaković, and the subjects did not differ much from the subjects which were taught in 1833.[114]

At the suggestion of Dimitrije Davidović, Minister of Education, prince Miloš transformed the *Viša škola* into a gymnasium in March 1835 and added to it one grade and one teacher. It was then officially the first gymnasium in Serbia to have four grades and four teachers.[115] Petar Radovanović's report of 1836, which has been previously mentioned, shows that this school was attended by eighty-five students. The first grade was attended by thirty-six, the second by twenty-three, the third by thirteen, and the fourth grade also by thirteen students.[116] The teachers were Serbs from Vojvodina: the first grade was taught by Petar Nikolić, who had an annual salary of 250 talers, the second by Grigorije Novaković with a salary of 300 talers, the third by Isidor Stojanović also with a salary of 300 talers, and the fourth by Atanasije Teodorović with an annual salary of 400 talers.[117]

Since it was the first gymnasium in Serbia it is necessary to mention the subjects that were taught. The first grade curriculum consisted of: Christian doctrine, Serbian grammar, Serbian and general history, nature study, mathematical and political geography, and mathematics; the second grade curriculum was: Christian doctrine, Slavic grammar, Serbian syntax, world history, political geography, anatomy and biology along with chemistry and mathematics; the third grade subjects were: rhetoric, mathematics, logic, psychology, general history, ethics, and Greek mytho-logy; and in the fourth grade: poetry, physics, mathematical geography, Roman antiquities, modern general history, stylistics, and Serbian history were taught.[118] A comparison of this subject list with the subjects taught in the *Viša škola* in 1833 will not reveal any great changes, but since in 1836 there were four teachers, it may be assumed that the subjects were taught more thoroughly. It is somewhat surprising that among the subjects not taught at the first gymnasium was the German language, which had been taught in the *Viša škola* for all the time of its existence.[119]

In the first Serbian gymnasium, a class received instruction in all subjects from a single teacher. The transition from this sort of teaching to having specialists in one or a number of related subjects began in 1839, and proceeded gradually.[120] This was, without any doubt, a significant step in teaching development because it brought Serbian education into line with the methods of the more progressive countries, especially those of Western Europe.

In the school year 1838-39, a fifth grade was added to the Serbian gymnasium and brought it one step closer to a regular gymnasium of that time, which had six grades. In order to improve teaching, the Ministry of Education issued a new curriculum for the gymnasium on September 26/October 8, 1838. It was the first document of that kind in Serbia and by it the following subjects were established: catechism; Slavic grammar; Serbian grammar and syntax; ancient, medieval, modern, Slavic and Serbian history; rhetoric; geography; zoology; botany; geology; anthro-pology; mathematics; arithmetic; German; and Greek.[121] As the curriculum shows, the number of subjects was significantly increased, and now for the first time in a Serbian school two foreign languages were taught. It has been pointed out that a knowledge of German was necessary, especially in commerce, but that was not the only reason for studying this language. A second, not so important and always forgotten, reason was that the gymnasium professors came from Vojvodina which was an integral part of the Austrian Empire so German was the language to which they were exposed and they were prepared to teach it without much effort. The introduction of modern Greek into the Serbian gymnasium, on the other hand, confirms that the Greeks still played an important role in the cultural and economic life of the country.

The gymnasium in Kragujevac was the only gymnasium in Serbia during Prince Miloš's reign. In addition to it, there also existed three principal schools (*glavne škole*), as they were called, or semi-gymnasiums (this name was officially given to them in the school year 1839-40). Instruction lasted for two years in the principal schools, and their graduates could enroll in the third grade of the gymnasium. They were located in Čačak, Šabac, and Zaječar in 1836 and 1837, and each of them had two elementary teachers.[122]

Prince Miloš, as has been mentioned, paid great attention to higher education because after graduating from higher schools, the students could immediately become officials who were indispensable to the state. In a letter to the *Soviet* dated June 25/July 7, 1836, which was most probably sent by Miloš, it was emphasized that greater care had to be taken of those schools which prepare officials.[123] He recommended to the *Soviet* that it consult with Petar Radovanović regarding how "to educate youth who would be necessary and useful to the country, especially those," he pointed out, "who would be necessary as educated men to the state."[124]

A further indication of how much Prince Miloš and the makers of educational policy were interested in the spread and improvement of higher education in Serbia is shown in the already-mentioned "Instructions to the Director of All Schools in the Principality of Serbia" of 1836. Article 6 of that document says that the director should identify "more capable children in elementary schools and enroll them into gymnasium and, in general, he will see to it that gymnasium gets a sufficient number of students every year."[125]

In addition to bureaucrats, every underdeveloped country has to have various specialists. Miloš was aware of this need when Serbia was created as a state. Despite enormous expenditures and small revenues, he began to open vocational schools. It seems that it was not his own idea, because after 1832 he almost completely modeled his educational policy after V.S. Karadžić's suggestion of 1832. In his previously cited letter to the Prince, Karadžić wrote: "Now, according to today's condition in Serbia, it would be useful to open three higher schools - one in Šumadija, a second one across the Morava River, and a third one across the Kolubara River, as well as one real gymnasium, and later, little by little, a lyceum and a university."[126]

Since the church played a very important role in the state, yet ecclesiastics had only the most rudimentary knowledge at best, consisting only of reading and writing, Prince Miloš, as early as 1818, tried to establish a theological seminary, turning for help to the Greek Metropolitan of Belgrade, Agathangelos. He planned to support such a seminary by people's contributions but the Metropolitan did not want to open it with such vague and insecure financial backing so Miloš's suggestion remained only an unrealized desire.[127] Prince Miloš did not give up his intention however; he still tried a few times to open such a school in 1822, for example, he sought advice from Lukijan Mušicki, Archimandrite of Šišatovac in Vojvodina. He received it and the next year, 1823, decided to open a seminary in Kragujevac. According to Miloš's conception, this school had to be supported by priests' contributions, by donations of prosperous laymen, and by monetary fines. Those people he suggested, who had committed grave transgressions and did not want to be subjected to corporal punishments had to free themselves by paying prescribed sums of money.[128] This, like other of Prince Miloš's plans, remained unrealized.

With the liberation of Serbia, favorable conditions for the opening of a seminary were created. According to the *Hatt-i-Şerif* of 1830, the Patriarch was obliged to recall both Greek bishops from Serbia, which he did in 1831, so the Serbs got their own hierarchs, and in January of 1832, a formal contract for the autonomy of the Serbian church was concluded.[129]

Archimandrite Melentije Pavlović was elected Serbian Metropolitan on August 18/30, 1831 - the first Serb from Serbia to be elected to that post. In addition, Archimandrite Nićifor Maksimović was elected the Bishop of Užice and Archimandrite Gerasim Djordjević the Bishop of Šabac.[130]

With these elections, the Serbian church obtained three Serbs at the head of its clergy, but unfortunately all three lacked education. About them, for instance, Lukijan Mušicki wrote the following to V.S. Karadžić on December 21, 1831/January 2, 1832:

> I think that it is not necessary to tell you that none
> of those three know anything except how to read
> poorly, and none of them know how to write in
> the true sense.[131]

When the heads of the Serbian church had such poor knowledge, it is not difficult to imagine what knowledge village priests could have had.

In 1833, Melentije Pavlović died and Pavle Jovanović, secretary of the Prince's chancery, was elected new Metropolitan; he received the monastic name Petar. After his election serious attention was paid to the establishment of a seminary. The Synod of Bishops, which was held in Kragujevac from January 30/February 11 to February 6/18, 1834, issued a decree establishing a theological seminary.[132] After long preparations, the first seminary in Serbia under the name of *"Klirikalna škola"* (Clerical School) was opened on September 1/13, 1836.[133] Initially, twenty-six students were enrolled, but because it was soon realized that instruction would last more than a year, twenty-one additional students were admitted so that in the first year the seminary was attended by forty-seven students.[134] Among them twenty-four were married. Since they were in a more difficult financial position than unmarried students, the Church Council tried to have them exempted from taxes and obligatory labor (*kuluk*) during the time of their studies. At the same time, the Council promised Prince Miloš that in the future married candidates would not be admitted. But the Prince did not accept this suggestion; he thought it would be unfair to exempt some seminary students from obligations toward the state, thus singling them out from the other citizens.[135]

Poor students did receive financial aid. For instance, by 1837, a year after its establishment, sixteen students were housed in the Metropolitan's residence, and "the military commissioner gave them every day *'Tayin* [ration] of bread' free."[136] Some students also received stipends.[137]

Although the Seminary was financed by the state, the Metropolitan had complete control over it until 1863. He selected professors, established the curriculum and disciplinary rules, supervised the school organization, and so on.

Metropolitan Petar Jovanović appointed two ecclesiastics as the first teachers in the Seminary - both were from Austria. They were Archsyncellus Likogen Mihailović from Dalmatia and Syncellus Gavrilo Popović from Baja in Bačka - monks who had been Court chaplains in Serbia before they were appointed seminary teachers. In the first two years, Mihailović had an annual salary of 350 talers and Popović of 300. After two years of teaching, beginning sometime in 1838, their salaries were increased annually by 50 talers.[138] Likogen Mihailović's salary was higher than the salary of Popović because he was a rector and in addition to his teaching obligation he had administrative duties.

According to Milan Dj. Milićević, who himself was a student at the Seminary in the 1840s, the following subjects were taught in the first years of its operation: Slavic grammar, church history with liturgy, dogmatics, and pastoral and moral theology (school year 1836-1837). The next school year, 1837-38, one more grade and the following subjects were added: teaching methods, rhetoric, and exegesis. In the following school year, 1838-39, the third grade, a preparatory grade, was opened and Pavle Popović was appointed its professor. In this grade general history, geography, and mathematics were taught.[139] It should be pointed out that in the same year pedagogy as a separate subject was introduced, because this school not only educated the first priests, but the first elementary school teachers as well, and any of its students who wanted to enter the teaching profession were obliged to study this subject.[140] There is no reliable evidence for the number of seminary graduates who became teachers before 1839, but it may be assumed that the number was quite large after church dignitaries introduced pedagogy as a teaching subject. From the list of subjects which were taught in the Seminary, it is apparent that the graduates who became teachers were narrowly trained, and for that reason they could not do well in the teaching profession. Yet, it should be emphasized that in spite of their one-sided and limited education, seminarians contributed greatly to the spread of literacy throughout Serbia. Furthermore, they were the first native teachers to graduate from a higher school which prepared them, if not completely, at least partly for the profession to which they devoted themselves.

At the end of 1838, the Seminary in its three grades had five professors (Tihomir Budić, Pajsije Popović, Gavrilo Popović, Gerasim Stojković, and Jevtimije Simeunović),[141] but it is not possible to establish either the number of students in that year, nor the number of students who graduated before 1838.[142]

To create a strong army was one of the chief tasks of Miloš's internal policy and he paid considerable attention to it. Aware that a strong army cannot be created without an educated commanding staff, he took the first step in that direction. As early as April 25/May 7, 1830, he established in Požarevac the so-called *Gvardiska škola* or the Guard School for the members of his guard, who were called cadets.[143] Unfortunately, more detailed information about the operation of this first military "school" in Serbia was not preserved. Three years later, in 1833, Prince Miloš took a significant step toward providing needed army officers by sending twelve young Serbian men to a military academy in Russia.[144] They returned to Serbia in 1836 and became the first native officers.

Despite the fact that Prince Miloš saw the need for a regular military academy immediately after the liberation of Serbia, it was not established until 1837. There are many reasons for that but, of course, one of the most important was the absence of a teaching staff. With the return of the first Serbian officers from Russia, this problem was partially solved and serious preparation for the opening of this school could begin. The Military Academy or *Knjažeskoserbska voenna akademija*, as it was officially called, was opened in Požarevac on December 15/27, 1837, and was attended by thirty-one students.[145] The first students were selected by a commission which consisted of: Ilija Hadži-Milutninović, Colonel and Chief of Military Police, Petar Radovanović, Director of all schools, and Stefan Hrkalović, a Serb and former Austrian army officer.[146] Most of them were selected from among the students who graduated from the gymnasium in 1836 and 1837, and the rest were selected from among the students who attended their final grade in the gymnasium during the 1837-38 school year.[147]

Stefan Hrkalović was the director of the Military Academy and the teacher of the theoretical subjects; the practical instruction was conducted by the Serbian officers who had been educated in Russia.[148] Besides military subjects and practical instruction, the following general subjects were taught: general history, geography, advanced mathematics, French, and German.[149]

The Military Academy did not remain in Požarevac for very long. On April 12/24, 1838, it was transferred to Belgrade where it remained only forty-three days, until May 25/June 6. From Belgrade it was transferred to Kragujevac, but there, too, it operated for only a very short time, until the middle of June when it was abolished.[150]

It is not known for sure why the Academy lasted for such a short time. There are different opinions but two of them - political tension in the state and the Porte's objection to this school - were probably the chief causes for its abolition.[151]

The intellectuals from Vojvodina were able to meet Serbia's needs for educated people for several years after her liberation. However, in time she became an organized state with a greatly increased apparatus and educated Serbs from Vojvodina could no longer completely meet those needs. The greatest need was for well-educated high state officials. In order to ease the existing problem, Serbia began to train her most promising native young men for the highest state positions. None of the existing schools could prepare personnel for the highest bureaucratic positions and therefore the government decided to establish a high school which would in time expand into a university.

On September 11/23, 1838, Stefan Stefanović-Tenka, Minister of Education, sent a letter to Prince Miloš, advising him "that **in place** of the abolished **Military Academy** to elevate the Gymnasium to the level of a lyceum and to bring capable people from Germany [Austria] to teach philosophical subjects and to whom decent annual salaries should be allocated."[152] According to Stefanović's estimation, the entire support of such a school would cost 9,500 talers per year.[153] This suggestion was accepted and after a short preparation in October of 1838, the Lyceum was opened in Kragujevac; it was the highest school in Serbia.[154] *Novine Srbske (The Serbian News)*, the only paper in Serbia, printed an article about the opening of the Lyceum on its front page.[155] The same article cited Prince Miloš's suggestion about the establishment of a fund to support it. In his opinion, such a fund had to be established and maintained by the people's donations; from it, the Gymnasium, Lyceum, and Seminary professors could be paid. In addition, such a fund could be used to support poor but talented students and poor and sick people. The author of this article also informed his readers that Prince Miloš had given 60,000 silver florins from his own budget for professors' salaries and for the support of poor students because he wished to spare the state budget.[156]

Instruction at the Lyceum was to last for two years and graduation from the gymnasium was a prerequisite for enrollment. In the first school year, 1838-1839, sixteen students were enrolled and after two years, thirteen of them graduated. The next school year, 1839-40, their number almost doubled to thirty-one students.[157]

Two professors from the gymnasium in Kragujevac, Petar Radovanović and Atanasije Teodorović, were appointed the first Lyceum professors because Prince Miloš did not succeed in his attempt to bring professors from Vojvodina.[158] After teaching only a short time they were replaced by Isidor Stojanović and Kosta Branković. Although better qualified than their predecessors, they also were not sufficiently qualified to be lyceum professors. Stojanović had graduated in philosophy and had begun to study law; Branković had studied law and had graduated from the Seminary in Sremski Karlovci.[159]

Like other Serbian schools, the Lyceum in Kragujevac was a copy of the Austro-Hungarian lyceums with some small adaptations to Serbian conditions. In order to prove this assertion it is sufficient to compare the curriculum of the Kragujevac lyceum for the first two years with the curriculum of the Budapest lyceum of 1806.[160] On September 18/30, 1838, the Minister of Education, Stefanović, presented the first curriculum for the Lyceum to Prince Miloš who accepted and confirmed it. This document defined the subjects which had to be taught in the Lyceum: philosophy, general history, mathematics, natural law, European statistics, drawing, German, French for beginners, and the Bible.[161]

The Kragujevac lyceum was not created as a direct result of a higher cultural impulse in Serbia at that time; it was a necessity. The main tasks of this institution, according to its founders' conception, were to be: the preparation of various kinds of specialists, the spread of education, and the training of future scientists and writers. In order to realize this conception, much better working conditions than Serbia could offer were needed. Since such did not exist in the beginning of its work, the Lyceum limited the scope of its work to the preparation of future bureaucrats. Although it had to be a high vocational school, the Lyceum in Kragujevac was not that in the first year of its existence because its instruction had a general character. Before 1840, it may be considered as a school for more or less general education or as a senior gymnasium. After 1840, when the Law Department was opened independent of the existing Department of Philosophy, the Lyceum of Kragujevac gradually began to function as a vocational high school.

Among the numerous schools which operated during the first reign of Prince Miloš, the so-called Court School (*Dvorska škola*) should be mentioned. As a matter of fact, it was not a real school at all. Its sole function was the private tutoring of the young princes Milan and Michael in the Prince's court. Quite probably the only reason it was called a "school" was because it was registered as such on the state budget.[162] Prince Miloš engaged very good professors for the tutoring of his sons. The best known among them were Dimitrije Isailović, Gligorije Zorić, and Konstantin Rano, who tutored them only in the French language.[163]

The absence of suitable textbooks was one of the most difficult problems in the secondary and higher schools. Most often the method of teaching in those schools was similar to the method used in the elementary schools - teachers dictated their subjects to the students who carefully wrote them down and then learned their notes by heart at home. Understandably, this method of teaching gave poor results so teachers, on their own initiative or by government order, began to write textbooks for their subjects. Before 1838 only a few textbooks for secondary and higher schools were published. Most often they were translations or adaptations of well-known foreign textbooks. Usually they were of poor quality because of bad translations or their adaptation fell short of making them suited to the needs and background of Serbian students. In spite of all these deficiencies, however, their publication was a big step forward in the development of education in Serbia.

Among the more important textbooks was *Francuskij bukvarj za upotreblenije učešće se mladeži u liceumu* (A French Elementary Reader for the Use of Lyceum Students) which was first published in Belgrade in

1839. This book was published without its author's name, but on the basis of the documents of the Ministry of Education, it may be concluded that its author was professor Aleksije Okoljski.[164] In the same year in Belgrade there was published a textbook under the title *Algebra ustrojena za upotreblenije slišatelja filozofije u liceum Knjažestva Serbije* (Algebra Written for the Use of Philosophy Students in the Lyceum of the Principality of Serbia).[165] Its author was Atanasije Nikolić, professor of mathematics at the same lyceum.

During Prince Miloš's first reign, in addition to being educated in Serbia, promising young men were sent as state scholarship holders to study abroad. As previously indicated, the first Serbian army officers were sent to Russia in 1833 to receive their training, but Russia, or rather St. Petersburg, was not the only place abroad where Serbian young men were educated. Even the scanty information that is available indicates that a certain number of them were sent to Budapest, Vienna, and Paris where they were prepared for various professions.[166] Most of them studied in military academies and polytechnical schools.[167] It is interesting to note that Prince Miloš, although illiterate, cultivated love for art and under his sole support, three young Serbs were sent abroad to study painting and lithography.[168]

There is no information as to how many young Serbs studied abroad before Prince Miloš's abdication in 1839. Presumably their number was not large because the state was faced with too many financial difficulties to be able to invest a large sum of money in education of its young men abroad. It is certain that the Serbian government and Prince Miloš, who made virtually all decisions, did not have any clearly defined plan for sending promising young men abroad to be educated.[169] Such decisions were made unexpectedly, sometimes as a result of state needs, sometimes on the basis of the suggestions of prominent persons (e.g., V.S. Karadžić), and sometimes as a result of Miloš's mood.

4.

For the educational and cultural development of any society, a printing press is not only one of the most important tools, but an indispensable one. Prince Miloš was aware of this and already in the first days after liberation he began to think seriously about buying a printing press which could satisfy the most basic needs of the state. It was not long before his intention was realized. By the end of 1830, the printing press needed for the opening of a publishing house was bought in St. Petersburg and delivered to Belgrade on May 21/June 2, 1831.[170]

The press began to work on September 9/21, 1831, when it printed a warning to citizens about the spread of cholera under the title *"Cholera morbus."*[171] Since 1831 was only the first year of its operation, the printing house did not print any serious work, all of its activity consisted of printing various office forms, registers, travel documents, advertisements, lottery tickets, and similar items.[172]

When the press was inaugurated, Serbia did not have any typographer and all qualified personnel had to be brought from Vienna and Budapest. After five years of operation, in 1836, native typographers began to be trained. According to the press manager, Cvetko Rajović, on February 14/26 of that year, there were twenty-one students on the staff, eleven of whom were being trained as typesetters and ten as printers.[173]

The press operated in Belgrade only for two years. After that it was transferred to Kragujevac. It operated there until June of 1835 when the printing press was returned to Belgrade where it remained.[174] It is not known why the press was moved.

Despite the fact that Serbia had its own government printing press, favorable conditions for a rich publishing activity did not exist because the number of literate people was small; moreover, some of them did not want to purchase published works and thus support the work of this establishment. Such an attitude is not surprising if we keep in mind that Serbia did not have a cultural tradition and that her education was still in its infancy. For example, in Serbia, which in 1834 had around 670,000 inhabitants, there were between two and three thousand literate people, barely half of whom could read without difficulty and who showed interest in published works.[175] The book publishers could count on, at the most, one thousand subscribers who were the entire reading public of Serbia at that time, consisting mainly of bureaucrats (50%) and ecclesiastics (23%), while the rest of the readers were from among the merchants, artisans, teachers, and peasants.[176] The largest city and cultural center of that time was Belgrade with a population of around 7,000; the second largest city was the capital Kragujevac, with around 2,200 inhabitants. Šabac, Požarevac, Smederevo, and Jagodina each had just over 2,000 people, while all the rest of the towns were considerably smaller.[177]

Under such conditions, every publishing activity was involved in serious financial difficulties if the state or some individual did not take the expenses of printing upon themselves. During the first reign of Prince

Miloš it was mainly the state that supported the printing house and financed its publishing activity.

In spite of the difficulties facing the publishing house, its publishing activity before 1839 was rather fruitful. In the relatively short period of only seven years, it published about one hundred books in the Serbian language; seventeen of these were published in Kragujevac.[178] About thirty books were published in foreign languages, notably German, Bulgarian, Greek, and old Hebrew.[179] One newspaper (*Novine Srbske* - Serbian News) was published and one calendar (*Mesecoslov* - Monthly Guide) was published from 1836 to 1939. In addition, four journals were also published: *Zabavnik* - Literary Journal (1833-1836), *Beogradska lira* - Belgrade Lyre (1833-1835), *Uranija* - Urania (1837-1838), and *Golubica* - Hen Pigeon (1839).[180]

The Serbian printing house did not have any plan concerning the publication of books. Various kinds were published from religious through popular to school textbooks. Yet, a free press did not exist because censorship was introduced almost as soon as the printing house began operation. As early as December 22, 1832/January 3, 1833, the Prince's chancery issued a decree on censoring books published in Serbia. The decree stated that no books could be published which wrote against God, Christianity, the Serbian government or any of its members, or foreign governments and their officials. Additionally, any book which disgraced or attacked any person and any book written in V.S. Karadžić's new orthography could not be published. Special attention was paid to this matter of orthography and it was emphasized that Serbian writers had to use their knowledge and talent to write new works which would help foster the development of education and culture, rather than waste their time in quarrels about orthography. "None of the other nations' orthographies, not French, English, or German, are more logical than Slavic orthography, and in spite of that their writers write all their books in them, and every branch of science blossoms in those countries."[181]

The first issue of the first newspaper in Serbia was published in March of 1832 under the name *Novine Srbske* (Serbian News) and it had only one page.[182] It was the only issue published at that time and the nation had to wait two more years for the regular publication of the *Serbian News*, which began in Kragujevac on January 5/17, 1834; this date may be considered the beginning of Serbian journalism.[183] The paper's first editor was Dimitrije Davidović, Prince Miloš's secretary, who had experience in the journalistic profession because he had published a newspaper of the same name in Vienna from 1813 until 1822.[184]

Like many things in Serbia at that time, the *Serbian News* was edited on the model of its Austro-Hungarian counterparts. The Vienna newspapers *Österreichischer Beobachter* and *Wiener Zeitung* were the models Davidović used for his editorial work on the *Serbian News*.[185] It was published weekly and featured such articles as, for example, political news from Serbia and abroad, including African, Asian, and the trans-Atlantic countries, the Prince's and governmental decrees, literary news, and anything else that could please or educate the population. Since the *Serbian News* did not have its own reporters and editor Davidović was not allowed to publish his commentaries, it used mainly translations from the foreign press, especially the Austrian press.

The publication of the *Serbian News* was greeted with acclaim, and it was one more success for the young Serbian state. The French diplomat Count Charles de Bois-le-Comte wrote in his reports from Serbia in 1834 that the *Serbian News* had 600 subscribers and noted that if the Austrian government had allowed its distribution in Austria, that number would have been doubled.[186]

It is difficult to believe there were so many subscribers during the first year of the newspaper's publication because in 1836 there were 300 subscribers, and in 1837 only 150; of these 100 were in Belgrade and 50 in other parts of Serbia.[187] Before 1837, the *Serbian News* was sold only in Serbia but after 1837 it was sold in Austria, too, although the Austrian government by various means disrupted and often prohibited its distribution.[188]

With the aim of increasing the number of newspaper readers and so decrease the expenses of its publication, in the middle of 1837 Prince Miloš issued a decree by which all officials, schools, monasteries, and coffee-houses were required to subscribe to the *Serbian News*. In addition, all fathers whose children had graduated from elementary school were advised to buy this newspaper so that their sons would have an opportunity to practice their reading and improve themselves. The last paragraph of this decree read:

> By reading the newspaper, the Serbian people will
> see what other people are doing and what is
> happening in the world. Thus they will be not
> only enriching their minds with current events but
> also acquiring for their benefit all the good and

> useful things that have been happening in the world, especially in their fatherland. In this way the newspaper will be a useful and instructive history.[189]

Dimitrije Davidović, first editor of the *Serbian News*, did not want this newspaper to be simply a means for the transmission of other people's opinions; he also desired the paper to express his own positions and views. But, when he tried to analyze the news instead of simply reporting it, he lost his editorial position; Prince Miloš did not wish his newspaper to attack any state or open a way for the penetration of advanced West European ideas. In order to make the *Serbian News* a government news-paper and to have complete control over it, on March 24/April 5, 1834, only two months after the beginning of its regular publication, he introduced censorship. This was the beginning of newspaper censorship in Serbia. Lazar Teodorović, Minister of Justice and Education, was appointed the first censor.[190] In a letter Prince Miloš ordered censor Teodorović to take special care of the following: (1) that the *Serbian News* does not carry any commentaries by native journalists about the policies of foreign states and that "free-thinking" does not creep into it, (2) that the *News* does not print anything that could offend foreign states, (3) that it may write about foreign states only what the foreign press writes about them, and (4) that in the *News* nothing will be written that would be contrary to domestic policy. This letter had the "power of an official act and it may be considered the first decree of press censorship in Serbia."[191]

Despite the fact that the *Serbian News* was the paper of the regime and full of defects, it still contributed greatly to Serbian educational and cultural development. It gradually opened the door to the world for the Serbian people and brought them into the maelstrom of international political events; it also partly acquainted them with the world's most important cultural achievements.

Before the liberation of 1830, Serbia had virtually no cultural institutions worthy of attention. Only after the liberation did they begin slowly to be created, but even then only in small numbers because there were not enough educated people to support their opening and operation. Besides, their work required large material resources which were hard to get from either the communes or the state since both levels of government were faced with big financial difficulties and showed only lukewarm interest in supporting such non-essential institutions. Everything that was done in that field was mainly the result of the initiative and investment of individuals, and the first cultural institutions worthy of notice were opened in Belgrade and Kragujevac, the most important cultural centers of Serbia at that time.

Serbia got her first bookstore in 1827; it was opened in Belgrade by Gligorije Vozarović, a Serb born in Zemun. In his bookstore he kept books in Serbian, German, and French, and newspapers in Serbian and German.[192] After the liberation, this bookstore was made into the first literary center in Serbia and was the only place where books could be borrowed. The most educated citizens of Belgrade, V.S. Karadžić, Dimitrije Davidović, Dimitrije Tirol, Lazar Arsenijević-Batalaka, to mention only a few, visited it and so did well-known merchants who dropped in almost every day to learn the latest news.[193] As a matter of fact, it was a literary meeting place of some kind, a forerunner of later cultural institutions. Therefore, it is not surprising that in this bookstore on February 15/27, 1832, the first public library in Serbia was opened under the name *Biblioteka varoši Beogradske* (The Library of the City of Belgrade), which had about 800 books at the time of its opening.[194] This number was gradually increased, mostly by donations of books sent by the Serbs of Vojvodina. It should be noted that questions concerning the Library of the City of Belgrade are not yet completely illuminated. For example, Gavrilo Kovijanić, in a comprehensive study, argues that this library existed as a part of the state publishing house from 1831 to 1838 as the only library in Belgrade and since it was nothing more than collection of books, "it is unfounded to attribute to it functions of a public and people's library, which it was not."[195]

In addition to the Library of the City of Belgrade, during the first rule of Prince Miloš there were still several smaller libraries which served the needs of other places and districts. Such a library was mentioned in Kragujevac in 1837, but unfortunately nothing more detailed about them is known.[196] There were also several private libraries of which Prince Miloš's library and the library of Josif Šlezinger (Joseph Schlesinger), military band-master, were the best known. Otto D. Pirch left a report about Miloš's library. It, he writes, mainly consisted of books "of juridical and political-economic content."[197] Schlesinger had only musical works in his library, and it was the first musical library in Serbia.[198]

The theatrical life also existed. Already in 1825 an amateur theatrical group under the leadership of teacher Djordje Jevdjenijević was formed in Kragujevac and it gave performances throughout Serbia.[199] Joakim Vujić's theater, which played in Kragujevac from 1835 to 1836, was the only theater in Serbia before 1839.[200] Its actors were amateurs, mainly students and bureaucrats. The performances of this theater were attended by a limited number of viewers: Prince Miloš with his family, his relatives, state officials, and richer merchants. It cannot be said that it played any large role in the cultural development of the state, but the memory of it contributed a great deal to the establishment of a theater in Belgrade in 1841.

In earlier Serbian and even later Yugoslav historiography, the predominant opinion was, with some exceptions, that Prince Miloš, with his autocratic rule, restrained the educational and cultural development of Serbia. On the contrary, on the basis of the material presented here it can be seen that during his reign much was done in that direction. If it is kept in mind that he ruled in autonomous Serbia for only slightly more than eight years, that the country was devastated by wars, that the Serbian people had to pay an annual tribute to the sultan, that Serbia had only a handful of educated and semi-educated men, that city life was in its infancy, that Serbia did not have an educational tradition, and that she was completely dependent on educated people from outside her boundaries, then the results of Miloš's educational and cultural policy is not only satisfactory but astonishing. Everyone who deeply thinks about it may rightly ask the following question: How could all that be achieved in only eight years in a state which began from nothing?

Although he was a dictator of a sort and a man without any formal education, Prince Miloš deserves special recognition. In a relatively short time he made a large advance in the educational and cultural policy of Serbia, creating a solid base for its further development. True, in his time Serbia did not develop her own natively-educated class but that is because there were almost no conditions favorable to its creation, from the general cultural atmosphere to the programs and methods of instruction of the existing schools. Yet, the first seeds were sown and for their fruit Serbia had only to wait for a certain time.

CHAPTER II

ELEMENTARY AND SECONDARY SCHOOLS

*Education is not preparation for life;
education is life itself.*

John Dewey

1.

To build an internal organization in Serbia according to the model of the West European states, the Constitutionalists needed a strong bureaucratic apparatus. Their intention was not only to take over all the important state positions, but also to assume complete responsibility for the welfare of the people who, according to the Constitutionalists' opinion, were not yet "politically ripe and capable of ruling themselves." "The people are pupils and the government is their tutor, and it ought to take care of them," said Jeremije Stanojević, a member of the *Soviet*, in an address to that body.[1]

With the aim of creating a completely dependable and effective bureaucratic apparatus, the Constitutionalists sought to control the judiciary, but they also placed emphasis on cultural and educational improvement. Special attention was paid to the secondary schools and to the lyceum, the highest school in Serbia at that time, because they were the institutions which prepared future members of the bureaucracy. The Ministry of Justice and Education (*Popečiteljstvo pravosudija i prosvešćenija*), which was established at the end of Prince Miloš's reign, had the principal task of helping the courts and schools achieve rapid and effective development. The fact that in the entire internal administration of Serbia only these two institutions had a separate ministry also confirms how much attention was paid to them. All other branches of the internal administration were under the Ministry of Internal Affairs. (*Popečiteljstvo vnutrenjih djela*).[2]

After they came into power, the Constitutionalists began to carry out numerous reforms in schools to make them capable of educating better personnel who were badly needed. As will be seen in the remainder of this chapter, a great number of the laws and decrees instituted at that time favorably affected the development of schools and improved the teaching, but some of them had the opposite effect.

The government did not pay special attention to elementary schools even though the successful development of secondary and higher education depended mainly on their quality. Through the Ministry of Education only the state retained control of the instructive supervisory aspect of primary education; the communes were left to bear the burden of financing old schools and opening new ones. As early as September 12/24, 1839, a decree was issued according to which the communes were obliged to support elementary schools from their own revenues. This action was confirmed by a law on "Organization of Public School Education" of September 23/October 5, 1844, but this new law added that the communes had to observe their obligations toward elementary schools "as long as a main established fund would not be able to come to the help of the communes."[3] This referred to a regulation issued on January 13/25, 1841, concerning the establishment of a school fund entitled "Decree on the Formation of a Main School Fund." This fund was to be supported by contributions from all the Serbian people, "either in ready cash, or natural products ... or in bonds." The income of this fund and interest on it were to be used for "the purpose of school support and general public education."[4] The government used various means to increase the school fund substantially and rapidly. For example, everyone who gave a contribution of 100 talers received a letter of thanks from the Ministry of Education and those who contributed 200 talers or more became honorary members of the "Deputation" (*Deputacija* - the management of the school fund). In addition, contributors' names were published in the *Serbian News*, were read in churches on the more important religious holidays, and so on.[5] Yet, all of these inducements failed to achieve the desired results because most Serbians did not appreciate the significance of schools, so their contributions were neither large nor frequent. For instance, almost a year after the School Fund was established, on December 30, 1841/January 11, 1842, the mayor of the Kragujevac district informed the Ministry of Education that in his district "nobody had either registered to give or had given anything to the School fund."[6] This attitude of the Serbian population toward school support was criticized by the *Serbian News* at the same time it pointed out the importance of schools and urged the population to help their development.

> Thus, he on whom the progress of the Serbian
> nationality fairly well depends [it wrote] should
> spare no effort and should do as much as he can,
> and much will be done. And so, with a common
> effort we shall be able to reach that level which
> many happy states reached a long time ago. It

should be our chief task, for when we achieve this
everything else will follow by itself.[7]

Since the attitude of a large number of people toward the School
Fund was more or less passive, the fund grew slowly and it was impossible
to support elementary schools from that fund alone.[8] For that reason, the
communes continued to bear the main financial burden. In order to satisfy
their schools' financial needs, they were forced to introduce various
surtaxes. Prosperous communes could cope with these difficulties but poor
ones were hardly able to do so. They could not open needed new schools
and occasionally they were forced to close some of the existing ones.[9] Petar
Radovanović and Milovan Spasić, the chief directors of all elementary
schools, suggested to higher authorities that they introduce a special surtax
from which the elementary school teachers could be paid.[10] Because of the
tension in the state due to the unsettled political conditions, the government
refused to introduce such an obligatory surtax until 1855. Then, on
December 14/25, a decree was issued by which all prior surtaxes for the
support of elementary schools were abolished and a uniform surtax of two
cvancigs [11] per year was introduced. This surtax had to be paid at the same
time that the tribute for the sultan was collected, and besides regular tax-
payers, "officials, pensioners, priests, teachers, village mayors, and all
other inhabitants of the fatherland who were permanent residents and had
regular means of support" were obliged to pay it.[12] The decree pointed out
that the surtax would be used to support elementary school teachers, "while
any surplus beyond the teachers' salaries had to be given to the Deputation
[management] of the Main School Fund, which was obliged to give a
certain sum to the agricultural school in Topčider [a part of Belgrade]
while the rest had to be deposited in the Fund as a basis for its increase."[13]
The school surtax hurt mostly the poor stratum of the population, of which
teachers were a part; ironically, they were obliged to pay the surtax to the
School Fund, even though that fund was used to pay their annual salaries.

With the decree introducing the school surtax, a significant step
toward a solution to the problem of the elementary school teachers' salaries
was made. The School Fund began to grow rapidly and after ten months, it
could almost completely support the elementary school teachers and thus
relieve communes of their heavy financial burdens. The responsibilities of
the School Fund were determined by a special decree entitled "The
Establishment of the Main School Fund," issued on September 15/27, 1856.
It pointed out that from the regular and additional incomes of the School

Fund "all the elementary school teachers of our fatherland and the Economic [agricultural] school in Topčider were to be supported, as well as a teacher-training school which is to be founded and in which elementary school teachers will be educated and trained."[14] This decree was a supplement to the decree of December 14/26, 1855. By it the list of persons who were obliged to pay the school surtax was enlarged to include the following groups: "bachelors who paid the tribute, Gypsies of both religions [probably the Christian Orthodox and the Moslem], *Šošoi* [feeble-minded persons] who were exempted from the tribute, beginning civil-service employees, and foreigners whose children attended schools."[15] In addition to the surtax, the School Fund was enriched by donations and by interest from a certain sum of money which was lent. In the beginning, the interest on it was 8 percent and later, 6 percent per year.[16]

Only the teachers of the regular elementary schools were paid from the Main School Fund. These were the schools in communes which had at least 400 households. Communes and villages with a smaller population could establish their own schools, but such schools were not considered regular ones and their teachers were paid by the communes, villages, and individuals who took it upon themselves "to build the schools and to supply them with all needs."[17] Some sources indicate that during the Constitutionalist period, in addition to communal and private schools, a few state schools existed as well, but it seems that their number was not large.[18]

Some years prior to the general surtax, however, a law governing public schools, which was promulgated on September 23/October 5, 1844, prescribed that the communes, besides supporting teachers, were obliged to build new school buildings, take care of old ones, provide inventory, and supply everything that was needed for the regular conduct of instruction. It was about that time that communes first received government instructions as to where to erect new schools, what building materials to use, and how to arrange class-rooms. The government directed that new schools be erected near churches, or on the crossroads which linked several villages. In addition, they were to be built in clean and healthy places, and to be as large and comfortable as possible.[19] One more decree with similar instructions was issued at the end of the Constitutionalists' reign on August 22/September 3, 1857.[20]

Although confronted with many other expenditures, the communes invested a great deal in order to open new schools, and the number of schools grew fairly rapidly during the Constitutionalist period. At the end of Prince Miloš's first reign, Serbia had 84 elementary schools with 2,316 pupils. As early as the middle of 1842, according to the report of Timotije Milašinović, director of elementary schools, she had 117 elementary schools. Five of these schools had three teachers each, eleven had two, and 101 had only one teacher. The number of pupils was 3,388, but the pupils of the Belgrade district were not taken into account.[21] According to official information, the number of elementary schools reached 232, and the number of pupils 6,830 in the school year 1846-47.[22] Among these schools there were three girls' schools (in Belgrade, Milanovac, and Ćuprija) and two Greek private schools in Belgrade.[23] A year before the Constitutionalists' downfall, the school year 1856-57, Serbia had 340 elementary schools with 11,237 pupils.[24] The data presented shows that during the Constitutionalist period the number of elementary schools was increased by 256 and the number of pupils by 8,321. It was a remarkable increase, especially since the newly opened schools were much better built and furnished, and since the communes and individuals had paid almost all expenses of their operation until the introduction of the obligatory school surtax at the end of 1855.

Despite the fact that improvement of the elementary school system was not a significant part of the Constitutionalists' educational policy, a great deal was done in that direction.

In order to strengthen its instructive supervisory control, the government divided Serbia into two school zones as early as September 23/October 5, 1839: the eastern zone extended from Belgrade to the Timok River, and the western one from Belgrade going toward the Drina River. Besides the existing director of elementary schools, Petar Radovanović, who afterward supervised the eastern zone, Gligorije Zorić was appointed the second director and he took control over the western zone.[25] The directors of the school zones were officially called "the chief superintendents of elementary schools." They worked in their zones independent of each other and at the end of a school year, they submitted reports on the condition of the schools, personnel reports, the knowledge gained by pupils, etc., to the Ministry of Education. They were also obliged to enclose lists of schools and teachers with the reports.[26] In order to increase control over schools, so-called "local superintendents" were appointed. The candidates were selected by the communes, which submitted their names to the school director of their district and he sent their list to the Ministry of Education for approval. However, neither laws nor decrees were issued to prescribe relations among communes, local superintendents, teachers, directors, police, and the Ministry of Education. Sometimes this deficiency caused misunderstandings among them and reduced the effectiveness of their activities.[27]

To promulgate a law for all existing schools in Serbia and to improve education were the most important tasks of the Constitutionalists' educational policy. The existing school decrees, the "Specification of Subjects" and the "Instruction to the Teachers" of August 11/23, 1838, were replaced on September 23/October 5, 1844, by a new law for elementary schools, business schools, the gymnasium and the lyceum, under the title "The Organization of Public School Education."[28] Its author was Jovan Sterija Popović, a well-known writer and cultural figure from Vojvodina who was then Chief of Personnel in the Ministry of Education in Serbia. If the "Constitution of Public Schools" of 1833, which probably never went into effect, is not taken into consideration, then "The Organization of Public School Education" may be considered the first general law for all schools in Serbia. There is no doubt that at the time it was the most important school law ever promulgated in Serbia because by it, a complete organization of all schools, from elementary to the highest, was introduced in Serbia for the first time. Later, it was supplemented and improved according to the needs of the state.

One section of the "Organization," under the subtitle *O učilištima osnovnim* (About Elementary Schools), gave detailed instructions concerning the operation of these schools. The beginning of this section emphasized that in time it would be necessary to open elementary schools throughout Serbia in which "those sons of the fatherland who would not otherwise have an opportunity to continue to study and to educate themselves, could learn enough so that in time they could be good Christians, honest men, and useful citizens."[29] Letters were sent to all district mayors which urged them to convince people of the need and usefulness of those schools.

This law also distinguished between village and town schools. It prescribed that village elementary schools were to have three grades with only one teacher for each school, and that town schools were to have four grades with two or three teachers for each school. If, for example, an elementary school of four grades had two teachers, each of them taught two grades. If, on the other hand, it had three teachers then two of them were to teach the first two and the third one the second two grades.[30] In addition, the "Organization of Public School Education" prescribed the subjects which were to be taught in elementary schools. The town schools taught the same subjects during the first three years as were taught in the village schools, but for the fourth grade the town schools taught the following subjects: Serbian grammar, Serbian history, stylistics (composition), mathematics, geography, and catechism with singing.[31]

In order to help teachers apply the section of the "Organization of Public School Education" which was concerned with elementary schools, on October 24/November 5, 1844, the Ministry of Education issued "Instructions for Elementary School Teachers" which were also written by Jovan S. Popović.[32]

The "Organization" and the "Instructions" of 1844 brought many novelties into Serbia's elementary schools. Besides the subjects which had to be taught up to that time, several new subjects were introduced: geography, Serbian grammar, stylistics, practical economy, Serbian history, and nature study, all under the name *Obšta znanja svakom Srbinu nužna* (General Knowledge Which Every Serb Needs). Considerable attention was paid to national history, and in the "Instructions" teachers were advised how to approach and teach it. "The history of the fatherland," the Instructions read, "is the center around which our love and feelings rotate. Here teachers will have ample opportunity to tell the children about the fate which befell our country, what kings, tsars, and despots we had, and in so doing to devote great attention to inspiring children with feelings and love for their fatherland."[33] The "Organization of Public School Education" did not prescribe the teaching of German and it was abolished in all elementary schools, except in the fourth grade of the Belgrade elementary school.[34]

Although the "Organization of Public School Education" in many ways was too far ahead of its time, still with its promulgation a significant step in the improvement of education in Serbia was made.

Since the curriculum for elementary schools prescribed by the "Organization" of 1844 was not in accordance with the educational capabilities of Serbia at that time, it was replaced with a new curriculum which was issued on July 30/August 11, 1850, under the title "The Distribution of Subjects which are Taught in Elementary Schools According to Grades and to Semesters." This curriculum, written in accordance with existing textbooks, was much smaller in size and therefore more acceptable than the curriculum of 1844. It was used for a full two decades.[35]

Regardless of how good they might be, school programs remain more or less a dead issue if there is no qualified and capable staff to carry them out effectively. Serbia did not yet have such a teaching cadre, and during the Constitutionalist period there was little effort made to create one. And yet, some progress was made toward opening a school exclusively to train elementary school teachers. The chief advocate of such a school was Milovan Spasić who after 1845, was the director of elementary schools in the western school zone. On his suggestion, the Educational Committee, of which he was a member, submitted an application to the Ministry of Education on December 29, 1846/January 10, 1847, asking for the opening of a teacher-training school in the interior of Serbia. The applicants stated they were convinced that Serbia would, "as had every well-organized state, make a big step toward the improvement of public education and for future generations, if she would establish a suitably organized and well-furnished institution for the education of teachers."[36] The Ministry of Education rejected this application in March, 1847, with the explanation that instruction in such a school would be similar to instruction in the gymnasium; consequently, Serbia would not benefit much by the opening of such a school.[37] This negative answer is surprising because it is known that it was written by Jovan S. Popović,the greatest reformer of schools in Serbia during the Constitutionalist period, and it came at a time when even the *Serbian News* had pointed out the need for a teacher-training school.[38] The government, too, in the "Establishment of the Main School Fund" of September 15/27, 1856, called for the opening of a "teacher-training school in which elementary school teachers would be educated and trained."[39] In spite of all these suggestions and even an official decision that a teacher-training school be opened, it was not inaugurated until 1870. Milovan Spasić points out that Metropolitan Petar Jovanović was the chief opponent to a teacher-training school because he was afraid that such a school would compete with the seminary whose graduates worked as teachers before receiving their parishes. "Will my seminarians," he used to ask, "when they graduate from the seminary, tend cattle until they receive their parishes?!"[40]

Various measures were used to create a qualified teachers' cadre. As early as 1846, special courses for teachers were held during school vacations. Usually teachers were instructed in school laws and decrees and teaching methods.[41] Although these courses were useful, they were not held for long because the government did not approve a budget for their further operation. In addition to those courses, the Ministry of Education instructed teachers by written communications which had the weight of decrees not only how to teach certain subjects, but also how to behave towards their pupils, how to dress themselves, how to communicate with their pupils' parents, etc.[42]

Since there were individuals among teachers who were completely incapable of performing their duty, the government took the necessary measures to remove them from teaching positions. Thus, for example, on August 7/19, 1846, the Ministry of Education informed Milovan Spasić that if he, as a director of elementary schools, thought that some teachers were incapable of performing their duties, he should send them to the Educational Committee which would test their knowledge by an examination. If the Educational Committee found that the director's opinion had been correct, those teachers would be fired from their positions.[43] The Educational Committee held examinations for the teachers who, according to the main elementary school directors, Petar Radovanović and Milovan Spasić, were incapable. But such examinations were easy, and teachers who showed the most elementary knowledge in reading, writing, and mathematics were allowed to resume their teaching positions. The chief, and, it may be said, the only reason for easy examinations was the continuing shortage of teachers; it was better to have any kind of teacher than to have none at all. Concerning the testing of incapable teachers, it is interesting to note a report of the Educational Committee to the Ministry of Education of August 31/September 12, 1846, which reads that the Committee, on Milovan Spasić's request, examined Milan Lukić, a teacher from Ribnik, and came to the conclusion "that the person examined does not have any capacity to be a teacher, but since he knows how to read and write fairly well, he could be used as a teacher in case of need."[44]

A diploma certifying graduation from school was not always a guarantee that its holder was indeed qualified to perform the task for which the diploma certified him, and some educated Serbs of the 1840s were aware of it. With the aim of improving the teachers' cadre, they suggested, following the promulgation of the "Organization of Public School Education," "that all of those who want to become teachers had to undergo a special examination."[45] Some examinations were to be held before a specially formed commission. Every candidate who passed that examination would receive a certificate, a so-called "Certificate of Proficiency," and only after that could he serve as a teacher.[46] The testing of a teacher's proficiency was not officially introduced until the Ministry of Education issued a decree entitled "The Organization of Elementary Schools in the Principality of Serbia" on August 22/September 3, 1857.[47] This decree caused widespread protest. Among the loudest protesters was, again, Metropolitan Petar Jovanović, who pointed out that this decree denied the value of the seminary. He intervened at the Ministry of Education to have this decree abolished or to have the seminary graduates exempted from the examination on the grounds that they already had certificates verifying their completed education. However, all his attempts were futile. The *Soviet* could not justify the exemption of seminarians because they, like many others, simply were not qualified to be teachers.[48]

In connection with this decree, an anonymous reporter from Belgrade wrote in an article published in *Srbski dnevnik* (*The Serbian Journal*) on June 29/July 10, 1858:

> I am for the law which prescribes examination, but it is not difficult for me to see that all strictness of formality is pouring out on poor teacher when in other occupations which are more important and much better paid, the door is wide open. Everyone who is looking for public service either as a teacher, or as a priest, or as a clerk should be subjected to an examination. Without it we shall never be without weeds.[49]

In spite of all attempts to see that elementary schools in Serbia got fairly capable teachers, little was achieved during the Constitutionalist period. There were many reasons for that but, of course, poor wages for teachers was one of the most important. Only those who could not find better jobs entered the teaching profession, and most often only temporarily: when they found better and better paying jobs, they usually left their teaching positions. There were some individuals who were aware that with such poor wages for teachers, Serbia could not get a better qualified cadre, and without such a cadre it was almost impossible to elevate elementary education to a higher level. They tried by various means not only to improve the teachers' material well-being, which was most important, but also to improve their treatment in society as well.

> Thus, what kind of teachers can we have [*Novine Čitališta Beogradskog* (*The Belgrade Reading Club News*) wrote] when we pay a teacher less than 50 talers per year? A common servant makes more, including food which his master gives to him, and a teacher should be an educated and an honest man; one entrusts to him that which is

dearest to him, his children and their happiness.[50]

In response to suggestions from the main elementary school directors, the press, and some individuals, the Ministry of Education tried certain measures to improve the teachers' condition and by that to attract better people to the teaching profession. However, these measures were ineffective and brought only temporary relief to the teachers' material condition. Most of them hardly made ends meet, and after their death their families were left in poverty without subsistence because teachers' pensions were not introduced in Serbia until 1871.[51] Sometimes the communes, which financed elementary schools, gave certain material help to a deceased teacher's family, but only richer communes could do that.

> The Belgrade commune [*The Belgrade Reading Club News* wrote in 1847] gave from its budget 80 talers to the family of deceased teacher Kosta Jovanović, who was in the teaching profession more than twenty years and who left his wife and children in poverty. With this gift, the Belgrade commune showed how much it respects the education of its children.[52]

In the first general school law of 1844, it was written that "only those who successfully graduated from the Seminary would be hired as elementary school teachers," and "later, also those can be teachers who have completed the gymnasium in accordance with the new curriculum, and who have studied pedagogy and teaching methods."[53] However, this law could not be completely applied because with the establishment of numerous new schools, the need for teachers grew rapidly and the two schools could not meet the demand with their graduates. Therefore, it was not rare that some communes were forced to hire as teachers those Seminary and gymnasium students who did not complete their education, and often even individuals who completed only elementary school.

Despite the many difficulties which confronted them, the Constitutionalists made a significant success of replacing teachers from Vojvodina with native ones who were in general better qualified than the teachers from Vojvodina. The largest number of teachers came from the Seminary, and it may be considered to be the semi-teacher training school of Serbia at that time. A report published in *The Belgrade Reading Club News* in 1847 shows the structure of the teachers' cadre in the middle of the Constitutionalist period. In the school year 1845-46, among 210 elementary school teachers, 61 were seminary graduates, 24 were seminary students, 6 were gymnasium graduates, 13 had graduated from teacher training schools in Austria, 14 were lower-gymnasium graduates, and 84 had only elementary school education.[54]

During the training of the teachers' cadre both in the Seminary and the gymnasium, no distinction was made between future village and town teachers. Even if such a distinction had been tried, it would have been extremely difficult to carry out. Firstly, most often students did not know until their last grade whether they wished to devote themselves to the teaching profession or not. Secondly, if they had determined to enter the teaching profession in the first year of their education, they did not know whether, upon graduation, they would get a teaching position in a village or in a town school. Thirdly, and most importantly, the material conditions of schools and the absence of a capable teachers' cadre made it impossible for them to introduce specialization of any kind. For that reason, the daily press criticized the Constitutionalists' elementary school educational policy.

> We believe [the *Serbian News* wrote] that it is wrong to organize town and village schools according to the same pattern and, therefore, it is also wrong to train village and city teachers according to the same pattern. Town schools, if we are not mistaken, should give us young men who will continue their higher education and who will be merchants and craftsmen. Village schools, on the other hand, should give us good village mayors and good landholders.[55]

In addition, the *Serbian News* pointed out that village schools had to have teachers who came from village cultures because those teachers would understand the peasant way of life, their conditions, and their needs. "Thus, we would need teachers," it emphasized, "who came from our simple habitats, and to whom city comfort is unknown."[56]

Except for an insignificant number, the capability of teachers was not satisfactory. Even the Seminary graduates, from whom much was expected, showed themselves to be incapable and disinterested in teaching. The chief directors of elementary schools often wrote to the Ministry of

Education about the incapability of the teaching seminarians. Thus, for example, Petar Radovanović in his report of June 24/July 6, 1844, wrote that seminarians achieved very poor results with their pupils, especially in mathematics. "And the cause is," he pointed out, "that these men neither know mathematics themselves, nor have they learned it well."[57] In the same report, Radovanović wrote that besides their poor knowledge, the teacher-seminarians did not show "that they had been diligent and eager, but that they had performed their duty only casually and as they pleased." The principal reason for their poor teaching, Radovanović saw, was that "a seminarian, though he might be the best, considers his teaching position as a room through which he has to pass in order to enter the room where his real profession [the priesthood] will be waiting for him after one, two or three years."[58]

Milovan Spasić, the second Chief Director of elementary schools, had a similar opinion. He wrote that with teacher-seminarians, "the schools gained hardly anything; first, because they were not trained to be teachers, and second, because they considered the teaching profession as a bridge across which, when the opportunity occurred, they would come to the rank of priest."[59]

Of the many difficulties which confronted elementary schools during the Constitutionalist period, it is necessary to mention two more problems which interrupted the normal process of teaching and had negative consequences on pupils' education. These were a certain anarchy surrounding the enrollment of children in school, and their frequent absence from school or the complete abandonment of their schooling. For example, in his report to the Ministry of Education of July 10/22, 1844, Petar Radovanović wrote that parents used to bring their children in to school whenever they wished, sometimes just before final examinations. If a teacher refused to enroll them, parents protested, quarreled with him, and sometimes cursed him. The parents usually said to a teacher: "I pay you and you must enroll my child in school when I want it; the school is mine, not yours."[60] In order to avoid those occurrences, Radovanović suggested to the Ministry of Education that it determine by decree certain times when children could be enrolled. This suggestion was accepted and, on October 24/November 5 of the same year, the "Instruction for Elementary School Teachers" prescribed that children not younger than six years of age had to be enrolled in school in the period between September 1 and 20 (O.S.) "so that disorder in teaching would not be caused."[61] A teacher was allowed to accept a child after that registration period, but in that case he was obliged to tutor him privately "until [that child] caught up with the regular students in grade subjects, and after that he had to be joined with them."[62] In spite of laws and decrees which presented the age and the period during which children could be enrolled in school, violations often occurred and negatively affected the effective execution of the curriculum and thus the children's education.

Absence from school was a frequent occurrence, especially in villages during the agricultural work seasons in the spring and in the fall when parents took their children out of school to help work the land. But it was not rare that a large number of children did not attend school during the winter months because of cold weather, long distances from children's homes to schools, impassable roads, and the like.[63] In his report to the Ministry of Education of July 21/August 2, 1850, Milovan Spasić wrote:

> This difficulty is greater in the summer than in the winter. In many places during my visits to schools I would not have found any pupils at all if the teacher had not asked their parents to send them to school so he would not be alone when I came. There were some places where I did not find any pupils in schools when I visited it.[64]

In order to stop this practice and to force parents to send their children regularly to school, the government, as early as 1853, introduced a fine, a so-called *štrof*, of the parents who did not enroll their children in school and for the parents who took their children out of school without any serious reason.[65] Later, the decree of 1857 on "The Organization of Elementary Schools in the Principality of Serbia" specified when parents would have to pay the fines and how much they would be. "For disorderly school conduct and school attendance," this decree stated, "the parents, heads of households, and guardians in general are responsible. And if satisfactory evidence for their excuse is not produced, they will be punished by an official warning, and if they do not respond, they will be obligated to pay a fine of one to three *cvancigs*."[66] However, absence from school could not be eliminated by laws and decrees because in many cases either the fines were not assessed when necessary or parents found a way to avoid paying them. Then, too, it was not rare that parents preferred paying the fines and putting their children to work in the household or the fields rather than send them to school. Similar practices were not just phenomena of the Constitutionalists' regime; to some extent they have occurred, especially in the villages of Serbia, almost to the present day.

In addition to irregular school attendance, it was a general phenomenon, again, especially in the villages, that a rather large number of pupils were enrolled in the first grade, while only a small number of them completed the third or fourth grade. For example, in the village schools, during the three years of curriculum, up to 80 percent of the enrolled pupils left school. In the towns, on the other hand, where elementary education lasted for four years, that percentage was significantly smaller at 30 percent.[67] The causes for this occurrence were various: the poverty of the pupils' parents, the great need for child labor, long distances between the schools and the pupils' homes (sometimes a two or three hour walk), etc.

The well-known Yugoslav historian of Serbian education, Živojin Djordjević, is of the opinion that the causes mentioned above are more or less of secondary importance and that the primary cause for the discontinuation of education lay in the instruction itself which not only did not attract children but actually repelled them. "Elementary school, with its instruction of primary literacy," writes Djordjević, "was more a torture-chamber than an educational institution for children."[68] A smaller number of town children left school at the beginning of their education because townsmen forced their children to endure the rigors of education whereas peasants did not do that. For example, peasants took their children out of school as soon as they noticed that they had difficulty learning or could not learn at all.[69]

Despite all efforts to improve the quality of elementary schools and the education of students, little progress was made during the Constitutionalist period. Only a very small number of elementary school graduates could "comprehensively read any Serbian book presented to them, put on paper their thoughts about daily work, or write in letters pleasing to the eyes."[70] Svetozar Marković, the first Serbian socialist, who graduated from such a school at the end of the Constitutionalists' regime, wrote about their poor education.

> When I graduated from the fourth grade [writes Marković] I read very well, I wrote rather poorly and I could understand with great difficulty the letters [handwritings] (according to the "class ranking" I was twelfth in it and there were about

> 50 of us.) In addition, I knew the four mathemati-
> cal operations; I was one of the best mathemati-
> cians in our school; an enormous majority knew
> only how to add and subtract.[71]

As this quotation indicates, Marković's knowledge was poor. We think that no further commentary about the knowledge of many pupils from his and older generations is necessary once we mention that Marković's father was a literate man, a district mayor, and that Svetozar learned how to read and write at home.

In order to stimulate pupils in their schoolwork, the educational administration awarded books to the best of them. However, this measure of stimulation did not bring the desired results because the poor quality of elementary school education was not the fault of the pupil alone but the result of numerous problems which schools had to face.[72]

In the first years of the Constitutionalist period, consideration was given to opening girls' schools. The Ministry of Education took the first step in that direction on November 16/28, 1840, by suggesting to the *Soviet* a program to establish girls' schools in Belgrade, Šabac, Kragujevac, and Smederevo. The *Soviet*, as was its practice, informed Prince Michael Obrenović about it. Michael was for the opening of girls' schools, but he stated in his letter to the *Soviet* of November 23/December 5, 1840, that such a school should first of all be opened in Belgrade so that, after a certain time, on the basis of its operation it could be concluded "whether it is worthwhile to develop this institution in other places."[73] But, for reasons unknown to us, this plan was not realized. Two years later, in 1842, the question of the establishment of a girls' school was again raised, this time by the Lekić sisters, who came to Belgrade from Vojvodina to open a private girls' school. They sent an application to Jovan Žujević, mayor of Belgrade, who approved it in agreement with the Ministry of Education. The Lekić sisters' school began to operate in the first half of the same year, but because of Toma Vučić-Peršić's revolt it discontinued its operation and never again resumed it.[74]

In the next year, 1843, in an article entitled "The Need and Usefulness of Girls' Schools," which was published in the supplement to the *Serbian News*, the so-called *Podunavka*, Jovan S. Popović explained the necessity for opening a girls' school. "The state is obliged," Popović wrote, "to take care of the public education of both male and female children."[75] Since the state did not take any quick action to open such a school, applications and suggestions were sent from all sides during the next two years. For example, Persida Djuričin applied to the Ministry of Education on June 28/July 10, 1844, to establish such a school but her application was rejected on July 15/27 of the same year without any explanation.[76] Petar Radovanović sent a letter to the same Ministry on January 5/17, 1845, and recommended the establishment of a girls' school; he suggested how such a school could be organized and the subjects which should be taught.[77] The Ministry of Education finally answered his letter affirmatively on February 24, 1845 (O.S.), and concluded it by saying: "The Ministry permits the opening of such a school with this stipulation, that it will issue the necessary regulations for such a school at its convenience."[78]

While the government was making preparation for the opening of such a school, newspapers continued to advocate its need. *Podunavka*, for instance, published an article on June 2/14, 1845, under the title "About Education" in which it said:

> He who only educates men and does not concern
> himself over the education of female children
> does well only to one half of mankind, and to the
> other half he does the greatest injustice.[79]

In September of the same year, a girls' school was opened in Paraćin. In numerous works of Serbian historiography, this school is considered the first girls' elementary school in Serbia. True, Paraćin's school was indeed the first girls' school established and financed by a commune, but it "does not yet represent a girls' school, different from a regular school for male children, a school organized according to a special plan and program for females."[80]

Finally, on July 3/15, 1846, after long preparation, the Ministry of Education issued a decree under the title "The Establishment of Girls' Schools." It prescribed that girls' schools consist of three grades, and that instruction in each grade last for two years; thus education for the girls' school lasted for six years. Only girls over five years of age could be admitted. Instruction was conducted for three hours in the morning and two hours in the afternoon during the winter, and three hours in the morning and three in the afternoon during the summer. General subjects were to be taught in the morning and home economics in the afternoon. The section "About the method for teaching the subjects" of that decree prescribed that this school teach the same subjects that were taught in the regular boys' elementary schools as defined by the "Instruction" of October 24/November 5, 1844, but the peculiarity of such a school had to be kept in mind. Therefore, it was recommended that instructresses observe the following rules: (1) to read carefully so that girls could immediately understand the meaning of the text; (2) although Serbian grammar was not prescribed for this school, still in the higher grades "syntax and composition" were to be taught; (3) girls had to learn the most elementary orthographic rules; and (4) only as much mathematics was to learned as was necessary for the management of a household, especially verbal arithmetic[81]

The first girls' elementary school set up according to this decree was opened in Belgrade on October 16/28, 1846. Immediately 134 girls were enrolled; this clearly shows how much parents were interested in the education of their female children.[82] Such a parental attitude is rather surprising when one realizes that Serbia still had a strongly patriarchal way of life and that only about ten years before this school was opened many parents had sharply opposed the education of **any** of their children.

Soon after the opening of this school, similar girls' schools were opened in other large Serbian population centers. In those areas where such schools could not be opened for lack of material support, girls attended elementary schools together with boys. Most of the girls' elementary schools were financed by the communes or by private persons, but in time they were equalized with regular elementary schools and financed from the Main School Fund. It is interesting to mention that the newspapers, whose correspondents were largely gymnasium and lyceum professors, continued to write about the need to open a greater number of girls' schools. With their articles they tried to encourage communes and individuals to establish them, and when such a school was opened somewhere, the newspapers expressed their joy in articles full of gratitude and enthusiasm. Thus, for example, after the opening of a girls' school in Aleksinac in 1850, the *Serbian News* wrote:

> The heart of every real Serb has to melt with joy
> when he sees girls' schools beside so many schools
> for the male children in his fatherland.... Serbian
> girls, the future mothers of young Serbs
> [concludes the writer of the article] should also
> receive enough moral education in school so that
> one day as mothers they will know what they are

and how to raise and educate the future citizens of
the fatherland in a real Serbian spirit and in the
Serbian nationality.[83]

The number of girls' schools grew rather quickly. Ten years after
the opening of the first such school in Belgrade, there were already twenty-
four of them, and at the end of the Constitutionalist period in the school
year 1857-58 that number reached thirty, attended by 894 school girls.[84]

Like regular elementary schools, the girls' schools were confronted
with many problems. Certainly, the absence of a qualified teachers' cadre
was one of the biggest. Because of the lack of native women teachers, the
state was forced to hire the more literate Serb women from Vojvodina.
Since most of them did not have qualifications for the teaching profession,
the Ministry of Education formed a commission composed of gymnasium
and lyceum professors with the task of examining the candidates before
they were hired. In spite of that, Serbia did not get enough qualified
women teachers because of the small number of candidates and her great
need fort hem. The examining commission was forced to pass every
candidate who showed the least elementary teaching ability. They were,
writes M. Spasić, "poor in reading and writing, and real ignoramuses in
mathematics. In home economics, on the other hand, they taught children
well, but they damaged our [Serbian] language, teaching children German
terms in home economics."[85]

The number of private schools in Belgrade gradually grew, and in
the school year 1857-58 there were seven of them: two for male and
female children and five exclusively for female children.[86] The most
important girls' school was "The Educational Institute for Female
Children" (*Vaspitatelno zavedenije za žensku decu*) which was established
by Leopold Spaček with permission of the Ministry of Education granted
on April 27/May 9, 1853.[87] Besides Spaček, the teachers in this schools
were: his wife for home economics and at one time or another Milan
Milićević, Djura Jakšić, Jovan Derok, and other eminent cultural figures.
Spaček's private school had the character of a prestigious girls' school and
it was attended by the children of Belgrade's most respectable families.

The Ministry of Education prescribed the rules for the operation of
this school at the same time that it issued permission for its opening. In
order to inform the public, they were published in the *Serbian News* on
May 14/26, 1853. According to those rules, only girls who were six years
old could be enrolled. In exceptional cases, younger ones could also be

enrolled, but they were treated as part-time, not regular, students of the school. The instruction lasted for five years, and besides home economics, general educational subjects were also taught, among which were German, Serbian grammar, physics, elements of psychology, ethics and esthetics, general history, and mythology. None of these subjects were taught in normal girls' schools. In addition to the regular subjects, those pupils who wished could study French, Italian, modern Greek, singing, piano, and dancing. The study of these subjects was not obligatory and those pupils who decided to take all or some of them had to pay extra fees. It should be indicated that in the rules for Spaček's school, the Ministry of Education emphasized that "literary subjects would regularly be taught in Serbian, but in higher grades one of them would be taught in a foreign language, too." Home economics, according to the same rules, was to be taught in Serbian and German only in the first grade, whereas in all other grades, the women teachers were to speak only in German "and with those [pupils] who study yet another foreign language also in it [or them.]"[88]

Spaček's school, like all the other elementary schools, was under the control of the Chief Director of Elementary Schools. This school was not only important because it was a kind of girls' high school but because it was also a school which produced the first native women teachers in Serbia.

Leopold Spaček's girls' school operated successfully and its results were praised in the daily press. "We have to be pleased with this institution," wrote the *Serbian News*, "which is the only one among private institutions where our fair sex can get well educated and, for our circumstances, quite appropriately educated."[89] Probably encouraged by his success, Spaček also wished to open a boys' private school and applied for permission to the Ministry of Education on March 5/17, 1858. Ordinarily we would not pay any special attention to this application, because it was neither the first nor the last, but Spaček requested that, besides a class for school-age children, he be allowed to open a special class for children from 4 to 6 years of age. As far as we know, his was the first such suggestion in Serbia. In his explanation, he pointed out that in such a class children could, through conversation, "while still very young, learn foreign languages and be prepared in them."[90] However, the Ministry of Education did not understand that it was a revolutionary suggestion in the history of Serbian education and that its acceptance could radically alter the course of elementary education in Serbia. Spaček's application was rejected on May 3/15, 1858, with the explanation that Belgrade had enough public schools for male children and "there is no need to open a private one for them."[91]

During the Constitutionalist period, Serbia took the first steps toward educating adults in the towns, who were mostly illiterate. The initiator of this idea was Atanasije Nikolić, chief of the Department of Police and Economy in the Ministry of Internal Affairs.[92] He and several of Belgrade's intellectuals applied to the Ministry of Education on June 12/24, 1845, for permission to open a school in which apprentices, journeymen, craftsmen, and house servants would be taught without charge the most necessary subjects, every Sunday afternoon. The Ministry of Education granted this request, and on July 5/17, 1845, it sent permission to Isidor Stojanović, rector of the Lyceum, for the opening of such a school.[93]

A curriculum for the Sunday school, under the title "The Program of the Sunday Schools," was issued on July 14/26 of the same year, and the operation of the school was organized according to its directions. Instruction in it was to last for three years and be conducted every Sunday from 2:00 PM to 4:00 PM, "according to the church clock." The school year had to start in the beginning of September and be concluded at the end of June. Examinations were to be held at the end of each school year, and authorized teachers were to issue certificates upon the student's request. Unlike regular elementary schools, which were under the control of the chief directors of elementary schools, the Sunday school was under the direct control of the Ministry of Education. The teachers of this school were to elect its principal every year from among themselves. The "Program" prescribed that the following subjects be taught: in the first grade, reading, writing, and the basics of Christian instruction "for those who have not had any instruction"; in the second grade, reading, writing, Christian teaching and mathematics "for those who have successfully completed the first grade, or to those who have attained that knowledge on their own"; and in the third grade, the duties of a citizen of Serbia, mathematics, and elementary knowledge about the world and nature "for those who have completed the first two grades, or for those who have studied the subjects of those grades on their own or in any other elementary school."[94]

The Sunday school began to operate on November 2/14, 1845, and in the first year, 400 students attended it.[95] Besides Atanasije Nikolić, its teachers were the lyceum professors: Janko Šafarik, Konstantin Branković, Isidor Stojanović, and Sergije Nikolić; the instructors were Archdeacon Teodosije Mraović, Syncellus Sava Jovšić, and Dimitrije Tomić, Chief of Personnel in the Ministry of Finance.[96]

In order to help teach adults how to read and write and some mathematics in the shortest possible time, Isidor Stojanović wrote *Brzouki bukvar* (The Quick-Learning Primer), which was published in 1846. Using this primer the students would, according to its author, be able "to read correctly in Serbian and the Church Slavic language, to write dictated texts fairly, and to do some arithmetic by heart."[97]

Although the Sunday school promised a great deal in the beginning, it did not fulfill expectations because it operated only until the spring of the following year, 1846, when it was officially abolished. A lack of students was the principal reason for its demise. As has been mentioned, in the beginning of its first school year, their number was surprisingly large and remained so during the winter months, "but when the spring came," writes Atanasije Nikolić, "our youth began to be absent, and by the end they were reduced to so few that it was not worthwhile to spend time on them. We had to abandon our good intentions without receiving any support in such a beneficial undertakings."[98]

The schools of foreign nationalities, which had existed in Serbia in Miloš's time, continued to exist in the Constitutionalist period. The Constitutionalists did not cherish any special affinity for foreign nationalities but in their schools foreign languages which were needed for the cultural and economic development of Serbia were taught, and most of those schools were open to Serbian children. During this period, Greek schools had the most important place among the foreign schools, mostly because of the language, since modern Greek was still one of the most used languages in Serbian commerce. The example of the Belgrade commune, which in 1840 took upon itself the financing of the existing Greek private school, shows how much attention was paid to the Greek schools.[99] The financing of this school from the communal budget lasted until the beginning of 1847 when private persons again had to take up the burden of its support.[100]

The change of financing for this school came about as the result of a campaign directed against its operation and even against its existence. On September 30/October 12, 1846, the Educational Committee directed that all its members state their opinion in writing about the existing communal Greek school. The opinions were varied. For example, in a report of October 6/18, 1846, Isidor Stojanović and Janko Šafarik, lyceum professors, expressed their dissatisfaction with the operation of this school because it was purely Greek and was controlled by Greeks from outside of Serbia. Under their influence it was unsuited to the needs of the Belgrade commune and its citizens.

> For those reasons the signers are of the opinion [it was emphasized in the report] that the Greek school established in Serbia by the Belgrade commune for the sons of Serbian citizens has to be a school of the Greek language for Serbs; thus, it has to think constantly about Serbian nationality and the Serbian fatherland so that children in it can learn Greek but at the same time learn that they are Serbs. Care should be taken that children studying Greek in that Greek school do not estrange themselves from their Serbian nationality; they should learn to understand themselves better. The children of Greeks who live here and who become a part of the Serbian population should also learn about Serbian nationality and their new fatherland.[101]

These lines clearly show a Serbian nationalism, the presence of which was more and more noticeable in the cultural and political live of Serbia.

Atanasije Nikolić, also a member of the Educational Committee, was much more critical in his report. He suggested abolishment of the Greek elementary school "since the government pays a Greek teacher in the Business School and those who desire to learn Greek because of commerce can study it there."[102] The other members of the Educational Committee, except Vasilije Lazić, mainly suggested some changes in the curriculum of the Greek school and that its teachers speak Serbian as well as Greek so Serbian children who attended that school would be able to understand them. Vasilije Lazić, book censor, was the greatest advocate of the existing Greek school and its use of only the Greek language. In his opinion, the Greek school had to continue its operation without using Serbian "and to be for the Serbian youth a **school for the Greek language**, and for the Greek youth **a small elementary school**." Further, in his report he pointed out that the Serbs did not have any reason to be afraid that their children would like their native country less if they studied Greek because Serbian children "also study French, German, and Latin, and they do not lose any love for their fatherland." Advocating the existing Greek school,

Lazić specially emphasized that it would be a great mistake for the Serbian government to force the Greeks to study Serbian "... to force someone to study a foreign language which he does not wish to learn," he wrote, "it seems to me to be not in accordance with the freedom of a man."[103]

Taking into consideration the opinions of all of the members of the Educational Committee, the Ministry of Education informed it on April 25/May 7, 1847, that in the future the Greek school would be considered a private institution "because the Greeks who live in this city [Belgrade] comprise a very small portion of its citizens. Every Serb has a choice if he wants his child to learn Greek. He can send him either to the Business School or he can entrust him to a private tutor."[104] Since future Serbian citizens were educated in this school, the Ministry of Education also informed the Educational Committee that it would assign one of the elementary school chief directors to supervise its operation.

As far as is known, Belgrade had one other Greek elementary school. It was established in 1843, as a private school, and as such was not supervised by the government.[105] Not much is known about its operation or how long it existed. It is, however, quite well known that it was in great competition with the regular Greek public school. In his report to the Ministry of Education of January 31/February 12, 1844, Petar Radovanović wrote: "It would be good to abolish the presently operating Greek private school so that children not be enticed from the public Greek school, because it disturbs the educational structure and harms children morally."[106]

It is known that on December 11/23, 1847, the Ministry of Education granted permission for still another Greek private school but it is not known whether or not it was actually opened.[107] Sources indicate that outside of Belgrade there was only one Greek private school. It was a school in Smederevo which was mentioned in 1842.[108]

The German school, which was established by the Evangelical community in Belgrade in 1854, was another foreign school which drew the attention of Serbian parents. In addition to German, the following subjects were taught: general history, geography, physics, geometry, analytical mathematics, drawing, and music. Its school year lasted ten months, and daily instruction lasted six hours. The only source which gives us information about the existence of this school says that its method of instruction was similar to that used in Germany, but it does not say anything specific about this. It may be assumed, however, that the school was very good because, according to the same source, "by that method every child, regardless of his gift, could learn correctly in half a year how to read and write."[109]

In the beginning of its operation, the German school was attended by German children only, but later Serbian children were enrolled as well. Those pupils who did not belong to the Evangelical community were obliged to pay one taler per month toward the teacher's salary. Since it was much cheaper for those parents who wished their children to learn German than to send them to Zemun, Pančevo, Sremska Mitrovica, or any other place in Vojvodina, the number of Serbian children in the school rapidly increased. Therefore, the representatives of the Evangelical community asked the Ministry of Education to take this school under its supervision. The only existing source shows that the Ministry accepted their request, but it is not known whether the Belgrade commune took it upon itself to finance it.[110] Also it is not known how long this German school operated and how many Serbs were educated in it.

It seems that during the Constitutionalist period there was a great interest in studying German in Serbia because some Serbs also wanted to open private schools for the German language. Thus, for example, on November 20/December 2, 1847, Petar Radovanović informed the Ministry of Education that "one Vikentije Filipović, a retired teacher from the Austrian state," wants "to open a private school for the German language here in Belgrade so that he might teach the youths and adults of this city that language and mathematics." This request was granted, but it is not known whether his school ever opened.[111] Materials in the archives mention one more case. It was Jovan Vasić's application of April 21/May 3, 1852.[112] It was also accepted but again there is no information that his school ever began operation.

Among schools of foreign nationalities in Serbia during the Constitutionalist period, there were also one Jewish school in Belgrade and twelve Turkish schools throughout the state, eight for males and four for female children.[113] However, they were not attended by Serbian children, and their role in the educational life of Serbia was insignificant.

2.

The number of lower gymnasiums and full gymnasiums was not increased during the Constitutionalist period. The only changes were that some lower gymnasiums switched the town of their operation and some of them were abolished only to be almost immediately replaced with new ones. Among the greatest improvement in the secondary schools were the addition of new grades and the introduction of several teaching plans and programs designed to improve instruction and to bring Serbian secondary schools more in line with Western European schools of the same kind and even to equalize them with those schools. The number of grades was gradually increased so that by the 1840s lower gymnasiums had four grades and really became full schools of that kind; the Gymnasium in Belgrade, then the only higher gymnasium in Serbia, got a seventh grade so that it needed only one grade more to be equal in number of grades with the gymnasiums of Western Europe.

As was indicated in the first chapter, in Prince Miloš's time, Serbia had three lower gymnasiums, located in Šabac, Čačak, and Zaječar. Each of them had only two grades and until the school year 1839-40, they were officially called *glavne škole* (the principal schools.). This name was replaced by the name *polugimnazije* (the junior, or lower gymnasiums.) The Šabac lower gymnasium, which was opened in the school year 1836-37, operated more or less normally, and in the school year 1846-47 it became a full lower gymnasium by opening a fourth grade.[114] The number of students gradually grew and together with them, the number of its professors grew as well. For example, according to Platon Simonović, the chief inspector of all schools in Serbia, in a report made on September 20/October 2, 1854, the Šabac lower gymnasium had sixty-two students in 1852, and in 1853 that number was increased to eighty-seven students.[115] If we can believe *Veliki beogradski kalendar* (The Great Calendar of Belgrade), this number of eighty-seven students was not changed until 1857, when it grew rapidly and reached 153 students.[116] It is difficult to believe that in only a year the number of its students almost doubled without any special reason, yet no such reason is known to us. In the last year of the Constitutionalists' reign, 1858, according to the same source, the lower gymnasium in Šabac had 160 students.[117]

After adding a fourth grade in the school year 1846-47, the lower gymnasium in Šabac usually had four regular professors and one or two clerics who gave instruction in Christianity. Its regular professors were both Serbs from Vojvodina and native Serbs, but toward the end of the Constitutionalist period the number of native professors gradually grew. For example, in 1855 two of the four regular Šabac lower gymnasium professors were Serbs from Serbia: Jovan Ilić, a native of Belgrade, and Stojan Bošković, a native of the district of Ćuprija. The former graduated from the Gymnasium, completed one year of philosophy at the Lyceum of

Belgrade, and studied physics in Vienna as a state fellowship holder. The latter graduated from the Department of Philosophy and Law at the Lyceum of Belgrade.[118]

Unlike the Šabac lower gymnasium which did not change its place of operation, the lower gymnasium of Čačak and Zaječar both changed their places of residence; in fact, the first one was completely abolished by a *Soviet* suggestion to the Regency of August 26/September 7, 1839. The Čačak lower gymnasium moved to Užice, where it operated until September 17/29, 1842, when it was returned to Čačak.[119] The person most responsible for the return of the lower gymnasium from Užice to Čačak, which was a much smaller town that Užice, was Bishop Nićifor Maksimović who, as early as October 6/18, 1840, asked Metropolitan Petar Jovanović to intervene so the Užice lower gymnasium be returned to Čačak, and the Metropolitan apparently did so.[120]

The Čačak lower gymnasium had a relatively small number of students. In the school year 1844-45, there were only thirty-two of them: twenty-three in the first grade, seven in the second, and only two in the third grade, whereas the fourth grade did not exist at that time.[121] It is not known whether it was because of the small number of students, or for another reason, but the Čačak lower gymnasium was closed in the middle of 1845 and was not reopened for a full twenty-four years. In 1869, at the request of the court of the Čačak commune, a gymnasium, the so-called *realka* (secondary school), with two grades was established in Čačak by a decree dated June 16/28, 1869.[122]

For some time, but especially during 1842, an unhealthy situation reigned in the Kragujevac gymnasium, the first gymnasium in Serbia. Quarrels spread among its professors, and a real state of anarchy existed. Some of its professors behaved in a vulgar and offensive fashion toward their students. A students' letter to the Ministry of Education nicely shows it:

> We, the poetry students [it said in the letter] when
> we were in the second grammar class and when
> we said something to Mr. Milovuk, or asked him
> to explain something to us, he would turn his rear
> toward us saying to it: tell them what they want to
> know.[123]

Because of the unwholesome relations in the school and the tense political conditions in the state, the Ministry of Education, by its ruling of September 17/29, 1842, abolished the operation of the Kragujevac gymnasium, and Kragujevac remained without a gymnasium until the second half of 1845. Since Kragujevac was one of the largest towns and cultural centers of Serbia, the desire to reopen the gymnasium became stronger and stronger, once the situation in Serbia had become relatively peaceful after the revolt of Toma Vučić-Peršić and Alexander Karadjordjević's accession to the throne. On July 9/21, 1845, the Kragujevac commune applied to the government for permission to reopen the gymnasium, and as early as August 1/13, 1845, Prince Alexander, in agreement with the *Soviet*, ruled "that the existing lower gymnasium in Čačak can be moved to Kragujevac."[124] By this resolution Kragujevac got, not a full gymnasium, but a lower gymnasium. It began to operate in the school year 1845-46 and had only three grades and three professors. The fourth grade was opened in the school year 1846-47 and had only six students. The Kragujevac lower gymnasium remained a four-year school until September of 1861. After that, every year a new grade was added to it until it became a full gymnasium.[125]

There is no reliable data regarding the size of Kragujevac's lower gymnasium before 1852, but it can be assumed that it was rather small because during the school year 1845-46, there were only seven students in the third grade.[126] The previously mentioned report of Platon Simonović contains the first official statistical data concerning the Kragujevac lower gymnasium that are available to us. It shows that in 1852, the school had 155 students, and in 1853, it had 158.[127] That number gradually grew. Thus, for example, in 1855 it was 175, and in 1856 there were 190 students.[128] With the opening of the fourth grade in the school year 1846-47, this lower gymnasium, too, had four regular professors. The roster of professors for 1854 and 1855 shows that only one of its four professors was a Serb from Serbia: he was Pavle Radovanović, who was born in Šabac. The rest of the teachers were from Vojvodina. Like most native lower-gymnasium professors, Radovanović graduated from the Department of Law of the Belgrade Lyceum, and before becoming a professor he was a beginning civil servant employee of the Appellate Court.[129]

The lower gymnasium in Zaječar was inaugurated at the end of 1836 and stayed there until the fall of 1839. Since in 1839 the bishop's residence was moved from Zaječar to Negotin, by a resolution of the Ministry of Education on August 25/September 5 of the same year, the lower gymnasium was also moved. It remained in Negotin until February 22, 1860 (O.S.) when, by Prince Miloš's order, it was returned to Zaječar.[130] As far as the number of students is concerned, the Negotin lower gymnasium was the smallest school of its kind in the period with which we are dealing. According to Platon Simonović's report, in 1852 it had fifty-five students, while a year later this number dropped considerably to thirty-six.[131] Later it gradually grew so that in 1855 it had fifty-two students.[132] The Negotin lower gymnasium also had four regular professors. The roster of professors shows that none of them was born in Serbia; they were all Serbs from Vojvodina.[133]

As has been indicated, before the Constitutionalists seized power, Serbia had three lower gymnasiums, but not yet with their full complement of grades. During the Constitutionalists' regime their number was not altered, but the number of their grades was increased, making them four-year schools or full lower gymnasiums. As far as the grades were concerned, they did not differ from schools of the same kind in the more developed countries of Europe. After 1845, when the Čačak lower gymnasium was moved to Kragujevac, there were no more changes of location so the schools continued to operate undisturbed in Šabac, Kragujevac, and Negotin.

Statistical data on the lower gymnasium students, as has been seen, is so contradictory that only an approximate estimation can be given. In order to have general picture of the students and professors of those schools, it is useful to present data which were published by a contemporary, Milovan Spasić. According to him, the three lower gymnasiums in Serbia in the school year 1845-46 had 151 students and 12 professors.[134] After a decade the number of their professors was increased by only three, so that at the end of the Constititutionalist period they had fifteen professors. It can be assumed that those three were not regular professors but ecclesiastics, because they were not mentioned in the rosters of professors. During the same period of time, however, the number of students in the three schools was significantly increased to 463, or 312 more than in the school year 1845-46.[135] If Spasić's data are compared with the data published in *Kalendar sa šematizmom za 1855 godinu* (The Calendar with Program for the Year 1855), there is a large discrepancy because, according to this calendar, in 1855 Serbia had only 314 students in all three lower gymnasiums.[136]

Spasić's data indicate that at the end of the Constitutionalists' reign, the number of lower gymnasium students decreased. In the school year

1857-58, there were 407 of them whereas the number of professors remained unchanged.[137] The *Calendar with Program* for this year did not publish the number of students for all lower gymnasiums and therefore a comparison with Spasić's data is not possible. But the report of the Ministry of Education for the school year 1856-57 exists, and it shows that in the three lower gymnasiums in Serbia there were 446 students and that each school had five professors.[138] Intensive research, especially in materials in archives, showed that it is almost impossible to establish correct statistical data for students and professors, not only in elementary schools and lower gymnasiums, but in all existing schools in Serbia as well. The official reports sent by various branches of the educational administration are, as has been shown in several examples, contradictory. We presented them, however, because they are useful in offering an approximate picture of lower gymnasiums.

Since lower gymnasiums belonged to the category of secondary schools, they were financed by the state. In order to give some idea of state expenditures for their support, we shall present a few examples. Serbia's national income for the year 1845 was 912,125 talers. The Ministry of Education was allocated the sum of 64,821 talers for all of its needs and spent 2,500 talers of this sum on lower gymnasiums.[139] After a decade, the national income was considerably greater; in 1854 it amounted to 1,188,206 41/60 talers. Yet the Ministry of Education was given less than for the 1845 - only 60,850 talers; however, the sum designated for the needs of lower gymna-siums was notably increased and amounted to 3,590 talers.[140] In 1858, the last year of the Constitutionalists' reign, the entire income of the Principality of Serbia amounted to 1,481,755 talers. From that income, 91,150 talers were allocated for all the expenses of the Ministry of Education, and the Ministry allotted 4,101 talers to lower gymnasiums.[141] Those examples show that the government significantly increased its support to lower gymnasiums despite the fact that their number remained unchanged and that the government supported all other higher schools and the Lyceum, which was expanded during this time period. The sum for the support of lower gymnasiums was increased not for the improvement of instruction but because the number of students increased. The number of professors increased as well, and their salaries, although low, absorbed the greater part of the schools' entire budgets.

After Prince Miloš's abdication on June 1/13, 1839, the transfer of the capital from Kragujevac to Belgrade became an active issue. It was obvious that as the future chief city of the state Belgrade could not be without a higher school; therefore, the Ministry of Education suggested to the Regency that a gymnasium be opened there in addition to the one at Kragujevac. As early as August 26/September 7, 1839, the Regency issued a decision for the opening of a gymnasium in Belgrade. It read in part:

> Upon the recommendation of the Ministry of Education, the Regency of His Serene Highness, in consonance with the *Soviet*, has been pleased to approve and confirm the inauguration of another gymnasium in Belgrade, in addition to the Gymnasium in Kragujevac, and that the first two grades of said gymnasium begin immediately with the start of the coming school year during the year 1839, so that it would be filled in all grades and that it would be able to get all needed competent professors within three years.[142]

In the first year of its operation, the Belgrade gymnasium had only two grades with 71 students; 44 students were enrolled in the first grade and 27 in the second grade. It began to operate on October 1/13, 1839, and its first professors were Mihail Popović, who taught the first grade, and Vasilije Berar, who taught the second. Their salaries were equal - 2,500 *groses* per year.[143] After the school year 1839-40, the Belgrade gymnasium added a new grade every year for two years which made it equal in grades to the Kragujevac gymnasium. Since the gymnasium in Kragujevac, as has been mentioned, was abolished in September of 1842, the Belgrade gymnasium remained the only gymnasium and the most important secondary school in Serbia for the next twenty years. In view of the fact that it was the only gymnasium, the number of its students rapidly increased, and with them, the number of professors as well. For example, in the school year 1845-46, it had 183 students.[144] By 1853, their number was almost doubled at 317[145] and in the school year 1856-57, there were 530 students.[146] However, the number of professors did not increase so rapidly. For instance, in the school year 1845-46, the Belgrade gymnasium had six professors[147]; a decade later in 1854 there were eleven of them, none of whom was a native Serb. Nine of them were from Vojvodina, while Antonije Šulc (Anton Schultz) was from Saxony and Karl Aren (Charles Aren) was from Toulon.[148] In the last year of the Constitutionalist reign, the school year 1857-58, according to Milovan Spasić, Serbia had fourteen gymnasium professors and again, none of them was born in Serbia.[149] Before 1858 Ljubomir Nenadović was the only professor of the Belgrade gymnasium who was born and educated in Serbia.[150] However, after two years of teaching he left his professorship and went over to the Ministry of Education where he soon became the Chief of Personnel.

Like Ljubomir Nenadović, a large number of future Serbian intellectuals stayed in the teaching profession for just a short time, usually only until they found a job in the civil service. Low and irregular teaching salaries were the main reasons for this practice. For example, in 1844, the approximate salary of a lower gymnasium professor was 250 talers,[151] and it was not increased for over ten years.[152] The annual salary of a gymnasium professor was somewhat higher; for instance, in 1854 it was approximately 350 talers.[153] A professor's salary was lower than the salary of many ordinary clerks. Such an inequity not only kept educated young people from seeking professorships but it also caused dissatisfaction among those who held such positions. Protests over the low salaries for gymnasium professors and applications for increases were numerous. One of the most important requests for the improvement of professors' material conditions was presented at the so-called Peter's Assembly (*Petrovska skupštna*) held in Kragujevac on St. Peter and Paul Day, on June 29/July 11, 1848.[154] After that, the government issued several decrees (1851, 1852, 1854, and 1858) regarding increases of professors' salaries, but they had little effect.

Stojan Bošković was undoubtedly one of the great organizers of cultural policy in Serbia during the Constitutionalist period and a powerful advocate for the improvement of the teaching cadre. In August of 1857, he published a series of articles in the *Serbian Journal* under the title "Concerning the Transformation of the Educational Profession in Serbia." In them, Bošković advocated the introduction of state examinations for all civil servants, the improvement of the material status of professors by making their salaries equal to the salaries of the other state officials, and requiring that all civil servants have the necessary qualifications.[155]

> Of what use is it [Bošković writes] that the cultural administration be organized in this way or that, that high schools be set up according to one new system or another, or that this or that new subject be introduced, when the instructors are not satisfied with their position, for they see how, in other branches of civil service, persons of much inferior knowledge and ability, who were their own children and pupils only yesterday, have easily attained high posts and increase in property and esteem with marvelous speed. It is for this reason that in recent times all our better young people avoid teaching posts instead of reaching for them and considering themselves fortunate to obtain them.... Another great obstacle to the rise

of public education and schools is the misfortune
that unschooled persons and ignoramuses are still
constantly being taken into the civil service,
persons who, either out of indolence and dullness
of mind or else out of poverty, have barely
learned anything beyond how to read and
write.[156]

With the aim of making the teaching profession more attractive to
native educated men and of improving the finances of existing professors,
the Constitutionalists introduced several rather important laws at the end of
their reign. For example, on September 15/27, 1857, the Ministry of
Education asked the *Soviet* to increase the salaries of the professors under
contract. This application was accepted by the *Soviet* on September
19/October 1, 1857, and confirmed by Prince Alexander on September
25/October 7 of the same year.[157] Later, he promulgated a much more
important law regarding the material status of professors on February
15/27, 1858.[158] By this law, the salaries of lower gymnasium professors
were equalized with the salaries of gymnasium and seminary professors and
amounted to 400 talers per year. According to this law, professors' salaries
increased by 100 talers in each of three periods. The first period was from
11 to 15 years of teaching, the second from 16 to 20, and the third one
from 21 to 25 years of teaching. The fourth or the last period was from 26
years of teaching until the end of a professor's activity and its increase
amounted to 150 talers.[159] This periodical increase of salaries did not apply
to temporary professors or to professors under limited contract. However, if
they became regular professors, this law automatically applied to them, and
the years which they "spent as temporary professors or professors under
limited contract" were also counted.[160] Article X was the most important
article of this law, and it reads: "A professor who has held a professorship
for thirty years has the right to be retired with the full salary which he
received in the last year of his teaching, regardless in what ... school [lower
gymnasium, gymnasium, or seminary] and how long he taught in each of
them."[161] It was the first law in the history of education in Serbia that
guaranteed a pension to the professors of secondary and higher schools.

The state invested a rather large sum for the support of the Belgrade
gymnasium and improvement of its instruction. With the rapid increase of
gymnasium students, the budget for its support was increased as well. For
example, the entire budget of the Ministry of Education for the budget year
1848 was 62,841 talers. From that sum, 2,650 talers were spent for the
Belgrade gymnasium, which then had six professors.[162] Ten years later, in

1858, the entire income of the Principality of Serbia amounted to 1,481,755 talers. Out of this sum, 91,150 talers were allocated for the needs of the Ministry of Education and the Belgrade gymnasium, which then had twelve professors, was given 6,200 talers of 3,550 talers more than ten years earlier.[163]

In its first years, the Belgrade Gymnasium operated according to the already mentioned plan and program for gymnasiums of September 26/October 8, 1838. Since the makers of educational policy were not entirely satisfied with that program, the Ministry of Education issued a new curriculum on August 24/September 5, 1843, under the name "The System of Subjects to be Taught."[164] However, this curriculum was used for only one year. As has been mentioned regarding elementary schools, on September 23/October 5, 1844, a law for all existing schools in Serbia, except the Seminary, which was under the control of Metropolitan Jovanović, was promulgated under the title "The Organization of Public School Education."[165] This "Organization" had a separate section concerning high schools, which contained all regulations and the curriculum not only for the gymnasium but for the lower gymnasium as well. This law prescribed that a lower gymnasium was to have four grades with four professors including its principal. The gymnasium, which until then had five grades, received a sixth grade. It was decreed that the gymnasium would have seven professors, not including a principal, and those professors would teach "not all subjects in a grade but each of them his subject or subjects in all grades."[166] The same subjects were prescribed for lower gymnasiums and the first four grades of the gymnasium, whereas for the fifth and sixth grades of the gymnasium, separate subjects were prescribed.

Since the gymnasium was the only school of that kind in Serbia, it is useful to list its prescribed subjects. They will help to give us a more complete picture of the beginning of organized secondary education in Serbia. After the school year 1844-45, in the lower gymnasium and in the Belgrade gymnasium, the following subjects were taught: in the first, or the so-called "grammar" grade, catechism, Serbian grammar, geography, nature study, mathematics, and penmanship; in the second grade, catechism, Serbian grammar, Latin grammar, German grammar, geography, nature study, history of the people of the Ottoman Empire, mathematics, and calligraphy; in the third grade, Biblical history, Latin grammar, German grammar, geography, the histories of the people of Serbia, Montenegro, and the Austrian lands, mathematics, and calligraphy; and in the fourth grade, the history of the Christian church, Latin grammar, German grammar, geography, the histories of the Russian, Polish, and Greek people, mathematics, and drawing (*načertanije*). Besides those, in the Belgrade gymnasium these subjects were also taught: in the fifth grade, or the so-called "grade of rhetoric," instructions in Christianity, rhetoric, Latin language with conversation, mythology, geography, history, algebra, and drawing; and in the sixth grade, or the so-called "grade of poetics," instructions in Christianity, poetry, interpretation of poets, Slavic, Greek, and Roman antiquities, geography, algebra, anthropology, ethics, and drawing. In addition to the listed subjects, the lower gymnasiums and the full gymnasium also taught physical education in all grades, and in the fifth and sixth grade of the Gymnasium, pedagogy with teaching methods "especially for those who wanted to devote themselves to the teaching profession and who would also be obliged to study church singing."[167] In the beginning of the next year, that is on January 29/February 11, 1845, a supplement to the "Organization" under the title "Instructions for Gymnasium and Lower-gymnasium Professors" was issued which elaborated in detail the section of the "Organization" concerning the Gymnasium, especially the curriculum prescribed by that law.[168]

By the "Organization" and the "Instruction," Serbian lower gymnasium and the gymnasium were to receive a national and classical-humanistic character. The "Instruction" pointed out that the Serbian language had "to have first place in the gymnasium."[169] However, such an emphasis never developed because more attention was paid to the Latin language, which was taught from the second to the sixth grade. Thus, it may rightly be said that after the promulgation of the school laws of 1844 and 1845, the lower gymnasiums in Serbia and the Belgrade gymnasium received a predominantly classical-humanistic direction. Paying great attention to the Latin language was not the result of an effort to meet a need of the still backward Serbian society, but rather an attempt to copy the Austrian schools system with its orientation toward the classics. Moreover, the classical character of the Belgrade gymnasium was increased still more with the optional study of classical Greek, which was introduced at the request of the Belgrade merchants, especially the Greeks.[170]

Latin had been taught in the gymnasium even earlier than 1844, and great attention was paid to it. The Ministry of Education, in its letters to the *Soviet*, pointed out its importance, especially for those students who should decide to study medicine.[171] Unfortunately, it was of little use for gymnasium students to read, for instance, Cicero, Caesar, and Tacitus, when conditions outside of the school were wretched and primitive because Belgrade at that time, was "full of depraved and debauched men and women" from Bosnia, Austria, Albania, and other regions.[172]

> After an hour spend in school where they were
> taught about the beautiful works of the classical
> writers or about "beautiful writing (*ukrašeno*

> *slovosačinenije - syntaxis ornata)*" our gymnasium
> students, candidates for the social sciences [writes
> Slobodan Jovanović], went to their wretched and
> poor lodgings which were run by "the most
> hideous persons (*najskaradnijeg lica*)" dropping in
> before that at a public kitchen (*aščinica*) or a
> *buregdžinica* (a small shop which sells only a type
> of pastry, usually filled with meat or cheese) for
> lunch where they could meet that rabble gathered
> in Belgrade from the entire Ottoman Empire.
> What, then, could they retain from that humanitar-
> ianism with which schools was obliged to ennoble
> them?[173]

German was the only living foreign language taught in all grades of lower gymnasium and in the Gymnasium. True, the "Organization" of 1844, as has been indicated, prescribed the teaching of German only in the final three grades of the lower gymnasiums and in the second, third, and fourth grade of the gymnasium, but it was changed by the "Instruction" of 1845 which prescribed its teaching in all grades of the lower gymnasiums and of the gymnasium.[174] Such an emphasis is understandable if it is known that a certain number of young men, such as the state fellowship holders, continued their higher education abroad, especially in Vienna and in Berlin, where a knowledge of German was indispensable to them.

It is surprising that the authors of the new curriculum did not find it necessary to introduce French as an obligatory subject, if not in lower gymnasiums at least in the Belgrade gymnasium, because it had a humanistic character, at least according to the new law. In addition, almost every year Serbia sent a few young men to Paris to be educated, and an elementary knowledge of French was necessary to them. It should be pointed out that great attention was paid to the spread of the French culture in Serbia from the beginning of the nineteenth century onward. Dositej Obradović had already publicized the need to study the French language and to adopt French culture. He was the first Serb of the nineteenth century to translate from the French and he "gave inspiration and motivation for the writing of textbooks for the French language."[175] Also, France was a model for many developing countries, and therefore it was not surprising that the Serbs tried to imitate the French in many things during the shaping of their independent state. Thus, for example, the Serbian Civil Code of 1844, the greatest legal work of the Constitutionalists' regime, was in fact a transla-tion of the German translation of the French Civil Code.[176]

French as an obligatory subject was first introduced in Serbia in the Military Academy in 1837, and in 1839, the Lyceum began requiring it as well. Several years later an attempt was made to introduce French as an obligatory subject in the Kragujevac and the Belgrade gymnasiums. On May 6/18, 1842, the Ministry of Education sent a letter to the *Soviet* asking that French might be introduced as an obligatory subject in the forenamed gymnasiums. The Ministry explained its request with the following words:

> It is generally known that we have very few published books in our native language and as far as the books for advanced subjects are concerned, almost none. Therefore, we have to use books in foreign languages, and they are, for now, written in French for scholarly and diplomatic subjects and in German, which is a neighboring language, for scholarly educational subjects. In them the most important works in all fields are written.[177]

The *Soviet* granted this request on May 14/26, and Prince Michael confirmed the decision on May 18/30, 1842.[178] However, because of the political tension in the country and the change of dynasty in the same year, the decision by the *Soviet* and Prince Michael did not go into effect. The Belgrade gymnasium had to wait nearly ten years before French would be introduced as an obligatory subject.

The "Organization" of 1844 with the "Instruction" of 1845 clearly shows that its authors, in agreement with most educated Serbs, desired that the Gymnasium, "with Latin and German as well as literature, elevate Šumadija's [a province in northern Serbia] peasant children to humanity, that is, to that ideal of education which was created in Western Europe in the time of an aristocratic culture."[179] But, it remained only an unrealized desire; the Serbian lower gymnasiums and especially the Belgrade gymnasium, were at that time still far from being humanistic schools.

In the new curriculum, the natural sciences were poorly represented. For the first time, physical education with military instruction was introduced in all grades, and pedagogy with teaching methods was introduced in the higher grades of the gymnasium. It was the main intention of the authors of the "Organization" and the "Instruction" to prepare the lower-gymnasium and gymnasium students for higher education and for various professions (officials, army officers, teachers, etc.) for which there were not yet special schools. However, that intention did not give the expected results.

Despite its numerous deficiencies, the "Organization" of 1844, with the "Instruction" of 1845, still contributed greatly to the development of secondary education in Serbia. This education did not remain unchanged but was altered to fit the needs of the society. However, the makers of Serbian educational policy had two reasons for working to improve the quality of gymnasium instruction: they wished not only to fit it to the conditions and the needs of the Serbian state, but they also tried to make the Belgrade gymnasium good enough to be recognized outside of Serbia's borders. To achieve that latter goal, many experiments were tried: foreign curricula were copied and numerous mistakes were made which negatively affected the desired outcome.

In order to give the entire educational program a new profile and to put it on a firm footing, the government decided to bring an experienced person from abroad and entrust to him that delicate job.

According to some of the educated Serbs from Vojvodina, the person most capable of modernizing education in Serbia was Platon Simonović from Russia, who knew the Serbian language and who had enormous experience in the educational profession. He was a Serb by birth, from Kamenac in Srem, and in 1851 when he was recommended to the *Soviet* and Prince Alexander for the position of inspector of all schools in Serbia, he lived on his estate in Odessa as a pensioner after twenty-five years of educational service. Before retiring, Simonović had been a full professor in the Richeliev Technical School in Odessa and the "Russian Imperial State Councillor."[180] On June 24/July 6, 1851, Prince Alexander, in agreement with the *Soviet*, informed the Ministry of Education that he favored inviting Platon Simonović from Russia.[181]

After Simonović accepted the offer and came to Serbia, the Prince appointed him "Acting Chief Inspector of All Schools in the Principality of Serbia" on January 22/February 3, 1853.[182] Several months later, on June 17/29, 1853, the government issued a decree titled "Instructions for the Chief Inspector of Schools" which prescribed Simonović's duties. On the basis of this decree, Platon Simonović became a middle man between the Ministry of Education, on one side, and the principals of all the schools, including also the Lyceum rector, on the other side, and he was responsible to the Ministry of Education.[183] In comparison with gymnasium and lyceum professors' salaries, Platon Simonović's annual salary was quite high: it amounted to 1,200 talers.[184] In order to get a more graphic conception of Simonović's salary, it is sufficient to state that at the time of his service in Serbia, the entire annual budget of the Business School amounted to 1,440 talers.[185]

During the first year of his stay in Serbia, Platon Simonović composed new curricula for the gymnasium and for the Lyceum which were based on his experience in Russia. His new curriculum for the gymnasium was issued on September 15/27, 1853, under the title "The Organization of the Gymnasium of the Principality of Serbia" and it brought about many changes in the organization of instruction, school administration, and the previous curriculum. In its first article, it pointed out that it was issued with the following intentions: (1) "to give a fairly solid education to those young men who did not plan to, or were not able to continue their education in the Lyceum" and (2) "to prepare for higher schools those young men who wish to devote themselves to higher education."[186] The Belgrade gymnasium was enlarged to seven grades and the number of professors was increased from seven to thirteen. It is important to note that there were some plans to enlarge the Belgrade gymnasium by two grades and thus, as far as the grades were concerned, to equalize it with European gymnasiums, which at that time had eight grades. They were not realized because some Lyceum professors opposed them, fearing that they would be moved from the Lyceum to the gymnasium, thus from the higher school to the lower one. The solution was found in opening only a seventh grade.[187] Simonović's "Organization" did not alter the number of grades in the lower gymnasiums; they remained four-year schools.

The "Organization" brought a great many changes in the existing curriculum. Greater emphasis was placed on the natural sciences by the introduction of physics as a new subject and by expanding mathematics to include geometry and trigonometry. Despite that, the Belgrade gymnasium not only retained its classical-humanistic character but even emphasized it more by adding new subjects from the humanities and social sciences. For example, Serbian and Slavic literature were introduced as new subjects, the teaching of general and Serbian history was expanded, and besides the existing two obligatory foreign languages, three more were introduced: classical Greek and Church-Slavonic, as classical languages, and French as a live language.[188] Djordje Maletić, once the principal of the Belgrade gymnasium, rightly said that after 1853, with five obligatory foreign languages, this gymnasium "became a school for learning **only lanuages.**"[189] Such a large number of foreign languages burdened students a great deal, and they were not able to learn any of them well, including their native language. They also did not have enough time for their other subjects.

The "Organization" of 1853 abolished pedagogy and teaching methods in the gymnasium, probably at the request of Metropolitan Petar, who feared that gymnasium graduates could be rivals to seminarians in the teaching profession.

The main purpose of Platon Simonović's "Organization" of 1853 was to modernize secondary education in Serbia. However, it brought to Serbian education more harm than good because Simonović, who did not sufficiently understand conditions in Serbia, tried to introduce in Serbian secondary schools an only slightly modified Russian curriculum which was unsuited for the educational and cultural conditions of Serbia at that time. After the issuing of his curriculum, "it needed ten full years of wandering and new difficulties to partly remove and partly adjust Platon Simonović's 'reforms' to our [Serbian] conditions."[190]

Because of his reforms, Simonović was sharply criticized in Serbia. Besides that, his incorrect and even willful behavior toward his subordinates, as well as toward his superiors, increased his unpopularity. The Ministry of Education even sent him a rather sharp letter on March 25/April 6, 1854, warning him that he was obliged to observe the existing state laws. The letter said that the Ministry was forced "to recommend to you that you remain within the limits of this country's laws, to which you are subject, and to avoid impolite expressions in your letters, as well as toward everything that you found established in Serbia."[191] It should be noted that the French and English governments were not pleased with Simonović's stay in Serbia. Since it was the time of the Crimean War (1853-1856), it could have been suspected that Platon Simonović was hiding himself behind the title of Chief Inspector of Schools while acting as a Russian agent in Serbia. At the end of March, 1854, Novi Sad's newspaper, the *Serbian Journal*, published the news that the English and French consuls in Belgrade had requested of the Serbian government that Simonović leave Serbia.[192] Because of that request, his unpopularity among educated Serbs in Serbia, and unsuccessful school reforms, Platon Simonović was relieved of his position on October 19/31, 1855.[193]

With his dismissal, the office of Chief Inspector of schools was abolished, and its functions again entrusted to the Ministry of Education. The experiment with the position of the chief inspector had shocked still more an already unstable system and the policy of wondering in the Serbian educational system.

When it was realized that Platon Simonović's "Organization" had been an almost complete failure, work was started to correct it. After long preparation, on June 9/21, 1856, a supplement to the "Organization" of 1853 was issued. By it, some changes in the scope of subjects taught were made, the time for studying foreign languages was shortened, and some changes of a more or less organizational and administrative character were carried out.[194] But, with all these changes, teaching the Gymnasium and lower gymnasiums was not stabilized; it would remain unstable and without a definite direction until 1863, when a new school law was passed.

In order to make possible the education of talented but poor children, the Constitutionalists' regime established the policy of awarding stipends to lower gymnasium students and especially to students of the Gymnasium. It is known, for instance, that about 30 percent of native-born secondary school students enjoyed state help.[195] We could not establish the amount of money which was annually allotted for the stipends of native-born secondary school students because the state annual budget reports contain only the combined sum which was set aside for the stipends of gymnasium and Lyceum students. How much from that sum was spent for the former and how much for the latter could only be established if complete fellowship holders' lists existed for both schools. Nevertheless, an article published in the *Serbian News* reports that in 1850, the government spent 1,870 talers for gymnasium students.[196] It was a large sum considering the entire annual budget of that school for the same year was only 2,790 talers.[197] In order to grant stipends to those who needed them most, as early as June 14/26, 1844, the Ministry of Education sent instructions to the Lyceum rector and to gymnasium principal requiring that every fellowship applicant supply his school with a statement of his parents' or guardians' financial status.[198]

The Serbian government expended a rather large sum of money for the education of young men from those Slavic provinces which were still under Turkish rule and who were educated in the Serbian secondary schools and Lyceum. After the implementation of Ilija Garašanin's *"Načertanije"* or plan for Serbian foreign policy in 1844, that sum was considerably increased. For example, in 1853, Serbia allocated 600 *grošes* for aid to students from Slavic provinces still under Turkish occupation, and five years later, in 1858, that sum was increased to 2,000 *grošes*.[199] It is important to point out that those students got financial help from the Serbian government more easily than native students and the help given to them was in larger amounts.[200]

Poor students were supported, not only by the government, but by prosperous and notable individuals as well. "In this time students enjoyed great respectability and, according to the attitude of that time, to help a poor student was not only '*seva*' [a Turkish word denoting a good deed worthy of a reward], but a patriotic gesture as well."[201]

Besides pecuniary aid, poor but good students received free textbooks, were exempted from school fees, enjoyed free health care, and received free medicines from the state pharmacy. Free medical care for poor students was first introduced in the Belgrade gymnasium in 1857. In that year, the Greek doctor, Dr. Panagiotis Papacostopoulos, was appointed professor of modern Greek, and in addition to his regular teaching, he was obliged to treat poor gymnasium students free of charge.[202]

With regard to the Constitutionalists' policy toward poor students, it is necessary to mention one more novelty. On January 15/27, 1849, Prince Alexander issued a decree that all Lyceum and gymnasium students who died were to be buried at the state's expense if their parents were unable to bear the expenses of their funerals, but it was emphasized that the sum spent for a funeral could not be more than the three-months stipend of a deceased student.[203]

As he wrote the "Organization" of 1844, Jovan S. Popović was aware that for the development of education in Serbia it was necessary to have not only a good curriculum but qualified professors as well. With the desire that lower gymnasiums and the Belgrade gymnasium have such professors, he stated in article 39 of the "Organization" that anyone who wishes to be hired as a lower gymnasium professor "has to be a graduate from the Department of Philosophy of the Lyceum of Belgrade with at least a good grade, that besides Serbian he must know one scholarly foreign language, especially the one which he would teach as a subject, and that he be of exemplary behavior."[204] True, a great number of professors did have high scholarly qualifications, but they did not particularly distinguish themselves as teachers and educators, and they did not show notable interest in the profession by which they supported themselves. For example, about Luka Pavlović, a professor of German and one-time principal of the Belgrade gymnasium, his former student Jovan Dragašević wrote: "How much he knew? I do not know, but he is not a pedagogue at all, which was then generally known. It seemed to me that he was made more for police work than for education."[205] Svetozar Marković also later remembered his professors and was very critical of them. "Our professors," he wrote, "did not know their job well. Instead of taking care to develop our minds, to stimulate us **to think** and by that means to awaken in us a curiosity for knowledge, they forced us to learn a pile of words whose sense we did not know."[206] Marković also criticized the method of teaching in the gymnasium which, according to him, was similar to the method used in elementary schools - "professor assigned 'from her to here' [*odavde-dovde*] and for the next time everybody was obliged to know it," but "professor did not require his students to know [understand] the material, but only be able to recite it by heart."[207] As for the moral education of the lower-gymnasium and gymnasium students during the Constitutionalists' reign, professors tried through punishment to implant obedience in their students "which was, in the professors' and the government's estimation, meant to guarantee an essential requirement for bureaucratic fitness."[208]

Disobedience by lower-gymnasium and gymnasium professors toward their superiors was not a rarity. For example, Vasilije Berar, acting principal of the Belgrade gymnasium, reported to the Ministry of Education by letter on January 27/February 8, 1842, about the professors' arrogance and willfulness. "So," he writes, "when I called a meeting in order to consult them regarding some matters, everybody found some excuse for not coming, or if I visited some of their classes in order to advise and to reprimand youths, some of them would protest."[209] Usually no disciplinary action was initiated against professors. "Professors refuse obedience to their principals," wrote Ilija Garašanin in 1856, "and instead of being advised to be obedient they are permitted to write in newspapers all kinds of nonsense defaming their superiors publicly."[210] In addition, because of the professors' low salaries, bribery became common in the secondary schools of Serbia. "In the lower gymnasiums in the interior of the country," wrote Ilija Garašanin, "professors already trade with their professions. Therefore, it is not necessary anymore that a student know his subjects well in order to pass to a higher grade, it is sufficient that his parent compensates the absence of the student's knowledge with several ducats, and it is safer than any knowledge."[211] It should be mentioned that during the illness of a professor, regardless of how long it lasted, his subject was not taught. All these and many other deficiencies, which have been discussed in this chapter, adversely affected the quality of students who graduated from those schools.

One of the biggest concerns of the Constitutionalists' regime regarding school policy was the preservation of the purity of the Serbian language. As early as June 3/15, 1844, the Ministry of Education sent a letter to the principal of the Belgrade gymnasium asking him to guard the purity of the Serbian language in his school and emphasizing that professors were the most competent to do this. The letter stressed that lately foreign words, usually Latin, were being introduced, "without need or reason ... and so they [have started] to create a complicated mixture in our language."[212] It was almost ridiculous to talk about the purity of the Serbian language even then because numerous words had been borrowed from other Slavic languages, especially Russian, and there was also borrowing from Turkish, Greek, German, and French. In fact, it may accurately be said that at this time the Serbian language was still in the formative stage. Moreover, the government's request that secondary school professors preserve the "purity" of the Serbian language was unrealistic because, as has been indicated, they were mostly Serbs from Vojvodina who most often did not know Serbian well themselves, and some of them were foreigners with even less knowledge of the Serbian language.

Since the Belgrade gymnasium was behind the gymnasiums of developed European countries in the number of its grades as well as in the quality of its instruction, its students had difficulty continuing their education abroad. Therefore, its professors and the Serbian government tried to gain its recognition outside of Serbia, but very little was achieved in that attempt. Because of its closeness, the largest number of Serbian students who decided to continue their higher education abroad went to Vienna, so intensive negotiations were conducted between the Serbian and the Austrian governments. Finally, in 1850, the status of the Serbian students who continued their education in Austria's schools was regulated. According to the agreement, a graduate of the Belgrade gymnasium, which at that time still had six grades, could be admitted in the seventh grade of Austria's gymnasiums after passing a special examination in subjects which were not taught in the Gymnasium of Belgrade. The students who wished to begin their education at an Austrian university were obliged, in addition to graduating from the Belgrade gymnasium, to complete three years in the Department of Philosophy at the Lyceum of Belgrade. However, this agreement applied only to Serbian citizens; the conditions for Austrian citizens who graduated from Serbian schools and wanted to continue their education in Austria were much more difficult because the Hapsburg monarchy tried to prevent education of its subjects, especially the Serbs, in Serbia.[213]

At the same time, Serbian schools did not enjoy as good a reputation in Russia, and it was not rare that a student who graduated from the Lyceum of Belgrade was accepted in the third or fourth grade of a Russian gymnasium. At that time, there was no agreement about the recognition of Serbian schools in Russia, probably because only an insignificant number of Serbian young men continued their education at Russian universities.[214]

During the twenty years of the Constitutionalists' regime, great efforts were made and a large sum of money from the poor state budget was invested in the improvement of secondary education in Serbia. In spite of that, no particularly impressive results were achieved. Nevertheless, improvements were made and a rather solid basis was laid for further progress in education. Due to financial difficulties and the loosely-specified requirements for employment in the bureaucracy, a large number of gymnasium students left school prematurely after completing several grades and found employment in state service. The general consequence of this practice was that the creation of a highly educated native class was slow and difficult.

CHAPTER III

PROFESSIONAL AND VOCATIONAL SCHOOLS

If a man empties his purse into his head,
no one can take it from him.

Benjamin Franklin

1.

The modernization of the Serbian state, which began during the Constitutionalist period, required various specialists. In order to supply those specialists, several professional and vocational schools were opened during this period. In addition to the seminary, which had existed during Prince Miloš's reign, business, engineering, military, and agricultural schools were opened. But most important among them was still the seminary, which is mentioned in documents under such various names as *Bogoslovija*, *Bogoslovno učilište*, and *Seminarija bogoslovska*. It was the oldest professional school, had a large number of students, and was the school which had the most important role in elementary education in Serbia. The seminary was the only Serbian school in Serbia which was not under the control of the Ministry of Education, although it was financed from the state budget. As in Prince Miloš's time, Metropolitan Petar Jovanović had full control over its operation; thus the numerous governmental laws and decrees which were issued during the Constitutionalists' regime do not refer to it. In official state school laws, the seminary is mentioned only once, and this was in Article 7 of "The Organization of Public School Education" of 1844, which read: "In addition to these schools [elementary, business, lower gymnasiums, gymnasium, and lyceum] there is a seminary at the Serbian Metropolitan's residence; the guidance and selection of needed professors has been entrusted to the Metropolitan, or to his deputy. Seminary youths will study theological disciplines needed for the ecclesiastical profession."[1]

Since Serbia had only a small number of students with more than an elementary education, it was impossible during the first years of the seminary's operation to institute strict entrance requirements for students; it was sufficient that candidates knew how to read and write, regardless of age. However, with the establishment of the gymnasiums in Kragujevac and in Belgrade, and of lower gymnasiums, the Metropolitan took certain measures to ensure that seminary students would be young and have a good educational background. As early as 1839 the Ministry of Education suggested to the Metropolitan that the seminary accept only young men who had completed at least three years of gymnasium education.[2] The initiative of the Ministry of Education did not go long without response. First, on July 15/27, 1840, Metropolitan Petar issued a decree stipulating that education in the seminary was to last for two years, instead of the prescribed three years, for those students "who know how to read, write, and sing well," as well as for young men who had graduated from the Lyceum or from the gymnasium with good grades "because for them it will not be necessary to attend the first grade of the seminary which has to be considered a preparatory grade."[3] In the same year, another decree stated that all candidates considered for admission to the seminary could not be older than seventeen years.[4] On May 3/15, 1841, the Synod of Bishops passed a resolution that all students admitted to the seminary had to graduate from a lower gymnasium "so that it will not be necessary, as it is now, to spend a whole year in order to prepare them to be able to study prescribed subjects; this year could then be used for a broad teaching of theological discipline."[5] But the resolution of the Synod of Bishops could not be completely implemented because only a small number of candidates with required school preparation decided to devote themselves to the study of theology. Even seven years after this resolution was adopted by the Synod of Bishops, the seminary commonly accepted students who had only an elementary education. Then, writes Alimpije Vasiljević in his *Uspomene* (Memoirs), "the seminary accepted [students] from elementary schools; only rarely did somebody come from the first or second grade of the gymnasium, and nobody came from the third [grade]."[6] Usually, very poor gymnasium students, "gymnasium rejects" (*gimnazijski škartovi*)[7] went over to the seminary, and it was not reasonable to expect much from them.

In the school year 1844-45, one more grade was added to the seminary and it became a four-year school. In addition, instruction by class was replaced by instruction by subject in order to improve the quality of teaching. With that the operation of this school was largely stabilized, and the following subjects were taught: catechism, Slavic grammar, biblical history, geography, general history, mathematics, logic, physics, anthropology, church rhetoric, church history, liturgy, pedagogy, pastoral and moral theology, hermeneutics, exegesis, singing, and church rules.[8] This curriculum was periodically altered to admit such new subjects, for instance, as psychology, homiletics, and the Russian language. The introduction of Russian into the seminary had great significance, not only for that school, but for the entire course of Serbian educational policy, because it expanded Russian influence on education in Serbia.

Although close relations between Serbia and Russia had lasted for centuries, and although since the downfall of Constantinople in 1453 Russia had considered herself the protectress of the Serbs, as indeed she was, the Russian language was introduced into Serbian schools relatively late as an obligatory subject. Moreover, before the 1850s, the influence of the Russian school system on the Serbian system was insignificant. It is difficult to find a principal cause for that unusual occurrence, yet we think there are two causes worth mentioning. First, there was political tension between Serbia and Russia in the first years of the Constitutionalists' reign. And second, the foreign policy of Serbia defined by Ilija Garašanin's *"Načertanije"* in 1844 opposed the spread of Russia's domination over Serbia and was against her influence in the shaping of the foreign and internal policies of the Serbian people.

At that time, as it had been for centuries, the Orthodox Church was one of the most important ties between the Russian and Serbian people, and that is the only reason the Russian language became a compulsory subject in the Serbian schools. According to Milan Dj. Milićević, who was a seminary student and the man who left the most detailed account of this time, Sima Milutinović-Sarajlija initiated the introduction of the Russian language and the bringing of Russian professors to the seminary when he took the first group of Serbian students to Kiev in 1846 in order that they might be educated there. On that occasion, writes Milićević, Milutinović visited Moscow and St. Petersburg and there "he stated to Russians that it would be good if some Russian professors came to Belgrade in order to teach Russian."[9] There are no official documents which confirm or deny Milićević's account, and if it was so, it is not known whether Milutinović took that action on his own initiative or if he was just carrying out the orders of the Serbian government. It is a fact, however, that shortly after Milutinović's return to Serbia, A. Fëderov, the Russian Acting Consul General, informed the Serbian Ministry of Foreign Affairs, on March 31/April 12, 1847, that Tsar Nicholas I had appointed two Russian professors who would come to the seminary in Belgrade to teach church history and the Old Church Slavonic language.[10] Shortly after that, on April 11/23, 1847, Prince Alexander informed the Ministry of Education of this decision by letter. "His Majesty, Supreme Emperor of Russia, graciously decreed that two teachers for Old Church Slavonic and its literature as well as for church history would be sent here [to Serbia], who would receive their salaries from the Russian clerical fund and who would teach our [Serbian] youth those subjects." In the same letter, the Prince recommended to the Ministry that it come to an agreement with the Metropolitan as to which subjects the Russian professors would teach.[11]

Vasili Teodorovich Verdysh and Dmitri Alekseevich Rudinskii were the first Russian professors assigned to teach in Serbia. Both of them were priests' sons and professors in the Kishinëv seminary. Verdysh was born in the province of Bessarabia and was thirty-one years old; Rudinskii was born in the region of Voronezh and was twenty-eight years old.[12] Although the Serbian government was informed of their arrival as early as March of 1847, they did not come until August of 1849.[13] It seems that the Revolution of 1848 was one of the main causes for their late arrival in Serbia. They began to perform their regular duties as seminary professors in the school year 1849-50 even though in the beginning they did not know the Serbian language. Verdysh taught biblical geography and Rudinskii, in addition to Old Church Slavonic and its literature, taught Russian in the final grades, paying special attention to those students who had been selected to continue their education in Kiev. In the next school year, 1850-51, Verdysh began to teach church history and Rudinskii taught only the Russian language and literature, which at that time were taught in the first and second grades. Sava Sretenović, who was among the first Serbs to graduate from a theological academy in Russia and one of the first native Serbs to become a professor in the seminary, took over the teaching of the Old Church Slavonic and its literature.[14]

Dmitri Rudinskii and Vasili Verdysh proved themselves to be good professors and their students liked them. "Both of them," writes M. Milićević, a seminary student of that time, "treated us students more nicely and more kindly than any other of our teachers."[15] In addition to teaching, these two professors also took part in other aspects of the educational and cultural life of Serbia.

Although employees of Serbia, Verdysh and Rudinskii were paid by the Russian government. Their salaries were very low; each of them had annually 257 rubles and 40 kopecks in silver, which was less than 200 talers.[16] Regarding their annual income, Prince Alexander made the resolution that, to supplement their regular salaries paid by the Russian government, each would receive 120 talers per year from the Serbian government. The Prince informed the Ministry of Education of his decision on October 18/30, 1849.[17] The Serbian government also paid for the lodging of these professors, which amounted to 2,282 *grošes* and 30 *paras*.[18]

Verdysh and Rudinskii stayed in Serbia only a few years. When the Crimean War between Turkey and Russia broke out in 1853, the Porte issued an order that Russian citizens and merchants could stay in the Ottoman Empire under Austrian protection for only six months; at the end of that term **"all such persons at the specified time have to leave the**

state and none of them can place himself under anyone's protection." According to that order, Verdysh and Rudinskii had to leave Serbia in February of 1854.[19]

Besides the Russians, Vasili Verdysh and Dmitri Rudinskii, in the school year 1849-50 the seminary got two native ecclesiastics who were educated in Kiev between 1846 and 1849 as state fellowship holders. They were the aforementioned Sava Sretenović and Dimitrije Nešić.[20] Their appointment was a very significant event in the educational history of Serbia because they were the first Serbs from Serbia to be given professorships in the Belgrade seminary. Before that, all of its professors, except Likogen Mihailović from Dalmatia, were Serbs from Vojvodina, graduates from the seminary in Sremski Karlovci.[21]

As early as May 12/24, 1839, the Synod of Bishops concluded "that seminary teachers must always be monks who distinguish themselves through their ability and honesty, that they must be appointed to that position by the Metropolitan, and that they must be under his administration all the time."[22] Despite the fact that the Synod of Bishops wanted the seminary to have capable professors, this was not always feasible; sometimes "teachers with problematic qualifications" had to be hired.[23]

The method of teaching used in the seminary did not differ much from the method used in other Serbian secondary schools. With the rather primitive method and the curriculum of that time, students could not be prepared "for the continuous, systematic work which was needed for the successful study of any subject, especially a foreign language."[24]

The Ministry of Education tried several times to take the seminary under its control and to issue a special law for it, but the Metropolitan always found reasons for postponement, pointing out that the school was still in the formative stage and therefore had to stay under his control for a certain time. He succeeded in retaining almost complete control over it for the entire Constitutionalist period. No special law for this school was promulgated, but at the end of 1854, the government issued a decree which resolved the question of its teaching staff. According to that decree, the seminary could have five professors and their salaries had to amount to 400 talers per year; it was to be increased by 50 talers after ten years of teaching, another 50 after fifteen years, and by 100 talers per year after twenty years of teaching. In addition, if the seminary professors left their positions and became civil officials, the years of their teaching were to be counted in their length of service. They were obliged to pay a prescribed sum of money to the so-called "Widows' Fund," and most important, their right to a pension was recognized. By this decree the seminary in Belgrade was given "a middle status between the lyceum and the gymnasium."[25]

After the decree of 1854, Metropolitan Petar Jovanović could not retain complete control over the seminary for much longer. On July 1/13, 1858, the *Soviet* passed a resolution that "all seminary professors, regardless whether they are laymen or ecclesiastics, have to be appointed by the Prince, on the basis of the Metropolitan's recommendation."[26] But this resolution only limited the Metropolitan's power; the seminary would remain largely under his control until 1863 when it, like all the other schools, would come under the complete control of the state. It is surprising that Serbia, which was strongly centralized and which did not allow other schools even to make their own schedules of classes or to change anything concerning their operation without the permission of the Ministry of Education, allowed the seminary to be outside government control. That fact is even more surprising if it is kept in mind that the seminary was financed by the state and a large number of its graduates got teaching positions in state schools.

Despite the fact that during the Constitutionalist period the number of seminary professors was mainly unchanged and the number of seminary students was not drastically altered, the sum for its support was gradually increased. For example, in the school year 1839-40, its expenditures were 1,810 talers.[27] Several years later, in 1845, that sum already amounted to 2,285 talers,[28] and in the last year of the Constitutionalists' reign it was increased to 3,652 talers.[29] It was a rather large sum, especially since the three lower gymnasiums, which had the same number of grades as the seminary, received only 4,101 talers for the same year.[30] We think that the seminary succeeded in keeping its independence for such a long time because of Metropolitan Petar's skillful policy toward the government and because of the great reputation that the church enjoyed in Serbian society.

Because of contradictory reports, it is almost impossible to establish exact statistical data about the seminary students. But we have used the most reliable source available to give a general picture of their enrollments and graduations. According to Metropolitan Petar's report, in the school year 1843-44, the Belgrade seminary had only 104 students.[31] That number was increased, but not every year because there were some years when the total enrollment was smaller than the previous year. For example, in the school year 1846-47, there were 153 students, but in the next several years the number dropped considerably. In the school year 1847-48 it dropped to 129, and in 1848-49 it dropped to a low of 118 students. Yet, a few years later the enrollment had noticeably increased; in the school year 1851-52 it reached 160 students, while in the last year of the Constitutionalist period, the seminary was attended by 161 students.[32] In addition to the young men from Serbia, a certain number of students from neighboring Slavic provinces were educated in the Belgrade seminary at the expense of the government.

Although indigent seminary students had free lodging, food, books, and medicines, and wealthier ones paid only an insignificant sum, only a small number of them completed their education.[33] Milan Milićević wrote that when he began to study in the seminary in 1846, about 80 students were enrolled in the first grade. Only 32 of them graduated from the fourth grade in 1850.[34] In the school year 1849-50, in all grades of the seminary, 126 students were enrolled, yet only 33 of them completed the same school year. In the school year 1853-54, the seminary enrolled 163 students, and only 36 of them completed the year.[35] The main causes for dropping out were similar to the causes already discussed with regard to other schools - poor educational background, the loosely-specified requirements for employment in the civil service, lack of discipline, and the like.

Like most schools in Serbia, the Seminary was faced with many problems, one of the biggest of which was the small classrooms. Milan Milićević left a picturesque description of the crowed conditions:

> There were many students and so few desks in the
> school that there were not enough seats for every-
> body. Those who were richer and more impudent
> occupied the seats at the desks. Not getting a seat,
> I stood next to a stove and took my notes on it
> when a professor dictated his lecture.[36]

We do not know how qualified the priests who graduated from the seminary in Belgrade were as priests, but as teachers they were, for the most part, very poor and uninterested in that profession.[37] Their attitude was a big drawback to the improvement of elementary education in Serbia during the Constitutionalists' regime because they comprised the bulk of the teaching cadre. It is not known for certain what percentage of the existing teachers were seminary graduates, but on the basis of available sources, it may be concluded with great safety that it was around seventy-five percent. As previously indicated, the chief directors of elementary schools sent unfavorable reports to the Ministry of Education about the teaching performance of these seminarians. Such reports infuriated some individuals, and they gave vent to their dissatisfaction in articles published in the *Serbian News*, in which they emphasized that the seminarians were the best available teachers and greatly in demand. Thus, for example, in 1852, the *Serbian News* published an article which raised the questions:

> How can it be that [a person] who completed three grades in the gymnasium and four grades in the seminary is not capable of teaching small children? Where have peddlers, fired band members, expelled soldiers, craftsmen who abandon their craft, and bankrupted merchants been prepared for the teaching profession? Where are their certificates of proficiency for the teaching profession? Where did they complete pedagogic disciplines?[38]

Such articles, probably written by ecclesiastics, were useless. If they indeed wished to defend the seminarians as teachers, they should have found better comparison because to compare them with "peddlers, bankrupted merchants, or expelled soldiers" who were hired as teachers because of the shortage of better ones was a great mistake. Such comparisons did nothing to refute the reports of the chief directors of elementary schools or to prove that the seminarians were capable and good teachers.

In spite of the fact that materials in the archives clearly show that the great majority of seminary graduates were incapable and indifferent teachers, Serbian historical accounts, especially the earlier ones, with few exceptions, praised their capability and the role they played in the educational life of Serbia. Thus, for example, Živojin Djordjević, well-known historian of Serbian education, wrote about the seminary: "This school [was] very important to early education in Serbia not only because it gave us the first educated priests but because it gave us the first good public school teachers as well."[39]

We completely agree that the seminary played a positive role in the educational life of Serbia, but in the backward Serbian state of that time, every existing school played a positive role in her educational and cultural development. Conversely, it is often forgotten that the existence of the seminary was the major factor preventing the development of a cadre of qualified teachers because Metropolitan Petar Jovanović, as has been indicated, was one of the strongest opponents to the opening of a teacher-training school. He feared that graduates of such a school would not only compete with seminarians for teaching positions, but that they would gradually push them completely out of the teaching profession. Already during the Constitutionalist period, the seminary school was rightly "denounced as an antiquated one" in need of all sorts of improvement.[40]

There is no doubt that the seminarians, though insufficiently qualified for the teaching profession, made a great contribution to elementary education in Serbia because it was better to have teachers with limited qualifications than to have teachers without any qualifications or no teachers at all. In addition, the seminarians were among the first native teachers educated in Serbia and they were better able to understand the mentality and needs of her young people.

2.

The need for a business school arose as early as Prince Miloš's reign, but because of the Prince's indifference, financial difficulties, and the absence of teachers, it was not established. However, in the beginning of the Constitutionalist period, when the economic development of Serbia was gathering speed, the need for starting such a school was almost undeniable. Yet, the initiator of its establishment was not the government, but a private person. Manojlo Solar, an educated man and an expert in commerce, applied on March 16/28, 1842, to the Ministry of Education for permission to open a private business school. Instruction in such a school, according to his conception, was to last for three years, and a mixture of general and professional subjects with modern Greek and German were to be taught.[41] It seems that the Ministry of Education was pleased with his plan because as early as March 18/30 of the same year, it assigned Dimitrije Isailović, Chief Inspector of all schools in Serbia, Dimitrije Tirol, a member of the State Department for History and Antiquities, and Timotije Milašinović, director of normal (elementary) schools, to examine Manojlo Solar's qualifications for opening a business school.[42] This commission completed its examination in several days, and on March 23/April 4, 1842, informed the Ministry of Education "that the aforenamed Manojlo Solar has enough knowledge necessary for commerce to enable him to teach successfully those children who will decide to study this branch of civil activity, if his old age does not prevent him from it."[43] On the basis of this report, on March 31/April 12 of the same year, the Ministry of Education informed the mayor's office of Belgrade that Manojlo Solar had permission to open a private business school.[44] Yet, despite the fact that he was granted a permit, he did not open such a school in 1842 for reasons which are unknown to us. Srećko Ćunković, professional counsel of the Pedagogic Museum in Belgrade, writes that on October 1/13, 1843, the Belgrade commune, with the merchants' financial help, "established a two-year business school with Manojlo Solar as a teacher."[45] However, among all the numerous documents in the archives, we could not find any source which would indicate that Solar's or any other business school existed in Serbia in 1843. Moreover, neither the prominent Serbian cultural figures of that time nor contemporary commentators mention the existence of such a school in that year. The documents in the archives show only that in 1843 the question about the opening of a business school with Manojlo Solar at its head with an annual salary of 150 talers was again raised, but the school was not opened.[46]

The establishment of a state-operated and controlled business school, under the name *"Posleno-trgovačko učilište"* was first officially proposed in the aforementioned "Organization of Public School Education" of 1844. This document revealed that the Business School was "opened to all who know how to read and write Serbian correctly and, in addition, have learned the four mathematical operations, and for those who are engaged in occupations such as commerce, crafts, and the like." The same document prescribes that the school will have three grades with four teachers "whom the Ministry of Education will choose and appoint, and who will teach subjects prescribed by the Ministry."[47] Jovan S. Popović wrote a supplement to the "Organization" which was published on November 24/ December 6, 1844, under the title "The Program of the Ministry of Education for the Business School" which explained in detail the section of the "Organization" which applied to that school.[48]

It is significant that the first decrees for the Business School allowed the enrollment of part-time students. The regular students were obliged to take examinations after each semester whereas the part-time students were exempted from all examinations. One of the greatest novelties in the short history of Serbian education was that on the day of registration in the Business School, the regular as well as the part-time students expressed their desires to the school principal as to which subjects they desired to study. Instructions were then adjusted to accommodate their desires, and it was made possible for students to study those subjects which they considered the most useful for an efficient performance in their present or future occupations.[49]

The Business School began to operate on February 1/13, 1845. Petar Radovanović, one of the chief directors of elementary schools, was appointed its first principal. In addition to his regular director's duty, he performed this function as well until December 14/26, 1848, when he was replaced by Jovan Gavrilović, Chief of Staff in the Ministry of Finance. He was very experienced in matters of theoretical and practical commerce, and he did a great deal to improve the operation of this school. But because of a misunderstanding with Platon Simonović, Gavrilović resigned in March of 1853. On April 1/13 of the same year, the principal of the Belgrade gymnasium, Luka Pavlović, was appointed the new principal of the Business School and so became the principal of both schools, a duty he performed for several years.[50]

Instruction in the Business School was conducted by subject, and the following subjects were taught: Serbian, German, modern Greek,

Christianity, and drawing, in all three grades; mathematics in the first two grades; geometry, bookkeeping, and "technology with physics and chemistry" only in the third grade; economy and technology only in the second grade; and geography and history only in the first grade.[51] This curriculum was used until August 25/September 6, 1853, when, on Platon Simonović's recommendation, the Ministry of Education issued a new one for the Business School. It did not differ radically from the previous curriculum; the biggest difference was that the new curriculum introduced some subjects which gave the school a more commercial orientation, for instance, commercial geography, history of commerce, commercial mathematics, and study of goods.[52]

The Business School professors were more of less mediocre and the results of their teaching were rather poor. They changed from time to time, but it is interesting that none of them, as far as we know, was a Serb from Serbia. For example, according to Petar Radovanović, principal of this school, on September 1/13, 1848, in the second semester of the school year, the school had only three professors and all there were foreigners. Konstantin Djordjević was born in Banat (Vojvodina), Konstantin Rano in Rumelia (Bulgaria), and Milutin Vukoslav Golub in Pakrac (Croatia). Each of them had an annual salary of 300 talers.[53] The list of professors for 1855 shows that the teaching staff of the Business School had completely changed, that it was enlarged by one professor, and that their salaries remained the same. The only exception was Jovan Derok, whose annual salary was 400 talers. Why his annual salary was higher by 100 talers than the salaries of the other professors is not known. Those professors were also from outside of Serbia: Ljudevit Španić was from Varaždin, Jovan Derok from Dubrovnik, Milan Milovuk from Budapest, and Evtimije Djordjević from Sremski Karlovci.[54] It should be emphasized that the fact that all professors of this school were foreigners is not as interesting as the fact that domination by the professors from Vojvodina began to decline in the Serbian schools and that gradually professorships were entrusted to foreigners who were not of the Orthodox faith.

With the aim of reducing and gradually eliminating completely foreigners in official positions, including elementary teaching and professorial positions, on May 8/20, 1844, Prince Alexander handed down a decision that all foreign citizens in the state service who wished to remain in Serbia would be obliged to accept Serbian citizenship within six months. It emphasized that those who would not fulfill their obligation in that time or who would not be willing to accept Serbian citizenship "would be deprived of all rights and benefits which a Serbian official enjoys from the moment when his prescribed term expires."[55] In regard to this decision, on May 25/ June 6, 1855, Prince Alexander issued rules governing the employment of foreigners and naturalized Serbs in Serbia. The first article of those rules is the most important and it reads: "A foreigner, that is a person who does not have Serbian citizenship, cannot be appointed as a regular and full-time civil service employee; however, with the *Soviet's* and the Prince's permission he can be appointed an employee under contract."[56] These examples show that the Serbian government during the Constitutionalists' regime took a decisive and risky step regarding foreign citizens because there was the potential danger that many of them would rather leave Serbia than to accept her citizenship. If this had happened, the educational and particularly the cultural life of Serbia would have been affected because in those fields, the presence of foreigners was still indispensable since the state did not have a sufficient number of natives who could take over their duties and perform them successfully. The Serbian government was aware of the fact that naturalized Serbs could not have a true patriotic feeling or know the mentality of the people as well as native Serbs did; but more important than that, the government was aware that those foreigners who accepted Serbian citizenship would be exclusively subject to Serbian laws and as Serbian citizens would not have any obligations toward the states they came from. In addition, by this action, foreign governments would be prevented from interfering in Serbian internal and even foreign policy on the pretext of protecting the rights of their citizens.

The small number of enrolled students and the still smaller number who completed their education was one of the biggest problems of the Business School. For example, according to its principal's report of February 2/14, 1845, that is, in the beginning of its operation, the school had only 16 students.[57] Only two months later, on April 28/May 10 of the same year, in a letter to the Ministry of Education, principal Radovanović expressed his concern about a rapid decline in the Business School which then had only 5 students. Some of the students had engaged themselves in trade, some had begun to learn various crafts, and some had returned to their homes.[58] Several years later, Radovanović's report of September 1/13, 1848, shows that low enrollment was still a problem. In the second semester of the school year 1847-48, there were only 56 students in all three grades of the Business School: 35 in the first, 12 in the second, and only 9 in the third.[59] That number dropped even lower. Platon Simonović's report of September 20/October 2, 1854, shows that in the school year 1853-54, the Business School had 47 students,[60] and a year before the downfall of the Constitutionalists, "The List of Schools in the Principality of Serbia for the school year 1856-57" shows that their number dropped to 25, but in spite of that, the school still employed four professors.[61]

Despite the wide fluctuation in enrollment, the sum for the financing of the Business School was not significantly changed. For example, for the first year of its operation, 1845-46, it received 1,200 talers.[62] A decade later, 1855-56, that sum was increased slightly to 1,440 talers,[63] and in the last year of the Constitutionalists' regime, 1858, it amounted to 1,110 talers.[64]

Since the Business School did not fulfill expectations, some changes had to be introduced. At the initiative of some Belgrade merchants, by a decree issued on May 27/June 9, 1858, and by the Prince's order of June 3/15 of the same year, the Business School was transformed into a commercial school with one preparatory and four regular grades. Filip Silvestar Nigris, former director of a commercial school in Vienna, was appointed its principal and, therefore, in the historical documents this school is sometimes referred to as "Nigris's School." Requirements for this school were somewhat stiff: to be admitted, every student had to have completed his elementary education and had to pass an entrance examination of some kind before the school's principal. The biggest change in its curriculum was that instead of modern Greek, the Italian language was introduced.[65]

In addition to the state business of commercial school in Belgrade, a private commercial school existed in Požarevac. It was inaugurated by Živan Kovačević, an elementary school teacher, in the school year 1850-51, according to a permit issued by the Ministry of Education on August 11/23, 1850. In the beginning of its operation, it had a very small number of students, only three, and they were obliged to take their final examination at the end of the school year in the Business School in Belgrade. All three took it and passed in August, 1851.[66]

Since instruction in that school lasted only one year, on September 22/October 4, 1852, Kovačević applied again to the Ministry of Education asking permission to continue the operation of his school and to extend the period of instruction to three years. This request was granted on September 26/October 8 of the same year. He was allowed to open the second grade in the school year 1852-53, and the third grade was to be introduced in the following school year, but there is no evidence that the third grade was ever opened.[67]

Živan Kovačević's commercial school was financed from tuition fees and by the merchants and craftsmen associations of the Požarevac district. For example, on April 27/May 8, 1853, the merchants guild from Požarevac promised to help the school with 30 talers per year; forty-three persons signed this obligation.[68] The grocers guild made a similar promise, but they did not specify the sum which they were willing to give. In this obligation, which was issued under the title "The Pledge of the Grocers' Guild," it was written:

> This sum [it was not specified in the document]
> which does not come from superfluous wealth, but
> is collected by your benefactors named below who
> earned it with their hard work and sweat, is
> intended for you, our dear youths, for your happi-
> ness and brighter future. Thus, let this small gift
> be a charge to you from which we all shall obtain
> a great benefit, and one day may you know how to
> do deserved honor to the shades of these donors.[69]

Kovačević's school was financed in this way until January, 1857, when the Požarevac commune took the financing upon itself. A report about it was sent to the *Serbian Journal* on January 17/29 of the same year which says that there had been some attempts to abolish this school, "but now," its author writes, "we are happy to announce that this school will remain permanently."[70]

The curriculum followed in this school differed from the curriculum in the similar school in Belgrade. In its first grade, the following subjects were taught: commerce, mathematics, Serbian grammar, German, commercial geography, composition in Serbian and German, drawing, and religious instruction; in the second grade the following were taught: commerce, commercial mathematics, German, elementary bookkeeping instruction, instruction in writing business and ordinary letters, dictated writing of Serbian and German, drawing, and religious instruction.[71] As this list shows, the instruction of this school emphasized professional subjects. Of foreign languages, only German was taught, probably because it was the only foreign language that Kovačević knew.

There is no statistical data about the number of students who attended Kovačević's school prior to 1855, but records exist for years following that date. In the school years 1855-56 and 1856-57 there were 28 students, but in 1857-58 their number declined considerably to only 15.[72]

It is not known what results the students of this school achieved, but it may be safely said that they were hardly on an enviable level. It would be unreasonable to expect a miracle from Živan Kovačević, an ordinary elementary school teacher in the role of a professional school instructor.

The need for business schools was caused by the rapid development of the Serbian economy. They were opened, but they were unable to meet the expectations of those for whom they were intended and those who invested in their operation. The chief cause of their poor success should be sought in the unpreparedness of Serbian society for that type of school. Yet, they made a definite contribution, no matter how modest, to the development of Serbian education in general, and to the economic life of the state, because as a result of their pioneer work, similar schools were built at a later time and the founders of those schools were able to avoid the mistakes made by their predecessors.

3.

After receiving her autonomy in 1830, Serbia began to carry out an intensive renovation. Old buildings were repaired, new one erected, roads and bridges built, agrarian reform executed, and so on. Since Serbia did not have a native cadre for these and similar jobs, she was forced to bring specialists from abroad, especially from Vojvodina. However, because of the increased economic development during the Constitutionalists' regime, those foreign specialists, who were often only skilled and talented workmen, could not continue to meet all the state's needs. Besides, it was very difficult to get good specialists. In order to solve this problem at least partly, the Ministry of Interior with Ilija Garašanin at its head began to advocate the education of native specialists who could gradually replace foreigners and be able to meet the needs of the state. On January 25/ February 6, 1846, the Ministry sent a letter to the *Soviet* explaining the difficulties concerning the hiring of foreign engineers. "This Ministry," the letter states, "encountered large obstacles while seeking engineers this year as well as last. It cannot fill all the engineering positions that were anticipated by the [State] budget because roads are being built all over Europe where engineers have well-paid jobs. Therefore, either because of the small salaries or because of unsuitable conditions, engineers do not wish to accept our invitation to come here." For that reason, the Ministry was of the opinion that the government "cannot suitably satisfy that need [for engineers] as long as it does not educate its [own] engineers from among our youth."[73] The *Soviet* accepted this suggestion and on May 29/June 10, 1846, decided that an engineering school would be opened in Belgrade. Prince Alexander confirmed it on June 19/July 1, 1846.[74]

On the basis of the Prince's letter to the Ministry of Interior, it may be concluded that the first engineering school in Serbia was to be an advanced school of some kind because every candidate who wanted to be admitted had to have completed two years in the Department of Philosophy at the Belgrade Lyceum. Its course of instruction was to last for three years, and in the beginning of its operation, only eight students were to be admitted. The school was to have three professors, but it was pointed out that later, when the school became bigger, two more professors would be hired. Capable officials of the Ministry of Interior were to be appointed its first professors. They were expected to perform their regular duties in the Ministry, while teaching in the engineering school was to be a part-time job for which each of them would receive 100 talers per year in addition to their regular salaries. But the Prince's letter to the Ministry of Interior states "if the prescribed number of professors cannot be found among the officials of this governmental office, our lyceum professors will be hired." Instruction was to be divided into two parts: theoretical and practical. Theoretical instruction was to be conducted in the winter. Practical geodesy was to be taught in the first year, mechanics in the second, and architecture in the third year. In addition to those professionally-oriented subjects, drawing and the German language were prescribed for all three years. "The German language will be taught," it was said in the letter, "so that the students of this school will be able to improve themselves by reading German books or those who would distinguish themselves in these [engineering] disciplines could be sent abroad in order to improve themselves more." Practical instruction could only be conducted in the summer, at which time the students worked with engineers "in order to practice surveying and building edifices and roads, and supervising and carrying out according to plans the building of various constructions." The engineering school was to be supported by the state with an estimated annual expenditure of 1,100 talers.[75]

According to Milan Milićević, the Engineering School or *Indžinirska škola*, as it was officially called, began to operate in September, 1846, and was closed, for reasons unknown to us, in the spring of 1849. It was attended, not by eight students as the Prince had prescribed, but by nine. However, only two of them devoted themselves to the engineering profession - Jovan K. Ristić and Nikola Jovanović. Four died, two while still students, and the rest became government officials. The professors of this school were foreigners: Atanasije Nikolić, Ignjat Stanimirović, August Cerman, and Nenole, whose first name is unknown to us.[76]

The contribution of the Engineering School to the development of Serbian society was so small that it is almost not worth mention. If its subjects and professors are taken into consideration, it cannot be considered in any case an advanced school. Furthermore, if the number of its students is taken into consideration, it could not even be included in the category of Serbian regular schools, despite the fact that it was opened on the basis of a decree issued by the government and was supported by the state. It can best be characterized as a three-year course designed partially to prepare a certain number of young men to be engineers. Although the demand for engineers was great, almost nothing significant was undertaken either to keep the Engineering School alive or to enlarge it.

4.

The Military Academy which was opened during Prince Miloš's first reign operated for only a very short time, but reopening it or founding a similar institution was not considered until the middle of the nineteenth century. Only the young men who attended lower gymnasiums or the gymnasium received elementary military training because such skills were included in the subject of physical education. However, in time it was realized that young men with such limited training could not successfully perform the duties of army officers. In addition, with the development of the state, the army grew, and demands for army officers became greater and greater. The shortage could only be alleviated by opening a military school in Serbia; this action was taken during the Revolution of 1848-49.

A Czech, Franjo Zah (František Zách), who was well known for his involvement in the political life of Serbia, played an important role in the founding of the military school. After spending some time outside of Serbia, he returned to Belgrade in 1849 where he was asked by the Serbian Voivoda Stevan Knićanin and other military leaders to make a plan indicating "how a young generation of the officer corps can be educated and trained in a special school" and to submit it to Ilija Garašanin, then the Prince's representative.[77] Zách made a plan which was favorably accepted by the government, and as early as March 6/18, 1850, a decree regarding the operating of a military school was issued. It was established in Belgrade under the official name of the "Artillery School" (*Artileriska škola*) and began to operate on September 6/18, 1850.[78]

The decree of 1850 prescribed that instruction in the Artillery School was to last for four years, but after the enrollment of the first class, this was extended to five years. Admission requirements for this school were more strict than for any other secondary school in Serbia. According to the aforementioned decree, only candidates with the following prerequisites could be admitted to the Artillery School: "(1) good behavior, (2) those who have graduated from the Department of Philosophy of the Belgrade Lyceum or from the gymnasium with good grades, or those who have prepared themselves somewhere else for such a school [Artillery], and (3) those who are in good physical shape so they can, if necessary, bear the hardship of war."[79] However, because the number of candidates significantly increased over the next several years, the admission requirements for this school were considerably stiffened. Thus, for example, admission requirements for the school year 1855-56 were: (1) every candidate had to be a Serb by birth or by naturalization, (2) he could be neither younger than 15 nor older than 18 years of age, (3) he had to be in good physical shape, (4) he had to complete three years of the gymnasium with very good grades, but the decree adds "if a sufficient number of capable students who graduated from higher grades classes will apply, the priority will be given to them. Exception will be made and a student from a lower grade will be admitted if it can be shown that he is more gifted than a student from a higher grade," and (5) all candidates were obliged to take an entrance examination before a committee selected by the Ministry of Interior. That examination covered the following subjects: history, geography, statistics, mathematics, Serbian grammar, and the German language.[80]

The Artillery School had a large number of candidates mostly because the state bore all the expenses of their education and, in addition to that, every candidate had a regular salary (it was more like pocket-money) of 8 *cvancigs* per month and a supplement of 3 talers.[81] It should be indicated that at that time to be an army officer was a great honor and they enjoyed not only various benefits but also special respect and influence in Serbian society. So prestigious was the army that in 1853 the state spent 12,882 talers, 3 *grošes*, and 17 and 1/16th *paras* for the support of the Artillery School;[82] in 1855, 16,000 talers were spent,[83] and in 1856, 16,738 talers and 39 *paras* were spent.[84] This was, indeed, a large sum to set aside from the state budget for the financing of a school, especially considering, for example, that in 1856 the state gave only 10,139 talers to the Lyceum, 4,862 to the Gymnasium, 1,440 to the Business School in Belgrade, 3,575 to the three lower gymnasiums, and 3,590 to the Seminary.[85] As can be seen, the sum given to the Artillery School was only slightly smaller than the sum spent on all schools in Serbia financed by the state.

During its first years of operation, the following subjects were taught in the Artillery School: artillery, mathematics, drawing, mechanics, physics, special chemistry, fortification, tactics, military geography, history, and French. In addition, there was practice in artillery drilling, laboratory work, riding, swimming, fencing, and manufacturing of cannons.[86] This curriculum was gradually changed so that at the end of the Constitutionalists' regime, in the school year 1856-57, the following subjects were taught: instructions in Christianity, artillery, theoretical and practical chemistry, mathematics, geometry, mechanics, elementary practical mathematics, physics, tactics, military administration and administration of general staff, field fortification, "military style," construction (architecture), descriptive geometry and drawing, military geography, history, riding, swimming, gymnastics, fighting (fencing), French and German.[87] The students of the Artillery School traveled through Serbia, most often to Kragujevac and Stragari, from twenty to twenty-eight days per year, to engage in field work.[88] It is interesting to note that the Russian language was not among the subjects taught, although the first Serbian army officers were educated in Russia.

As in all other Serbian schools, a Western influence was noticed in the Artillery School. This was especially true after 1852 when the state scholarship holders educated in well-known military academies of Western Europe, most often in Berlin and Paris, began to return to Serbia, and some of them became professors at the Artillery School. Petar Protić-Sokoljanin and Ranko Alimpić were the most important of these. Alimpić was the first Serb from Serbia appointed principal of the Artillery School. He replaced František Zách at the end of 1858.

Zách was the first principal of the Artillery School. In the beginning he performed his duty as a civilian because he was not an army officer by profession, but on June 8/20, 1850, he was given the rank of artillery captain, and on November 30/December 12, 1857, he was promoted to the rank of major.[89] As principal, Zách had close ties with Army headquarters concerning professionally-oriented subjects and with the Ministry of Education concerning general subjects. Although he was not an officer by profession, he performed his duties well. The chief reasons for his replacement were political tension in Serbia and the change of dynasties that took place at the so-called Saint Andrew's Assembly.

In spite of its name, the Artillery School did not prepare only artillery officers, but officers for all branches of the army. It admitted a limited number of students, approximately 22, and they had to be the best.[90] The number of professors was gradually increased. When it began to operate in the school year 1850-51, the Artillery School had only three professors, but by 1857-58, they already numbered eleven and among them there were several Serbs who had completed their education in the best military academies of Western Europe.[91] Since it had relatively favorable conditions for its operation, good students, capable professors, and solid financial support, the Artillery School achieved the best results of all the existing professional schools in Serbia, and it seems to us that the author of an article published in the *Serbian Journal* did not exaggerate when he wrote: "We can say that it is now the best organized institution for the education of youths in Serbia."[92]

5.

Serbia was predominantly an agricultural country in which agriculture was rather primitive. In order to elevate agricultural production it was necessary to acquaint a certain number of people with the latest farming techniques so that they could later convey their knowledge and experience to peasants throughout Serbia. Such agricultural experts could only be trained in a special school. In the 1850s, initiatives for the opening of such a school in Serbia began to come from various sources. For example, at the end of 1850, the *Serbian News* published an article on its front page advocating the opening of an agricultural school. "Besides people's lower schools," the author of this articles writes, "we immediately need **people's agricultural-economic schools. Let us beautify our cultivated fields, our parks, our forests, our cattle -- then we shall light up the best and the most pleasant candle to God and to ourselves.**"[93] Two years later, a similar suggestion was given by a government representative. On November 11/23, 1852, Aleksa Simić, Minister of Interior, sent a letter to the *Soviet* asking to establish an agricultural school "in which farm youths will have opportunity to learn how to till land and to raise cattle."[94] The *Soviet* granted this request on December 1/13 of the same year,[95] and Prince Alexander endorsed the decision to open such an agricultural school on January 10/22, 1853.[96] The instructions for its opening, entitled "The Establishment of an Agricultural School in Topčider" was issued on the same day.[97] The preliminary estimate for the support of this school was 224,060 *grošes* and 28 *paras*.[98]

The "Establishment" of 1853 prescribed that every year the Agricultural School would admit one student from every district, which meant 55 students per year because Serbia then had 55 districts. The candidates were to be at least sixteen years of age, were to have completed their elementary education with good grades, and were to be in good physical condition so they would be able to do all agricultural tasks. Each district chose the student it would send, and they did not pay anything for their education. All the school's expenses were paid by a special surtax of one *groš* per year which every taxpayer was obliged to pay. That was the manner of financing until 1856 when the expense of its support fell to the Main School Fund. Besides the chosen students from every district, any child could attend the Agricultural School if his parents were willing to pay all his expenses except the tuition fee. The students lived in the boarding school, which was in the same building as the classrooms, and they were rather strictly controlled. For example, they had to get up at 4 AM in the summer as well as in the winter, and they went to bed at 9 PM.[99]

The Agricultural School in Topčider opened in May, 1853. Its course of instruction lasted two years and was divided into theoretical and practical studies. The following subjects were taught: instruction in Christianity, reading and writing, mathematics, agriculture, viniculture, fruit growing, forestry, cattle-breeding, apiculture, sericulture, military training, architecture, carpentry, and practical agricultural work.[100] The school had only a few instructors. Undoubtedly Atanasije Nikolić was the most important instructor of this school, and he may be considered its "spiritual creator and organizer."[101] According to the press of that time, the Agricultural School in Topčider showed good results. "Indeed," the *Serbian Journal* wrote, "Prince Alexander Karadjordjević can be proud of Topčider, and he will live to see his institution [the Agricultural School] will sooner or later be a model to the neighboring states."[102] The school had a "remarkable collection of fruit trees" and after final examinations, fairs were held to display cattle, agricultural tools, and agricultural products.[103]

Despite the progress they seemed to be making in their education, the Agricultural School students were dissatisfied with their hard life, and on December 16/28, 1858, they told the Saint Andrew's Assembly about it. In a letter they pointed out that their life in the schools was "one hundred times uglier and worse than [the life] of prisoners and convicts" and asked the Assembly to do something to make their life bearable.[104] Atanasije Nikolić officially denied the students' complaints. He wrote in his "*Biografija*" (Biography):

> I boldly deny that the senders [of that letter] could
> have sufficient knowledge and experience to judge
> the operation of this school. The senders gave as
> their own report that Vladimir Jovanović,[105] a
> known communist, had written for them because
> they were attracted to that movement which
> already in that time longed for a republic....[106]

But after reviewing the students' complaints, a member of the Saint Andrew's Assembly established "that no area, no district, no commune, no home in the country had any benefit from ... the Agricultural School."[107] The Agricultural School in Topčider, the first school of that kind in Serbia, was officially abolished on January 9/21, 1859.[108] At the time of its opening much was expected from it, but those hopes were only partly fulfilled because a large number of its graduates did not devote themselves to agriculture. Most of them chose more lucrative bureaucratic occupations.

In order to complete the discussion of professional and vocational schools in Serbia during the Constitutionalist period, it should be mentioned that on March 14/26, 1854, Prince Alexander decided that a three-year vocational school was to be established in Kragujevac. It was to be under the control of the cannon factory director, but it is not known if that school was ever opened.[109]

6.

Because of a textbook shortage, teachers in the Serbian school system were forced to dictate their lectures for the greater part of the Constitutionalist period. This method not only took much of the teachers' teaching time but negatively affected students' learning as well. The subjects were usually dictated with virtually no explanation, and the knowledge obtained by that method was of very little use.

The need for textbooks was felt during Miloš's first reign, at which time steps were taken to alleviate the shortage by publishing the first native textbooks. Their publication was continued during the Constitutionalists' regime, and it was considerably expanded after the issuing of the new school plan and program in 1844. In that field, as in many other fields of educational work, Jovan S. Popović made a large contribution. He not only advocated the publishing of new textbooks, but he wrote some of them himself.

Before the 1840s, the Serbian government did not have any defined policy regarding the publication of textbooks. Activities were usually limited to pointing out the need for high quality school books, rewarding their authors, and inviting professors to write textbooks for their subjects. However, this action did not show significant results since the professors' response was lukewarm, mainly because only a small number of them were capable of writing adequate textbooks. In addition to their limited knowledge, most of them did not have a good command of the Serbian language because they were mainly educated in Hungarian and Austrian schools. Milovan Spasić's case best illustrates the deficiency. He had a doctorate, and for a long time he was one of the chief directors of elementary schools in Serbia. Yet, in his report of January 26/February 7, 1847, which contained one thousand words, he made some five hundred mistakes. When this report was published in the *Belgrade Reading Club News*, a member of the Reading Club criticized Spasić for his poor writing and the editor of the paper, Pavle A. Popović, because he allowed the publication of articles with so many errors. "I leave aside logical mistakes," he wrote, "but at least let the grammar be accurate and correct, because newspapers are published so that people can learn something and not to destroy that which is already known."[110]

After the introduction of the new curriculum in 1844, greater attention was paid to the publication of textbooks, and this became an integral part of government educational policy. The task of reviewing prepared manuscripts and publishing approved ones was originally entrusted to the first Serbian learned society, the so-called *"Družstvo Srbske Slovesnosti"* (The Serbian Literary Society.) Later the tasks were assigned to special committees of the Ministry of Education.

Since the Serbian Literary Society was engaged in various activities and was not a constituent part of the Ministry of Education, consideration was given to the creation of a special school committee which would oversee the publication of textbooks. Such a committee, called the Educational Committee, was established by Prince Alexander's decree of July 3/15, 1845.[111] This decree prescribed that the committee was to be composed of nine members. They were to be chosen by the Ministry of Education from among the most educated people, and recommended to the Prince, who was to appoint them. Their mandate was to last for three years, and they could be reappointed.[112] However, officials of the Ministry of Education could not be members of this committee. Its first members were appointed on July 28/August 9, 1845, and they were Gavrilo Popović, archimandrite of Vraćevšnica Monastery; Dimitrije Isailović, gymnasium inspector, Atanasije Nikolić, chief of staff in the Department of Police and Economy; Petar Radovanović and Milovan Spasić, chief directors of elementary schools; Isidor Stojanović, Sergije Nikolić, and Janko Šafařik, lyceum professors; and Vasilije Lazić, literary censor. In addition to their regular salaries, each of these men received an extra 180 talers per year for their work on the Educational Committee.[113]

The chief tasks of the Educational Committee were to work on the improvement of curricula, review and approve the manuscripts of new textbooks, certify the proficiency of teachers and professors who applied for teaching positions, and so on.[114]

The Committee was given a rather large amount of power. For example, its charter stated that in case of a disagreement between the Committee and the Ministry of Education, the Prince would make the final decision.[115] Thus, the rather great power of the Committee had the effect of weakening the power of the Ministry. This caused relations between the two groups to be tense from the very beginning; thus, in spite of its good performance, at the request of the Ministry of Education, the Educational Committee was abolished on October 30/November 11, 1847, because "it does not serve the purpose for which it was established."[116]

Two years later, at the end of 1849, the question regarding the establishment of a committee which would make the Ministry of Education's task easier was raised again; this time, the Ministry itself was the initiator. On October 21/November 2, 1849, its acting minister, Lazar Arsenijević-Batalaka, suggested to the *Soviet* that it establish a school committee whose main tasks would be "writing and reviewing [textbooks] for all subjects, especially books for elementary schools ... and in general helping the Ministry of Education in matters of public education whenever the Committee finds it to be necessary."[117] This suggestion was accepted and on November 25/December 7 of the same year, Prince Alexander allowed the Ministry of Education to establish such a committee.[118] It was established at the beginning of 1850, under the name "The School Committee." In the first months of its operation, it had thirteen members, but that number was gradually increased. The main tasks of this Committee were to review the manuscripts of textbooks prepared for publication and to assign one of its members, or to hire someone outside of the Committee, to write textbooks if a need for them arose. In addition, if the Committee recommended a manuscript for publication, it was obliged "to give its opinion to the Ministry of Education as to what compensation an author deserves if he allows his work to be published at the government's expense and for its benefit."[119]

On February 7, 1850 (O.S.), the *Serbian News* published an article about the establishment and duties of the School Committee, emphasizing that "no school book, old or new, will be used or given to youths in elementary schools or in higher school institutions, if the Committee does not review and approve it."[120]

As far as its tasks were concerned, the School Committee was similar to the Educational Committee, but not as far as its authority and power were concerned. It could only make suggestions and present its opinions, while the Ministry of Education made final decisions. Besides, its members did not receive any compensation for their work on the Committee; occasional gifts in the form of books published in Serbia were their only reward.[121]

In spite of the limitation on its authority, the School Committee was very active, and in numerous cases it initiated changes in government educational policy. Since its main task was the publication of textbooks, it achieved the most noteworthy results in that field. Under its direction and control, numerous school books were published, and their quality improved every year. However, the improvement in textbook quality was not entirely the result of the Committee's conscientious and diligent work; in great part the improvement was due to the return of the first Serbs educated abroad. These returning Serbs, who were pioneers in scholarly work in Serbia, wrote the best textbooks written during the Constitutionalist period.

The School Committee was composed of leading Serbian experts who reviewed the manuscripts of new textbooks in their fields of specialization. Usually they did their work independently, though it was not rare that some manuscripts were read before the full Committee, and all members voted whether they should be published or not. The requirements for publication were rather strict; thus, many manuscripts had to be partly or completely revised while others were rejected outright. Thus, for example, in the spring of 1850, *Mitologija Grka i Rimljana* (Greek and Roman Mythology), a translation from French by Jovan Nikolić, a principal of the Negotin lower gymnasium, was rejected with the note "that this work cannot be published as a school book unless it is completely retranslated."[122]

Due to the numerous publications of textbooks, on September 15/27, 1853, the makers of educational policy forbade the dictation of subjects in the gymnasium and the Lyceum.[123] It is not known how carefully the professors observed that prohibition or how much it affected students' knowledge.

For several reasons it is almost impossible to establish how many textbooks for elementary, secondary, professional, and vocational schools were published during the Constitutionalist period. Often it is hard to tell from the title what books were used as textbooks. As far as we know, there are not lists of published textbooks in Serbia prior to the late 1850s. Reports concerning new textbooks published in newspapers and journals are not complete. Yet, on the basis of *Srpska bibliografija* (Serbian Bibliography) by Stojan Novaković, the well-known Serbian historian in the second half of the nineteenth century, a rather reliable picture can be obtained.[124] According to his *Srpska bibliografija*, in the Serbia of the Constitutionalist period, about forty textbooks and reference books were published for elementary school use, and about fifty were published for secondary, professional, and vocational school use.[125]

Most of the textbooks published in Serbia were written by foreigners, especially Serbs from Vojvodina, while only a few of them were written by native Serbs. Yet, *Srbska grammatika za osnovne škole* (The Serbian Grammar for Elementary Schools) by Ljubomir Cukić and *Srbska istorija za osnovne srbske škole* (The History of Serbia for the Serbian Elementary Schools) by Ljubomir Nenadović, both published in 1850, were among the most significant textbooks of the Constitutionalist period written by native Serbs.[126] On the whole, the textbooks produced during this period for elementary and secondary schools were of low quality and written in a relatively poor style. Most often they were translations or adaptations of foreign textbooks, or they were written on the model of foreign textbooks, especially Austrian ones.

Journals and newspapers were often used as supplements to textbooks; through them students could become acquainted with the latest political and cultural news as well as with well-known literary works, which were often published in installments. *Vospitatelj ženskij* (Women's Instructor), compiled by Lyceum professor Matija Ban, was one of the most important journals of that time; Prince Alexander allowed its publication by a decree of February 1/13, 1847, and its first and only issue was published in the middle of 1847.[127] *The Women's Instructor* does not deserve mention for exceptional quality but because it was the first journal exclusively intended for young females or for "the fair sex of the Yugoslav people," as Ban wrote on its front page.[128] It is worth mentioning that on January 17/29, 1853, the *Serbian News* began to publish in installments the then very popular book *Uncle Tom's Cabin* by Harriet Beecher Stowe under the title "Uncle Tom's Cabin or Slavery in a Free Country," only a year after its first publication in the United States. It was excellently received by the small reading public of Serbia so that its translation was published as a book twice in 1854 alone.[129] Later on, especially in the 1860s, it had a significant influence on Serbian liberal youth. For instance, young Svetozar Marković was so enthusiastic about it that he even tried to write a drama based on it.[130]

The publication of textbooks was one of the main tasks in the government's educational policy, and a great deal was done to publish them in as large a quantity as possible and to improve their quality. Unfortunately, no notable success was achieved, but nevertheless, significant steps were made. Textbooks were published for almost all the subjects of elementary, secondary, professional, and vocational schools. With their publication, the practice of dictation gradually disappeared from the Serbian schools and the quality of instruction improved.

The development of education took an important place in the Constitutionalists' internal policy. Serbian historians usually point out that the great need for officials who could effectively carry out their policy was the chief reason that the Constitutionalists paid special attention to education. This opinion is only partly correct. The materials presented show that for the twenty years of their reign, there was no increase in the number of secondary schools, even though the main task of such schools was to prepare a bureaucratic cadre. On the other hand, the number of professional and vocational schools was considerably increased, mainly due to the spontaneous economic development of the state. True, a large number of their graduates became employed as officials and clerks, but there is no evidence that the Constitutionalists opened those schools just to prepare bureaucrats who would execute their policy. If that was the result, it was not their intent; graduates often chose civil service careers for objective reasons - government service was very lucrative and advancement in it was rapid.

CHAPTER IV

HIGHER EDUCATION

Crafty men contemn studies;
simple men admire them;
and wise men use them.

Francis Bacon

The Lyceum, which was opened as part of the Kragujevac gymnasium in the academic year 1838-39, continued to operate throughout the Constitutionalists' regime. A great deal of money was spent to cover its expenditures as well as to improve its instruction, because it was the only institution in Serbia which prepared individuals to perform the highest functions in political, economic, and cultural life of the country or to continue their higher education abroad. In time it lost the character of a school for general education and became a higher professional school, "the germ of a university," as some educated Serbs proudly called it.[1]

Significant changes in its operation were already noticeable in the academic year 1839-40. In addition to the two existing professors, Isidor Stojanović and Konstantin Branković, several new professors were appointed. They were Atanasije Nikolić, Antonije Arnot, Aleksije Okoljski, and Archsyncellus Gavrilo Popović.[2] Since the Lyceum now contained two years, the subjects to be taught in the second year were defined, and some changes in the curriculum for the first year were made. According to the new curriculum, which was first used in the academic year 1839-40, the following subjects were taught: Christianity and the Gospel, and the Eastern Orthodox religion, introduction to philosophy, logic, mathematics, general European history, and geodesy; the second year subjects were: instruction in Christianity, philosophy, physics, practical geometry, general history, and agricultural economy. German, French, and drawing were taught in both years. The subjects natural law and statistics of Europe were not taught in the first year of its operation, 1838-39, though the first curriculum for the Lyceum, that of September 18/30, 1838, had prescribed them.[3]

In the first year of its operation, the Lyceum was under the direct control of the Ministry of Education. However, in the next academic year, that is 1839-40, direct control was entrusted to a professor whose official title was that of "rector." Ordinarily the rector was elected every year by his fellow lyceum professors and confirmed by the Prince, but the first rector, Atanasije Nikolić, was appointed by the Ministry of Education.[4] On October 1/13, 1839, on the first day of classes, he made a speech to a group, made up of students, professors, officials, and ordinary citizens. He began it with the motto: "Stand, stand with fear because the place on which you are standing is sacred!"[5] His speech was permeated with Serbian patriotism even though he was not a Serb from Serbia, but a Serb from Vojvodina. Among other things, he also said:

> We shall spare no effort, we shall spare no sacrifice, we shall use all means to bring and to direct you, dear hope of our fatherland, to a real way of benefaction. Our greatest happiness will be to see you in this country inspired by good deeds and adorned with wreaths of great wisdom, and to hand you over as such glorious young men to our dear fatherland and into your parents' arms .... Your dear parents handed you to us from their arms and now we are your father and mother. If you are willing to be useful to our dearest fatherland, and to yourselves, and to be a comfort, happiness, and help to your parents, have full confidence in us and follow our counsel.[6]

Future rectors of the Lyceum followed Atanasije Nikolić's example and greeted new students in the beginning of every school year. In time it became a tradition of this institution.

In the first two years of its operation, the Lyceum did not have a separate building but shared one with the gymnasium. This arrangement lasted until the end of the academic year 1839-40, when the Lyceum was moved to a former military arsenal.[7]

As the capital of Serbia, Kragujevac played a primary role in her cultural life until 1839. Then, the capital was shifted to Belgrade and the move virtually destroyed the cultural life of the former capital. Belgrade quickly became the main cultural center of Serbia and almost all cultural institutions were located there. For that reason, the professors of the Kragujevac Lyceum wished to move it to Belgrade. In order to support their request, they gave many reasons. Among the most important were: the existence of the printing house in Belgrade, the greater ease in getting necessary books because Belgrade had a larger collection than Kragujevac, they as well as their students could have the opportunity to be in the company of educated people and learn a great deal from them, and it would be easier for them to publish articles in the *Serbian News* as well as in its supplement, *Podunavka*.[8] They did not have to wait very long before their request was granted. As early as May 27/June 8, 1841, the Ministry of

Education suggested to Prince Michael to move the Lyceum from Kragujevac to Belgrade. Michael accepted it and on June 25/July 7 of the same year, he made a resolution that the Lyceum be moved to Belgrade at the end of the academic year 1840-41. It was moved in the beginning of August, 1841.[9] For the first three years it operated in a communal house, but in 1844 it was moved to Princess Ljubica's palace where it remained until 1863.[10]

In July 1840, thirteen students completed their second year in the Department of Philosophy at the Kragujevac Lyceum, and at the same time, their education in this institution because its course of instruction lasted only for two years. With the desire of preparing this first generation as well as possibly for numerous administrative jobs in the state, especially for juridical positions, Stefan Radićević, Minister of Justice and Education, suggested to the *Soviet* on August 1/13 of the same year, to open a class for the philosophy graduates in which the discipline of law would be taught "in order to improve and extend that knowledge which they received 'til now so they would become excellent and educated members of the fatherland."[11] The *Soviet* accepted this suggestion and on September 3/15, 1840, it informed Prince Michael of its resolution, recommending that he appoint two professors for the discipline of law with an annual salary of 700 talers each. The Prince approved the *Soviet's* resolution and on September 6/18 of the same year, he decreed the opening of a one-year course in law and political science at the Kragujevac Lyceum.[12] This decision is not only important because with the opening of the Department of Law the foundation of the future Law School was laid, but because with its establishment, the Lyceum began to lose the character of an institution for general education and became a higher professional institution. After 1840, it was indeed "the germ of a university."

Since Serbia did not have anyone among her people who could teach law and political science, she had to find new professors outside of her borders. Jovan Raić, renowned attorney from Novi Sad, was elected the first professor of the new department. His name was known to educational administrators in Serbia because he should have come to the Lyceum in 1839 to be a professor in the second year of its Department of Philosophy, but he had not come because of political tensions and unrest in Serbia.[13] In order to fill the position of the second professor, an open competition was announced in the *Serbian News* of August 3/15, 1840. It was the first open competition of that kind to be announced in the Serbian press. It pointed out that candidates had to have a law degree and juridical experience. In addition, every candidate was required to indicate in his application "his religion, how old he was, his morality, and his previous occupations."[14] Three lawyers from Vojvodina - Jovan Sterija Popović and Dimitrije Nešić from Vršac, and Marko Marinković from Sremski Karlovci - applied for that position.[15] Jovan S. Popović, who had the best qualifications, was elected and approved. His application showed that he had graduated in philosophy and Hungarian law with excellent grades, had passed the bar examination with honors, had studied Austrian law since 1835 as a certified attorney, and had presented lawsuits. In addition, he pointed out in his application that his literary activity of sixteen years in the Serbian and the Latin languages, in addition to his professional qualification and legal experience, confirmed his ability to become a professor in the Kragujevac Lyceum.[16] Popović's selection benefited Serbia a great deal because he played a very important role in her educational policy and cultural life, first as a lyceum professor and, after 1842, as a personnel chief in the Ministry of Education.

Jovan Popović began to teach his course in natural law on November 1/13, 1840. However, Jovan Raić did not begin to teach his courses in social science until the next academic year, that is, 1841-42. In the meantime, Ignjat Stanimirović was his substitute, offering a course in statistics. He was appointed temporary professor of statistics by the Prince's order on September 6/18, 1840, with the salary of 700 talers per year, the same salary as Popović had. Stanimirović was also from Vojvodina with a solid education. He had completed the gymnasium in his native city, Subotica, and graduated from the Faculty of Philosophy and from the Law School in Kežmarok in Hungary (today in Czechoslovakia).[17]

Popović's report of June 21/July 3, 1841, shows that in the first semester of the academic year 1840-41, in the Department of Law of the Kragujevac Lyceum, the following subjects were taught: natural public law, civil court procedure (*kurijalni štil*), and the French language.[18] Natural law was the most important subject in this department, or "*Pravoslovno odelenije*," as it was called. The manuscript of Popović's lectures in this subject was preserved and Radovan D. Lukić, Law School Professor at the University of Belgrade, has studied and analyzed it in detail. He concluded that Jovan S. Popović was "a follower of the school of natural law and of the then-popular variant which considered that virtually the entire substance of law can be directly shown from human reason." In Professor Lukić's opinion, Popović was "basically a liberal." "It can be seen," he points out, "from his understanding of freedom of thought, his view on the limits of state power, the responsibilities of employees, the right of defense, international relations, parental power, and many other viewpoints."[19]

Ten students completed their first year in the Department of Law at the Kragujevac Lyceum and immediately all of them received high government jobs. Those first native lawyers educated in Serbia were: Andrija Stamenković, Gruica Jovanović, David Rašić, Dimitrije Matić,

Jovan Dimitrijević, Jovan Nikolić (senior), Jovan Nikolić (junior), Nikola Tasić, Stoica Ivanković, and Teodor Grujović.[20]

Since the demand for well-educated lawyers was great, consideration was given to extending instruction in the Department of Law to two years after the first year of its operation. However, because of numerous difficulties which Serbia had to face, the second year of this department was not opened until the academic year 1843-44. In the first semester of the second year of the Department of Law, the following subjects were taught: Roman law, criminal law, and court procedure. The teaching of Roman law was discontinued as early as the second semester of the same academic year because the students' background, especially in Latin, was so poor that they could not study this subject successfully. Instead of Roman law, the Serbian Civil Code, the first law of that sort in Serbia, whose author was Jovan Hadžić (Miloš Svetić) from Vojvodina, began to be taught. That subject was entrusted to Maksim Simonović; Sergije Nikolić, who had taught Roman law, would later become a professor of public economy.[21]

With the opening of the second year in the Department of Law, instruction at the Kragujevac Lyceum lasted for four years - two years in the Department of Philosophy and two years in the Department of Law. Since the Department of Philosophy had a general education character, everyone who wished to study in the Department of Law was obliged to graduate from the Department of Philosophy in order to receive a firm foundation for the study of purely legal disciplines.

It is interesting to note that on November 20/December 2, 1839, Professor Atanasije Nikolić opened a drawing school at the Lyceum.[22] There is no information about its operation. It is only known that it discontinued operation on October 29/November 10, 1842.[23]

Before 1844, when the first of the more important laws concerning the Lyceum was promulgated, no significant changes were made in its teaching plan and program. There were some attempts to introduce several new subjects in the Department of Philosophy, but they remained only attempts. For example, on February 25, 1841 (O.S.), the Ministry of Education sent a letter to the *Soviet* pointing out the need to introduce "esthetics, as the subject of refined and beautiful taste, moral philosophy in a general sense, and Slavic grammar" into the Lyceum.[24] The *Soviet* answered this letter on March 4/16, 1841. It agreed with the Ministry that these subjects "could be useful enough but because of the condition of our finances," it was pointed in its answer, "it is now impossible for the *Soviet* to approve this suggestion of the Ministry."[25]

The first law concerning both departments of the Lyceum was issued in the already mentioned "Organization of Public School Education" of September 23/October 5, 1844, under the title *"Liceum ili veliko učilište"*

(Lyceum or Great School). Its author was a former professor of this institution, Jovan S. Popović.[26] This law prescribed the subjects which were to be taught. In the first year of the Department of Philosophy they were: instruction in Christianity, basic philosophy, logic, general history, mathematics, esthetics, general philology, and French; and in the second year they were: instruction in Christianity, metaphysics, ethics, general history, history of Serbia, advanced mathematics, architecture, Slavic philology with esthetics, physics, and the French language.[27] If this curriculum is compared with the curriculum for the academic year 1839-40, considerable changes can be seen. In the first year of study, two new subjects, esthetics and philology, were introduced, and in the second year, five new subjects were introduced: metaphysics, ethics, history of Serbia, architecture, and Slavic philology with esthetics. Geodesy and the art of drawing were not taught anymore in the first year. It is not known why the curriculum of 1844 did not include the German language. In that time, its teaching in the Lyceum was indispensable because after 1839, the Serbian government sent the most promising Lyceum graduates to Austria and Germany for further education. In addition, because of the absence of textbooks and other literature in Serbian, the Lyceum students had most often to use books written in German.

For the first year of the Department of Law the following subjects were prescribed: natural law, political science, public economy, statistics of main European states and Serbia, public law of Serbia, canon law of the Eastern (Orthodox) Church, and French; during the second year, the subjects were: Serbian civil law, criminal law, court, civil and criminal procedures, and public law.[28]

This Lyceum curriculum, especially for the Department of Law, like the first curriculum of the Kragujevac Lyceum for the academic year 1838-39, was more or less a copy, with certain adaptations to the Serbian conditions, of the 1806 curriculum of the Budapest Lyceum. For example, the subjects prescribed for the Department of Law are almost identical with the subjects prescribed by this Hungarian curriculum. The only difference was that in the Budapest Lyceum, those subjects were taught in three years, while in the Belgrade Lyceum, they were condensed in two years and Hungarian law was omitted.[29] It would have been natural to replace the study of Hungarian law with Serbian law, but that could not be done because the law of Serbia was still in the formative stage.

The law for the Lyceum of 1844 determined that nine professors were to teach all the prescribed subjects; one instructed in Christianity and canon law, one in the French language, four taught all subjects in the Department of Philosophy, and three taught all subjects in the Department of Law. The same law points out that the Ministry of Education would distribute the subjects among the professors of both departments.[30] Instruction according to the new curriculum began in the academic year 1844-45, and by a resolution of the Ministry of Education, the following professors carried it out: Sava Jovšić taught instruction in Christianity and canon law, Aleksije Okoljski the French language, Janko Šafařik physics, Konstantin Branković philosophy, Isidor Stojanović general history, Simon Prica mathematics, Sergije Nikolić natural law, Maksim Simonović Serbian civil law, and Ignjat Stanimirović statistics.[31] All of them, except Šafařik and Okoljski, were by birth from Vojvodina. Janko Šafařik was born in Kisörös, a small town near Budapest, and Aleksije Okoljski in Popowo in Poland.[32] As can be seen, Serbia had to hire foreigners as professors in her highest educational institution because she did not yet have capable native people to whom those positions could be entrusted.

The curriculum of the Belgrade Lyceum was not significantly altered until July 28/August 9, 1848. Then Prince Alexander decreed that a new course entitled "Political economy, finance, and business disciplines" had to be introduced in the Department of Law in the academic year 1848-49, with one professor whose annual salary would be 600 talers.[33] The course was entrusted to Konstantin P.L. Cukić by the Prince's decree of July 31/August 12, 1848.[34] This appointment was significant for the history of higher education in Serbia because Cukić was the first Serb from Serbia to whom such a high teaching position was entrusted. Konstantin Cukić was born in Karanovac, today's Kraljevo, in 1826. He attended elementary school in his native city and in Kruševac. The first three grades of gymnasium were completed privately in Kragujevac, and the other three in Vienna. He studied philosophy in Vienna and political science and economy at the University of Heidelberg, where he received his doctorate. He supported himself until the last year of his study. Then, he became a scholarship holder of the Serbian government with an annual scholarship of 300 talers. In addition, the Serbian government sent 100 talers to him for his travel expenses from Germany to Serbia.[35]

During the Constitutionalist period, and before it, too, it was custom in Serbia that every official, before entering civil service, take an oath before a clergyman of the Orthodox Church. Konstantin Cukić also took this oath before the Belgrade priest, Mihailo Popović, on August 30/ September 11, 1848. Since he was the first native Lyceum professor in Serbia, it is interesting to cite his oath, the original of which is kept in the Serbian Archives in Belgrade. In it he said:

> I, Kosta P.L. Cukić, entering into the teaching
> profession as a professor of political-economic
> subjects in the Lyceum of the Principality of

> Serbia, swear to Almighty God, before the Holy
> Cross, and on the Gospel that I will be faithful to
> the reigning Serbian Prince, Alexander
> Karadjordjević, and obedient to the constitution of
> the country; that I will perform the duties of this
> my profession correctly, diligently, and conscien-
> tiously according to the stipulated regulations and
> the legal orders of my superiors; that I will firmly
> keep any official secret and that I will avoid every
> action which would be against the interests of the
> Government and the interests of the people. So
> may the Lord God help me to be able to give a
> good account at His last judgment![36]

By the Prince's decree of July 30/August 11 of the same year, Dimitrije Matić, who like Cukić had studied at some of the well-known universities of Western Europe, was appointed professor of Serbian Civil Code, civil court procedure, and public law.[37] Although he was not born in Serbia, Matić can be considered one of the first native Lyceum professors because he received his higher education in Serbia, was a scholarship holder of the Serbian government during his studies abroad, and considered Serbia his homeland. He was born in Ruma (Srem) in 1821. He started the gymnasium in Sremski Karlovci, and completed it in Kragujevac. He graduated in philosophy and law from the Kragujevac Lyceum and was one of the first lawyers to receive a law degree from this school. After that, he entered civil service where he stayed until 1845 when, as a scholarship holder of the Serbian government, he was sent to Germany to continue his education. He studied law and philosophy at the University of Berlin, and received his doctorate in philosophy from the University of Leipzig.[38]

While still a student in Germany, Matić dreamed about a professorial position in the Belgrade Lyceum. When his desire became a reality, he wrote in his "Diary" on August 1/13, 1848:

> So, my wish is fulfilled, I am also confirmed by
> the Prince to be a professor of my fatherland here
> at the Serbian lyceum. Thus, from now on I will
> work with young Serbian souls; they are the field
> of my work, oh indeed, a blessed field.[39]

The Ministry of Education informed the Professorial Board of the Lyceum by letter about Cukić's and Matić's appointment on August 23/ September 4, 1848. The letter concluded with the following words: "The

Ministry confidently hopes that you have conscientious, diligent, and tireless coworkers in your difficult and useful occupation."[40] Indeed, through their work and devotion, the young professors fulfilled all the hopes placed in them. They brought innovation into the Lyceum operation, introducing various new methods of teaching with which they had become acquainted during their studies in the West. But, even in the beginning of their work they indicated to their superiors that they wished to teach their courses freely and to acquaint their students with the latest results in their fields and philosophy, "especially practical philosophy."[41]

> I began my course [Matić writes in his "Diary"] yesterday at 3 o'clock in the afternoon. Besides my regular students, my colleagues and friends who returned home from their studies [abroad] also came. I opened my lecture with a word which, I think, fits the spirit of the present time. I said that from now on I would live for my profession and that I would perform my duty conscientiously regardless whether somebody would like it and regardless of the consequences.[42]

From the very beginning of their work, these "young and liberal Lyceum professors were brining modern ideas and political principles into those ugly conflicts of court intrigues, bureaucratic discords, and family hatreds by which Serbia was torn."[43] With their liberal ideas they attracted the special attention of the lyceum students; this did not please the Constitutionalist oligarchy, which opposed the penetration of liberalism into Serbia. In order to limit their influence among young people, the government relieved them of their professorial duties and gave them higher administrative positions in the middle of 1851. On July 14/26, 1851, Dimitrije Matić was appointed secretary at the Appellate Court, and on August 17/29 of the same year, Konstantin Cukić was appointed secretary in the Ministry of Education.[44] Two years later, in December, 1853, Cukić was again given a professorship in the Lyceum. He retained that position until January 29/February 9, 1856, when, by Prince Alexander's decree, he was appointed personnel chief in the Ministry of Foreign Affairs.[45] However, Matić, who liked the professorial profession so much, was never again given an opportunity to stand before his students and to convey to them the knowledge and ideas which he had brought from the West. He had to be satisfied with the position of a high civil servant, and to convey his knowledge, experience, and ideas to the younger generation through his scholarly and literary works.

By the transfer of the first native professors educated at the West European universities, the penetration of liberal ideas was slowed down, but it was not stopped. These ideas found their way to the young intellectuals, most often through returnees from the West European universities who wanted "to inspire Serbian youths with the same ideas which stirred their interest."[46]

By the end of the Constitutionalists' regime in 1858, several more native intellectuals educated at the West European universities as scholarship holders of the Serbian government or at their own expense worked as the Lyceum professors: Djordje Cenić, Rajko Lešjanin, Vladimir Jakšić, Filip Hristović, and others.[47] But their professorial careers, too, with few exceptions, did not have a long duration. Most often they were transferred to administrative positions and their teaching positions were filled by foreigners, usually Serbs from Vojvodina.[48] The Belgrade Lyceum benefited a great deal from the hiring of native professors because they were young men full of enthusiasm for work, with a solid education and a liberal understanding; they were also advocates of modern teaching methods. In addition, they were closer to the students and understood their problems, needs, and abilities better because they had had to cope with similar difficulties and problems before they went to study abroad.

At the end of 1848, the students of the Belgrade Lyceum tried to make some changes in the curriculum. As far as we know, it was the first attempt of that kind in this institution. On October 7/19, 1848, a group of the second year law students applied to the Ministry of Education to be exempted from the study of the French language since "in the past three years," they indicated in their application, "we did not achieve hardly any result because the professors of French were often changed, and their methods of teaching differed." The application further reads: "... so the esteemed Ministry will not think that we want by this means to have more free time, we have unanimously concluded that the prescribed French classes be replaced by civil and criminal law, as the disciplines of the greatest importance."[49] The Ministry of Education, however, refused this request on October 8/20 of the same year, with the explanation that the students do not have sufficient reasons to change the existing curriculum, and it emphasized that the importance of a knowledge of French, regardless of how limited it was, especially for those students who wished continue their education abroad.[50]

With the development of the Serbian state, the need for qualified lawyers became greater and greater. In order to meet that need fairly well, the Ministry of Education suggested to the *Soviet* on December 10/22, 1848, the introduction of the following new course in the Department of Law: "Justinian's Institutes, abbreviated Justinian's *Pandects*,[51] people's law, administrative law or discipline about the state administration, and Serbian public law." In addition, it proposed the extension of instruction in the Department of Law from two to three years, because the Ministry emphasized in its proposal, "the disciplines prescribed by the existing curriculum, especially since the new political economic disciplines were introduced, could not be completed in only a two-year course."[52] After a brief study, the Ministry's proposal was accepted. Prince Alexander decided on February 4/16, 1848, that the proposed courses were to be introduced in the Department of Law, that for the new courses a professor with an annual salary of 600 talers was to be hired, and that the course of law in the Lyceum was to be extended to three years.[53]

Although the budget for the hiring of a professor was approved, the Ministry of Education decided not to hire anyone but to wait for the state scholarship holder, Rajko Lešjanin, to complete his studies abroad. In the meantime, by the order of the same Ministry, the professors in the Department of Law had to distribute the new courses among themselves. There is no complete evidence as to how those courses were distributed before 1850 when Lešjanin returned from Paris and by the Prince's decree of August 31/September 12 was appointed the professor for the new courses.[54] He was, like the other native Lyceum professors, well educated. He had studied law in Belgrade, Heidelberg, and Paris.[55]

After 1850, the course of French, which was one of the poorest in the Belgrade Lyceum, was considerably improved due to Matija Ban, who was appointed the professor of French at the same time that Rajko Lešjanin was appointed to his professorship.[56] Ban was a very educated man. He was born in Dubrovnik in 1818 where he was trained for an ecclesiastical vocation. However, he instead devoted himself to educational work. Before receiving this professorship in the Belgrade Lyceum, he held various positions. At one time or another, he taught Italian literature and French in Greece and Constantinople, was the tutor of Prince Alexander Karadjordjević's daughter, and wrote propaganda with the aim of liberating the Slavic people who were still under Turkish rule.[57]

Matija Ban succeeded in persuading the makers of educational policy to increase the weekly number of hours for the teaching of French. However, he still was not completely satisfied with the program and, after a short time, he asked the Ministry of Education to be allowed to teach French literature in addition to the French language. He presented three main arguments to justify his request. First, that knowledge of a great European literature such as the French would be useful to Serbian students. Furthermore, it would help them to develop their taste and to improve their writing abilities because at that time, Serbia did not yet have a sufficiently native literature. Second, he argued that in the higher schools of all culturally developed countries, both foreign languages and the literature written in them were taught. His third, and probably most persuasive, argument for the introduction of French literature as a compulsory course in the Lyceum was that Serbia would be the first and the only South Slavic country with a chair of the French language and literature. The third year Lyceum students supported Ban's request. They also sent an application to the Ministry of Education asking that French literature be included into the regular curriculum and be taught two hours per week.[58] The request of Ban and his students was granted, and on October 1/13, 1851, the Ministry of Education informed the Lyceum rector, Konstantin Branković, that it allowed Professor Ban, in addition to French, to teach French literature, but in French, and only in the third year "and so well and briefly," it said in the letter, "that with two hours per week it can be completed in a year."[59] Matija Ban officially began to teach French literature in the beginning of 1852, not in French as the Ministry of Education had recommended, but in Serbian "because he thought that he would be playing a comedy to speak in French to an audience which could not understand him well."[60] This novelty of the Belgrade Lyceum did not remain unnoticed by the Serbian press. The *Serbian News*, which always stimulated Serbian educational and cultural development, greeted the introduction of the new chair and proudly pointed out: "This is the first chair of foreign literature in Serbia, over which we rejoice as a significant advance in our chief educational institution."[61]

With the expansion of the Lyceum and with the sending of students abroad to continue their education, the need to introduce the German language became greater and greater. Konstantin Branković, the Lyceum rector for the academic year 1851-52, was the initiator of such a chair. On October 16/28, 1851, he asked the Ministry of Education to establish the optional study of the German language at the Lyceum "so that those Lyceum students and all other students as well who studied this language in the gymnasium and achieved any success could further improve themselves [in it]."[62] Prince Alexander issued the order on November 29/December 11 of the same year "that a special chair of the German language was to be established at our Lyceum with an annual salary, as the Ministry of Education suggests, of 100 talers."[63] It was inaugurated on December 2/14, 1851, and in the beginning of its operation, twenty-seven persons were enrolled, twenty-four Lyceum students and four government officials.[64] Antonije Šulc (Anton Schultz), the Professor of German in the Belgrade gymnasium, was appointed its first professor.[65] After two years, that is, in 1853, the German language became a compulsory subject for all Lyceum students.[66]

It is an interesting fact that before the end of 1851, serious thought was not given to the introduction of a chair for the Serbian language, literature, and history in the Belgrade Lyceum, though these were subjects which could inflame the same nationalism among the students as that which, after the Revolution of 1848 in neighboring Vojvodina, was more and more present in the political and cultural life of Serbia. The architects of the Serbian educational policy were aware that such a chair would be useful to the Serbian youths, but they pointed out that it was too early to establish such a course since the disciplines which should have been taught in it were not yet developed enough.

Aleksa Vukomanović, young, educated, and a great patriot who had studied in Russia, returned to Serbia in the fall of 1851. He loved his homeland above all. His correspondence shows that during his studies in Russia he dreamed about his native parts, and sometimes it seemed to him that Belgrade and the Rudnik Mountain called to him. In those difficult moments, he swore that neither pleasant life, nor devoted friends, nor beautiful Polish women would prevent him of his return when he realized his goal and completed his education.[67] Returning to Serbia, he wanted to convey his knowledge to his younger countrymen and to develop in them a special love for Serbia. His desire could be realized only if a chair of national subjects which he would teach could be established in the Lyceum. In order that this desire would not remain only a desire, immediately after his return to Serbia, Vukomanović took certain measures to realize it. First of all, he turned for help to Lazar Arsenijević-Batalaka, member of the *Soviet* and one of the first Serbian national historians. Arsenijević-Batalaka did not believe that he could do much and advised him to write to Prince Alexander. Vukomanović did so on October 29/November 11, 1851. In his letter he pointed out that among the many subjects taught in the Lyceum, there were no subjects "which would acquaint the students with our people's life" and suggested to the Prince the introduction of the Serbian language, national history, and national literature in the Lyceum curriculum, all subjects which he could teach.[68] Although some members of the School Committee and of the Ministry of Education opposed his suggestion, it was accepted, and the Prince's decree of December 18/30, 1851, established one more chair in the Belgrade Lyceum.[69] It was the chair of the "History of the Serbian people and the literature of Serbia." By the Prince's decree of January 11/23, 1852, Aleksa Vukomanović was appointed its first professor.[70] He was born in the village of Srezojevci in the Rudnik district. He completed the gymnasium in Odessa, and studied history and philology at the Imperial University of "St. Vladimir" in Kiev.[71]

The instructions of the new courses did not begin until September 9/21, 1852. Three days before their beginning, the *Serbian News* informed its readers that Aleksa Vukomanović would begin to teach in the Lyceum, the "history of the Serbian people and Serbian literature in relation with the short history of people and literature of the other Slavs" and added: "since attendance of classes in our Lyceum is free, everybody who is willing may freely, at the prescribed hours, attend Mr. A. Vukomanović's lectures."[72]

Vukomanović was well acquainted with Serbian school policy and did not expect much from his students. This is nicely shown in a letter which he sent to Vuk Stefanović Karadžić after his first lectures. "Until now everything is going rather well," he wrote, "the students listen to and take notes of what is said to them, and what more can I ask from our students who are anyway poorly prepared in everything?"[73]

As previously indicated, Platon Simonović, the chief inspector of all schools, made numerous changes in the Serbian school system. Besides the laws for the Belgrade gymnasium and lower gymnasiums, a new law for the Lyceum under the title "The Organization of the Lyceum of the Serbian Principality" was promulgated on September 15/27, 1853.[74] By this law, the Lyceum was reorganized and some changes were made in its curriculum. It was to be an advanced school with the task of preparing specialists "for all branches of the country's work." It prescribed that the Lyceum have three departments: the Department of Law, the Department of Natural Science and Technology, and the Department of General Education. In fact, the Lyceum had only two departments which prepared specialists because the Department of General Education had the task of enlarging students' general knowledge. All students in the Department of Law and in the Department of Natural Science and Technology were obliged "at the same time to take prescribed course in the Department of General Education" (the new name for the transformed Department of Philosophy.) The students were no longer obliged to study for two years in the Department of Philosophy (General Education) in order to be allowed to study in the Department of Law or in the Department of Natural Science and Technology, but every student who completed the gymnasium could be enrolled in one or the other department. In both departments, instruction lasted for three years. It is interesting to note that Platon Simonović, who probably was the author of the new law, wanted it to be in effect for a rather long time because the sixth article in the first chapter of the "Organization" reads: "After six years of trial with this 'Organization' the Lyceum Council may suggest changes of those of its rules which will be shown to be deficient."[75]

The law of 1853 prescribes the following subjects in the Department of General Education: instruction in Christianity, psychology, logic, "theory of literature (philology with philosophical grammar and criticism)," esthetics, history of Serbian, Slavic, and the literatures of the major

European nations, general history, history of the Serbian people, statistics, state economy, finance, "political mathematics," French, and German. The Department of Law was to teach: survey of law and history of legal knowledge, Roman law, administrative law, international law, Serbian public law, criminal law, and Serbian civil and criminal court procedures. In the new established Department of Natural Science and Technology, the following subjects were to be studied: physics, physical geography and meteorology, nature study, mineralogy with geognosy, botany, zoology, chemistry, technology, civil architecture, commerce with bookkeeping, agronomy, and a brief survey of Serbian administrative and public law. In addition to those subjects, both the Department of Law and the Department of Natural Science and Technology offered optional courses in advanced mathematics, practical geometry, mechanics, and pedagogy; the "Organization" reads "only those who wish to devote themselves to the teaching profession will study this last subject."[76] All these subjects were to be distributed "among thirteen, and if necessary among fourteen professors and two language teachers," who had to be gymnasium professors.[77]

The "Organization" of 1853 brought some changes into the administration of the Lyceum. One of the most important was that from then on, the Lyceum Council elected its rector from among the professors, no longer every year, but every three years and, as before, he had to be confirmed by the Prince.[78]

"The Organization of the Lyceum of the Serbian Principality" was the last law enacted during the Constitutionalist period which made significant changes in the structure and curriculum of the Belgrade Lyceum. From 1853 until the downfall of the Constitutionalists in 1858, the only noticeable changes were made in the teaching of the exact sciences, and rather great attention was paid to them, due mostly to the efforts of their professors, especially Josif Pančić.

During the Constitutionalists' regime, significant progress was made in the development and operation of the Lyceum. It grew from a higher school of general education with only two professors in the academic year 1838-39 to an advanced professional school with one general and two professional departments which required fifteen professors in the academic year 1857-58.[79] Since the Lyceum was the only advanced school in Serbia which prepared specialists for all branches of civil service, the government, in spite of the low national income, increased the budget for its expansion and the improvement of its instruction from year to year. For example, the national income of Serbia for the fiscal year 1845 amounted to 912,125 talers. From that income, 64,821 talers were allocated for all the expenses of the Ministry of Education, while the Ministry allotted 5,122 talers to the Lyceum.[80] Serbia's national income gradually increased, and in 1854, the year when the Lyceum began to operate with the newly established Department of Natural Science and Technology, the national income amounted to 1,123,405 talers. Yet, the Ministry of Education was allocated only 60,244 talers, 4.597 talers less than in 1845. Despite that fact, however, the Ministry of Education gave the Lyceum 7,706 talers, 2.584 talers more than in 1845.[81] In the last year of the Constitutionalists' regime, that is, in 1858, that sum was considerably increased so that the budget for the institution's needs amounted to 10,861 talers.[82] It should be noted that the sums allocated for scholarships to poor students, for teaching aids, various collections, cabinets, and libraries were not included in these budgets.

The Ministry of Education tried to get people with a solid education and good morals for Lyceum professors. It was usually successful in that effort, especially after 1848, when the first groups of native intellectuals educated at well-known European universities began to return to Serbia. It is very difficult to establish how many native professors taught in the Lyceum because some of them, as was indicated, enjoyed their professorships for only a short time. Nevertheless, on the basis of numerous archive documents, we tried to establish the number of native intellectuals who held professorial positions in the Belgrade Lyceum during the Constitutionalists' regime. The results of our research show that the Serbian government entrusted professorships in her highest school to ten native young men and they were: Konstantin Cukić, Dimitrije Matić, Djordje Cenić, Rajko Lešjanin, Vladimir Jakšić, Filip Hristović, Milovan Janković, Aleksa Vukomanović, Stojan Veljković, and Kosta Jovanović.[83] All of them, except Aleksa Vukomanović, were educated at the West European universities. Vukomanović, as already mentioned, was educated in Russia. This number is surprising in light of the fact that in the same period, the Belgrade gymnasium had only one native professor (Ljubomir Nenadović) and even he was engaged only a short time. A larger number of the Lyceum professors were Serbs from Vojvodina, but they were gradually replaced, either by native professors or professors from other neighboring states and provinces, such as, for example, Janko Šafařik from Hungary, Matija Ban from Dalmatia, Josif Pančić from the Croatian Littoral, and others.

Among the Belgrade Lyceum professors, there were five physicians: Vuk Marinković, Josif Pančić, Janko Šafařik, Georgije Mušicki, and the Bulgarian Djordje Atanasijević. Inasmuch as the Serbia of that time had only a limited number of physicians and that the professorial position was poorly paid, there is a question as to why those physicians did not devote themselves to the medical profession. We could not find the answer to that question, except perhaps in the case of Josif Pančić, who had almost no financial success in the beginning of his medical career.[84]

The salaries of Lyceum professors were considerably higher than the salaries of secondary school professors; their average was around 600 talers per year, though there were cases where the salaries of some professors were notably lower.[85] For example, Djordje Cenić's annual salary was only 300 talers.[86] The matter of the Lyceum professors' salaries was officially raised at the St. Peter's Assembly, on June 29/July 11, 1848, by the professors' representative, Isidor Stojanović, who was also a Lyceum professor. Thereafter, several decrees were issued concerning professorial salaries, not only for the Lyceum professors but for all the professors in Serbia. The last such decree was passed on February 15/27, 1858, and it was more or less a supplement to similar decrees issued in 1851, 1852, and 1854. It confirmed that the Lyceum professors' salaries were to be increased in four periods. The first period was to begin after ten years of teaching and lasted until the end of the fifteenth year, the second from the beginning of the sixteenth year until the end of the twentieth, the third from the beginning of the twenty-first year until the end of the twenty-fifth, and the fourth from the beginning of the twenty-sixth year until the end of the teaching career. At the end of the first period, their salaries were to be increased by 100 talers, at the end of the second and third by 150, and at the end of the fourth period by 200 talers. If, for instance, a Lyceum professor had 600 talers per year in the beginning of his teaching career, he could conclude it with the annual salary of 1,200 talers, as much as his pension had to be if he worked in the professorial profession for thirty years. This decree, however, did not apply to those professors who were not permanently employed.[87] If these salaries are compared with the Minister of Education's annual salary, which was 1,000 talers, the impression is that professors were paid very well.[88] However, that was not the case because during the Constitutionalist period there were very few Lyceum professors whose salaries could be increased on the basis of the years of teaching, because as has been indicated, a large number of them held their professorships for a short time. In addition, the Minister of Education was not particularly well paid if his annual salary is compared with the annual salary of the Serbian archbishop and Metropolitan, which was 5,000 talers.[89]

There is no doubt that professors' salaries, not only of the Lyceum, but of the secondary schools as well, were poor and that this cadre did not enjoy any special respect in Serbian society during the Constitutionalist period. "How the professorial condition and profession is rejected and despised in Serbia," writes Stojan Bošković, who was himself a secondary school professor in this period, " can be judged when I mention one among many examples. A professor, friend of mine, complained to me that he had proposed marriage to a girl, but was rejected with the excuse that the professorial occupation does not have any prospect for the future."[90] Yugoslav historians and pedagogues, especially contemporary ones, who have written about the development of education in Serbia before 1858, consider the Constitutionalists the chief culprits for the material difficulties which faced Serbian educators. Numerous examples, however, do not support this opinion. True, there were many vague areas in the financial policy of this regime, but we do not get the impression that this significantly damaged educational policy. Indeed, great attention was devoted to education, and large sums of money from the poor state treasury were invested in its advancement. In addition to the examples already presented, a comparison of the Ministry of Education budget with the budgets of other ministries and branches of the state administration confirms this statement. For example, Serbia's national income for the fiscal year 1851 amounted to 949, 092 and 19/42 talers. From that sum, 57,597 talers were allocated for all the expenses of the Ministry of Education, 48,840 for the *Soviet*, 41,642 and 4/10ths for the Prince's Office and the Ministry of Foreign Affairs, 106,759 talers for the Ministry of Justice, and so on.[91] Seven years later, in 1858, from the entire national budget, which amounted to 1,481,755 talers, the sum of 91,150 talers was allotted to the Ministry of Education, 58,934 to the *Soviet*, 40,844 to the Prince's Office and the Ministry of Foreign Affairs, 152,070 talers to the Ministry of Justice, and so forth.[92] These data show that in the last seven years of the Constitutionalists' regime, the annual budget of the Ministry of Education was increased by 33,553 talers, not including periodical financial help to the individual Lyceum chairs; over the same period, the budget of the *Soviet* was increased by only 10,094 talers, that of the Prince's Office and the Ministry of Foreign Affairs was decreased by 798 and 4/10ths, and that of the Ministry of Justice was increased by 45,311 talers. We think that it is correct to state that the difficult material condition of professors during the Constitutionalist period was more the result of an aggregation of problems, especially financial ones which Serbia had to face, than the result of the educational policy of the regime itself.

Prior to the academic year 1848-49, the Belgrade Lyceum was not recognized in Austria. In the beginning of the next academic year, the newly appointed professor, Dimitrije Matić, suggested to the Professorial Board that the Lyceum be elevated to the level of an academy, and that the government be asked "to make an agreement with Austria that it recognize the competency of the Serbian Lyceum."[93] At first the Lyceum professors did not pay much attention to this suggestion, but as the number of students began to decline noticeably, Matić's proposal drew their attention at the end of the same academic year. On June 25/July 7, 1850, the Lyceum rector, Emilijan Josimović, informed the Ministry of Education of the decline in enrollment. In his opinion, the number of students could be considerably increased "when the youth of other Slavic peoples, especially the South Slavic youth and the Serbs from Vojvodina, could come and study at our institution."[94] In order to get those youths to study at the Belgrade Lyceum, it had to be recognized by Austria, because students usually continued their education in her advanced schools and universities. Therefore, Josimović asked the Ministry of Education to intercede with the Austrian government to recognize officially the Belgrade Lyceum so that its graduates could easily continue their education in Austria. "Our institution," Josimović wrote, "accepts proper school certificates issued by the learned institutions of foreign countries, and the professors think that it would be right that other states recognize and respect our institution as a good one, so that the **principle of mutuality** is recognized."[95] The Serbian government negotiated with Austria regarding this question, but her negotiations did not bear fruit. The Department of Philosophy was recognized by Austria as an extension of the Belgrade gymnasium, and the Department of Law was not recognized at all.[96] We do not have evidence as to whether the Serbian government negotiated again with the government of Austria after 1850 concerning the recognition of her highest school, but it seems that during the Constitutionalist period, the Belgrade Lyceum was not recognized outside of Serbia. Its operation, however, was not unknown outside of Serbia's borders. For example, on July 31/August 12, 1844, the Association of Hungarian Physicians and Biologists invited the Lyceum professorial board to send its delegates to a formal convention of Hungarian physicians and biologists held in Kolozsvár (Cluj) in Transylvania.[97]

On the whole, the Lyceum professors of the Constitutionalist period were capable, although none of them had been trained for the professorial profession. The quality of teaching gradually improved, especially in the exact sciences, by the establishment of the chemistry, physics, and the so-called *"prirodnjački* (nature study)" laboratories and by the introduction of the first scientific expeditions in the 1850s. Among the Lyceum professors there were several who achieved notable results not only as teachers, but as scholars as well. Josif Pančić was undoubtedly the best known among them, and his scholarly works in botany, zoology, and geology were also known outside of Serbia. Although he was born in the Croatian Littoral, Pančić is considered the pioneer of Serbian science because he began and ended his scholarly work in Serbia. "Yes, although by birth Pančić is from a small Croatian village...," said Aleksandar Belić, the president of the Serbian Royal Academy, at the formal session on the fiftieth anniversary of Pančić's death, "he did not consider that he said an untruth when he called Serbia his home country and when he invested all of his ability in order to make Serbian science well-known."[98]

Even in his lifetime, Josif Pančić was respected as a professor as well as a scholar. The words of his student, Vladan Djordjević, physician and well-known historian of Serbia in the second half of the nineteenth century, which he spoke on February 26, 1888 (O.S.), at the cathedral in Belgrade during the funeral service of his former professor confirms it.

> Dear teacher [he said],
> My soul is weeping and yet I must speak.... Feelings when they are so powerful, have only one, but irrepressible expression - tears .... But I have to strengthen my heart, I must not weep. I must try to console your children, your students, hundreds of your admirers, a whole nation who are weeping because they lost you.[99]

Besides their teaching duties and scholarly works, the Lyceum professors also made their contribution to the building, enlightenment, and modernization of the young Serbian state. For example, Maksim Simonović, law professor, lectured after the end of 1843 on the Serbian Constitution of 1838 for all students, without pay; Vuk Marinković, professor of physics, lecture after the end of 1850 on natural history one hour per week to the interested Lyceum students; Janko Šafarik, professor of physics and Slavic philology, lectured on Slavic philology, both to students and to citizens who wanted to know more about the philology of other Slavic people, etc.[100] However, most often the government assigned them to duties where their knowledge and experience were needed. For example, in the beginning of 1857, Mihailo Rašković, professor of chemistry, was assigned with the state pharmacist, Pavle Ilić, to examine mineral waters in the country; Djordje Cenić and Stojan Veljković, law professors, were assigned in April of 1857 to a commission "for making rules of procedure with convicts during their imprisonment, forced labor, or captitivty"; in May, 1858, Vladimir Jakšić, professor of statistics, was assigned to a commission to inspect the Majdanpek mine, and so forth.[101] In addition, some Lyceum professors published various articles in the daily press and journals, and some of them started their own newspapers.

The small number of students was one of the biggest problems of the Lyceum during the Constitutionalist period. While the number of students in the lower gymnasiums and in the Belgrade gymnasium rapidly grew, at the Lyceum, in spite of the new laws and decrees, the establishment of new departments and chairs, the improvement of teaching, and the financial help to the poor students, the enrollment remained very small. There were even some academic years, for instance 1846-47, when, on average, every professor had fewer than three students.[102] In the second year of its operation, that is in the academic year 1839-40, the Lyceum had thirty-one students. By the academic year 1845-46, when it began to operate according to the new law of 1844, this number doubled and sixty-one students were enrolled, thirty-nine in the Department of Philosophy, and twenty-three in the Department of Law.[103] It was the first and the last academic year during the Constitutionalist period that the Lyceum had so many students. Several years later, their number suddenly dropped so that, for instance, in the academic year 1849-50, the Lyceum had only thirty-four students.[104] With the promulgation of the new law and the inauguration of the Department of Natural Science and Technology in the academic year 1853-54, their number again increased and amounted to fifty-nine.[105] From then until the downfall of the Constitutionalist regime in 1858, their number gradually decreased until, in the academic year 1857-58, the Belgrade Lyceum had only thirty-nine students.[106] It is important to note that the Belgrade gymnasium, the completion of which was a requirement for enrollment in the Lyceum, had 530 students in the same academic year.[107] The annual influx into Serbian society of young men who had completed their education in the highest native school was a drop of water in the ocean because according to the census of 1859, Serbia had 1,078,281 inhabitants.[108]

The question as to why a certain number of the Lyceum students discontinued their studies after a short time was treated directly or indirectly by the contemporaries of the Constitutionalist regime as well as in the Serbian and in the Yugoslav historiography. The general theory was, and some historians still support it, that these occurrences were the result of a great need for civil servants, coupled with a poorly defined policy for hiring civil servants. This explanation is partially correct. True, the need for civil servants was great and it was not rare that some got bureaucratic positions after only a few completed grades in the Gymnasium. The Lyceum students, however, had difficulty getting any government job prior to completing their education because the government wished them to graduate from its highest school so that it could entrust to them high and responsible administrative duties. Thus, for example, on January 29/February 10, 1840, Stefan Stefanović-Tenka, the Minister of Education and Justice, asked the *Soviet* "that none of the enrolled Lyceum or Gymnasium students will be given either full or part-time jobs in any governmental office until they complete all prescribed subjects, so they could prepare themselves to be proficient and perfect for every occupation."[109] The *Soviet* granted this request and required that all students complete their education in order to be hired for civil service. However, this requirement was not strictly observed in the case of Gymnasium students, though for Lyceum students it was. A letter from the Ministry of Education to the Lyceum's rector, Ignjat Stanimirović, on September 7/19, 1843, informing him that the applications of several law students for any position in the state service were declined, confirms this. "Therefore, the rector is directed," the letter reads, "to inform those applicants that their requests cannot be granted, but they should earnestly and diligently try to achieve success in their studies in order to show they are worthy of the Ministry's favor in receiving positions."[110]

Various sources, especially the documents in the archives, indicate that the chief cause of the small number of Lyceum students was not a great need for civil servants and the state employment policy, but the poverty of the gymnasium as well as of the Lyceum students. It is sufficient to mention just a few examples. In the academic year 1848-49 of fifty-two regular students, twenty-two received financial help;[111] five years later, in 1853-54, thirty-one of fifty-nine students enjoyed the same help,[112] or, for instance, on September 3/15, 1843, a group of Lyceum students applied to the Ministry of Education for any government part-time job in order to be able to continue their studies, because they were in a very difficult material condition.[113]

In addition to stipends, the poor Lyceum students enjoyed free medical treatment, and consideration was given to building a hospital for them.[114] Financial help, however, which was the most important to them, averaged only about 3 talers per month and it was not nearly enough for even their most basic needs.[115]

It should be noted that in 1844, the Ministry of Education informed the Lyceum rector and the Gymnasium principal that the children of foreign citizens employed in Serbia could attend schools free, and even receive stipends from the Serbian government, but "they should not expect to get any government position."[116] It is not known why the Ministry of Education made this decision, but it can be assumed that it was a supplement to the government decree of May 8/20, 1844, which required that all state officials had to have Serbian citizenship.

How much the Lyceum students learned during the Constitutionalists' regime is more or less unknown because their examinations were usually oral, and the number of their written compositions which have been preserved is insignificant and fragmentary. True, there are a large number of newspaper reports and reports by professors and rectors, but they are not reliable. The tendency, especially of the *Serbian News*, was to present the results of the examinations favorably. If it is assumed that these reports were accurate, which is hard to believe, the question of how much they really knew still remains unanswered, because in many instances, as is very well known, the result of an examination is not always a true measure of a student's knowledge. We are of the opinion that on the whole, the knowledge of the Lyceum students was poor in comparison to the knowledge of students gained in similar West European institutions. The notices, letters, official documents and memoirs of the state scholarship holders educated in the West confirm this view. Petar Protić wrote: "When in October of 1846 I came to Berlin, I could not understand one word of German."[117] In view of the fact that a large number of students lived under very difficult conditions, that the environment in which they moved and spent their spare time was still primitive, that curriculums and professors were often altered, that students had a poor educational background, that they were burdened with a large number of subjects, that their professors did not possess a solid pedagogic knowledge, and that students' textbooks were small in number and most often of poor quality, it is plain that not much could be expected of the Lyceum students.

As early as the 1850s, the Lyceum students began to observe critically the society in which they lived. Most often they stated their opinions in the press or presented them in their literary society. But, there were some cases when they expressed their opinions in their compositions. An example is a composition entitled "Home rule and Forms of its Development in England with a Special Look at the Home rule of the Slavs," written by an anonymous author in 1855. The topic is rather extensively covered and its author wanted to demonstrate the existence of home rule in almost all larger European states. Dealing with Serbia he wrote: "It is impossible to talk about home rule ... where we Serbs live; where we live the conditions in which it can be implemented do not exist. By home rule educated people meant when a nation completely freely governs itself and that is free only when it rules itself and fully understands its role."[118]

During the Constitutionalist period, great attention was devoted to the discipline and moral education of the Lyceum students; one of the principal aims of the Serbian government was to make them well-bred, religious, and obedient officials. Already in the first months of the Lyceum operation, Stojan Simić, the president of the *Soviet*, directed a letter to the Prince's Regency asking it to hire a man with a monthly salary of 5-6 talers "who will live in the school building [Gymnasium and Lyceum] in order to take care of it." The letter further reads: "His task will also be to secretly and publicly supervise students' behavior and to see to it that students do not roam lanes, taverns, and coffeehouses at night or during the day." In addition, he was also to be obliged to punish violators.[119] Incarceration for several days was the most frequent form of punishment, though corporal punishment was not rare. Among numerous examples, the case of Nikola

Tasić, a second year philosophy student, may be mentioned. When he received news from home that his mother was on her deathbed, he asked the rector for permission to go home for several days, but his request was not granted. Receiving a second letter which informed him that his mother wanted to see him, he went home without the rector's permission. When, after a few days, he returned to the Lyceum, the rector ordered him to whipped in front of all the philosophy students so cruelly "that two sticks were broken on him."[120] Before the 1850s, the students more or less obediently accepted all the decisions of their superiors. However, after the 1850s, they ceased to be obedient lambs and no longer submissively received decrees and orders issued by the Lyceum council. For example, when the "School Rules for the Students of the Serbian Principality Lyceum" were issued on August 31/September 12, 1851, the students boycotted classes for several days in the beginning of the academic year 1851-52, and some of them even left the school.[121] The chief reason for their dissatisfaction was that these rules were rather more strict than similar rules issued on August 19/September 1, 1849.[122]

The government used all necessary measures in order to have complete control over students. It is sufficient to cite a few examples. In the second year of the Lyceum's operation, on October 13/25, 1839, the Minister of Education and Justice, Stefan Stefanović-Tenka, informed the Lyceum rector, Atanasije Nikolić, that the Lyceum and gymnasium students were forbidden to lodge in taverns because, he wrote: "they will have opportunity to hear and see there, all sorts of ugliness which is not in accordance with school and general education."[123] Several years later, on September 24/October 6, 1841, the same Ministry informed the new rector, Konstantin Branković, that students could not change their lodgings without the permission of the Lyceum council.[124] It should be noted that these and similar orders were not always strictly observed.

Before the Revolution of 1848, which also spilled over into neighboring Vojvodina, the Lyceum students were mainly politically passive. After 1848, however, until the downfall of the Constitutionalists, their political activity which was manifested in various forms, became more and more noticeable. Already in 1848 when he returned to Serbia after several years spent abroad, Dimitrije Matić noticed the political awareness of the Serbian students. The beginning of the Lyceum students' political activities excited the liberally-oriented Matić, and he wrote in his "Diary": "I specially note that youth who attend schools are ardent and burn with the zeal of patriotism and honesty. They promise a great deal to Serbian nationalism."[125] Their first important political activity was at the previously mentioned St. Peter's Assembly of 1848, where several of them wrote "petitions, requests, and complaints for the delegates of some districts which they submitted to the government."[126] In time, their political activities became more organized. For example, when the Crimean War broke out in 1853, the first student demonstration, as far as we know, was organized in Serbia. Dimitrije Marinković, then a Lyceum students, left a valuable record of it.

> From 1853 [writes Marinković] we, students, began to discuss politics. At least I began to be interested in politics, and not in internal but in foreign. All of us students were for the Russians and only one of our friends, one Aleksa Ostojić... was a Francophile or as we called him *Frncuzan*.... We, students, organized a demonstration in Russia's benefit. Namely, on St. Demetrius Day we celebrated the *Slava* [Serbian family feast for its patron saint] at the home of our friend, Jevrem Veljković, and from there, slightly drunk, we went toward our school and big church [the cathedral] shouting on the way "Long live Tsar Nicholas!"[127]

The biggest demonstrations during the Constitutionalist period that were organized by the Lyceum students at the beginning of 1854 were against Professor Matija Ban, and their cause was not of an educational but a political nature. The specific issue was that in Novi Sad's journal *Sedmica* (Week), No. 7 of February 20, 1854, Ban published an ode entitled "To Sultan Abdülmecid, Founder of Civil Equality in the Ottoman Empire, Educator of the East, and Friend of Humanity" in which he glorified the Sultan and his merits. "A Serb," he wrote regarding this ode, " has need to sing the praises of that man who insured people's rights in Serbia, now and for centuries to come and who always shows himself to be a protector of Christians in the true sense of the word."[128] The Lyceum students, who were anti-Turkish, considered glorification of the Sultan by a professor of the Serbian Lyceum an insult to the Serbian people and decided to boycott his classes. They marched through Belgrade streets and sang these verses:

> *Proud Istanbul, sink into the sea*
> *Powerful is the hand which drives you!*

from the poem *Stambolu* (To Istanbul) by Ljubomir Nenadović, then an already known Serbian poet, writer, and journalist. Numerous citizens joined them. This demonstration was by no means harmless. Matija Ban did not teach for more than a week after that; he was even afraid to leave his apartment for some time, and a policeman was assigned to guard the building in which he lived.[129]

Before the 1840s, Serbia was relatively immune to foreign influence. But after 1840, with the expansion of the Lyceum, the coming of foreign professors, the opening of public reading clubs, and the return of the first native men educated abroad, she could no longer remain immune, and foreign influence began to be more and more noticeable in almost every aspect of Serbian life, especially in cultural and political matters. The Lyceum professors and state scholarship holders educated abroad were the original and most influential bearers of new ideas, and students were their executors and propagators. They were inspired by the new ideas and spread them with youthful naivete and enthusiasm, believing that in the general acceptance, spread and adaptation of these ideas lay the progress of Serbia and the prosperity of her people. They were most excited by the ideas of national liberalism and the ideas of Panslavism or *"Slavjanstvo,"* as they were called in Serbia. Native professors educated abroad acquainted them with the former; they were acquainted with the latter by professors from Vojvodina who were influenced by the teachings of the great Czech writer and Panslavist, Jan Kollár (1793-1852), and the well-known Slovak writer and Slavophile, L'udovit Štúr (1815-1856), during their studies in Budapest or in Pozsony (Bratislava).[130]

Under those influences, Lyceum students became more and more active in cultural and political life. On Professor Sergije Nikolić's initiative, they established an association under the name *"Družina Mladeži Srbske"* (Society of Serbian Youth) on June 15/27, 1847 - St. Vitus Day and an important Serbian national holiday. In the beginning, it had about twenty members among whom Milovan Janković, Jevrem Grujić, Petar Protić-Sokoljanin, and Dimitrije Petrović were the best known. Their number gradually grew and shortly before its end in 1851, the Society had about fifty regular members.[131] Secondary school students, state officials, and Professor Rajko Lešjanin were also among them. Undoubtedly, among the state officials who were the members of this society, Andrija Stamenković, member of the Appellate Court, was the most active and influential.[132]

In addition to its regular members, the Society of Serbian Youth also had a rather large number of honorary members. They were mainly prominent citizens of Belgrade: for instance, Jovan Ilić, Ljubomir Nenadović, Dimitrije Matić, Konstantin Cukić, and others. Metropolitan Petar Jovanović was also among them.[133] Numerous citizens and members of the government welcomed the establishment of this society, and some of them helped it financially. For example, Stojan Simić, President of the

Soviet, donated 500 *groses*. Toma Vučić-Perišić also gave a sum of money, but it is unknown how large his donation was.[143]

The Society of Serbian Youth was established as a literary society in which members could read and discuss their works. This is clearly shown by the first article of the Society's rules written by the Lyceum rector, Konstantin Branković, and issued on June 21/July 3, 1847. "The aim of the Serbian Society as a volunteer society," it read, "will be to practice written, oral, poetic, and prose forms of the Serbian language."[135] The same rules prescribed that regular meetings of the Society were to be held "every other Sunday after religious services." There were to be annual meetings at the end of every academic year, and persons "outside of the Lyceum" were allowed to attend them. Those provisions were altered on June 6/18, 1848; from then on the Society held its meetings every Sunday with the annual meeting held every year on St. Vitus Day.[136]

In the beginning, the Society's work was mainly literary. At every meeting the literary attempts of its members were read, discussed, and their authors praised or criticized. They were mostly youthful poetic outpourings permeated with patriotism and sometimes with Slavophilism as well. There was little originality in them. Most of their authors were under the influence of "pseudo-classical poetry, old German Romanticism, and a little bit under the influence of Serbian folk poetry."[137] In addition, under the influence of the Panslavic movement, they translated several articles concerning the Slavs from some of the Slavic languages or from German.[138]

From the very beginning, the Society of Serbian Youth made connections with similar Serbian youth societies in Vojvodina and Hungary; they were especially influenced by the Pozsony youths, with their Panslavic policy.[139] The Serbian youths of Pozsony founded their society under the name *"Mladež Požunska"* (The Youths of Pozsony) in 1845, and as early as 1847 they had published their own magazine, *Slavjanka* (literally, "Slavic Woman"), in which they published their own works as well as works by young Serbs from other provinces and states. The articles in the magazine were written in the spirit of Panslavism. For example, Svetozar Miletić, then one of the best known leaders of the youth movement in Vojvodina, published in it a poem in which he wrote, among other things: "I am a Serb of the Slavic race; my heart is longing for a new Slavic life. Ho Slavs, dear brothers, our hour has come." Jovan Ilić, a well-known Serbian poet and, as has been mentioned, an honorary member of the Society of Serbian Youths, also published in *Slavjanka*; his poems did not significantly differ in their content from Miletić's poems. He wrote: "Let the firmament echo, God, please bless, bless our dear Slavic race."[140]

The cooperation between the Lyceum youths of Serbia with other Serbian youths did not end with the exchange of literary works and support for the Panslavic movement; in time it manifested other forms as well. For example, in April, 1848, Svetozar Miletić came to Belgrade and, with the members of the Society of Serbian Youth, tried to organize an uprising. The attempt, however, was thwarted in time, and Miletić had to leave Serbia immediately.[141]

The sphere of activities of the Society of Serbian Youth was gradually expanded until it reached its peak during that turbulent revolutionary year, 1848. Then, under the influence of the revolutions in West and Central Europe, especially in Hungary and Vojvodina, these Lyceum youths, who until then were more or less apolitical, became politically active. "The Lyceum students study hardly anything," Jevrem Grujić wrote to his friend, Miloš Petrović, in March of 1848, "one hardly hears anything except hurrah, hurrah, hurrah, long live Serbian liberty and independence, long live the King [sic] of Serbia!"[142] The presence of revolutions near the Serbian border and the revolutionary mood in Serbia itself led the Constitutionalist government to be tolerant toward many things in order to preserve peace in the country. The members of the Society of Serbian Youth under the leadership of their new president, Jevrem Grujić, took advantage of this situation and began more freely to expand their political activity within the country as well as outside of her borders. For example, a certain number of them attended the so-called May Assembly held in Sremski Karlovci in 1848, a rather large number of them joined volunteer detachments in Vojvodina, they advocated freedom of the press, and so on.[143]

During 1848, the Society of Serbian Youth developed from an ordinary student literary group into a strong association of secondary school and lyceum students. It was no longer preoccupied only with the ideas of nationalism and Panslavism, but it became a champion of liberal and humanitarian ideas as well as the first sharp critic of the regime.

With the desire of making literate those Belgrade men who did not have an opportunity to attend school regularly, such as apprentices and journeymen, the members of the Society of Serbian Youth applied to the Ministry of Education on January 2/14, 1849, asking to be allowed to teach in a Sunday school.

> Our literature is still on a very low level and it has
> to be [they wrote] when our people - a mass of
> them - do not yet have a basic elementary
> education. In order that it begin to bloom and that
> the general progress of the people be sped up, the

mass of our people has to be taught the basics of
elementary education, that is, how to read, write,
and count. The Society of Serbian Youth has
taken note of this need and has decided to help as
much as it can.[144]

The Ministry of Education did not inform the Society of its decision
regarding this request, but it did inform the Lyceum rector on January
11/23 of the same year. It pointed out that the "desire and intention of the
Society's members are without question noble and praiseworthy" but that it
could not grant their request until it saw the results of their final examinations in June. Then, it wrote in its answer, the Ministry would make a
decision as to whether the applicants "can take some of their valuable time
and use it to educate others without hurting themselves."[145] As far as we
know, this request was not re-examined at the end of the academic year
1848-49 and the "noble and praiseworthy" desire of the Society's members
remained unrealized.

The Society of Serbian Youth participated in several other activities;
for instance, it tried to popularize peasant costumes, collected old coins,
gave books to gymnasium students and to the small public reading clubs in
the interior of the country, corresponded with its former members who
studied abroad, and the like.[146]

The publication of their literary works in book form under the title
Neven-Sloga was, undoubtedly, one of its greatest successes. The book was
permeated with ideas of nationalism, Panslavism, and liberalism, and as
such it may be considered a mirror of the Society's political orientation. Its
publication was considered as early as the spring of 1848, but at first the
Society's members could not agree what was to be included - one group
favored poetry, and another prose. Fearing that this disagreement might
weaken the Society, its president, Jevrem Grujić, advocated a compromise.
In a speech made in March of 1848, he said:

Thus, I am concluding [the presentation] of my
opinion by saying that poetic as well as prose
works should be published in order to preserve our
unity which is now necessary, absolutely necessary
to us if we do not want to see Serbian people who
have begun to liberate themselves remain in
slavery as a result of dissension. Let St. Vitus Day
teach us.[147]

How much Grujić's words helped the group to reach a compromise is unknown, but a compromise was reached and 1,500 copies of the first and last collective work of the Society of Serbian Youth, *Neven-Sloga*, was published in Zemun in 1849.[148] The Society decided to publish it there because the censorship in Austrian Zemun was not as strict as the censorship in Serbian Belgrade.[149]

Neven-Sloga had 181 pages, 131 pages of poetry (29 poems) and 50 pages of prose (4 articles). The authors were: Petar Protić-Sokoljanin, Jovan Ilić, Jovan Ristić, Teodor Bojović, Miloš M. Mačvanin, Stevan P. Crnogorac, Pavle Petronijević, Toma Cincar-Janković, Živko Jovanović, Milan A. Petronijević, and Jevrem Grujić.[150] On the back of this anthology the following verse was printed:

> *Oh! sing loudly, Serb,*
> *Go quickly to the Mother of glory,*
> *Tell clearly to the whole world,*
> *That you wish to die in liberty.*

The lines were a reflection of the Society's policy and its mood during the revolutionary year 1848.

The best and the most important work during the Society's activity was published in *Neven-Sloga* under the title "Obzor Države" (The State of the Nation) by Jevrem Grujić, who was not only one of the best known members of the Society, but also one of the most active; he was also the best known and most liberal young man of the Constitutionalist period. Grujić's article was written critically, courageously, and in the spirit of the national liberalism of 1848. The lectures of the first Serbian liberal professors, Dimitrije Matic's and Konstantin Cukić's in particular, had significant influence on young Grujić, and "with a great deal of probability it may be concluded that his article, "The State of the Nation," was a "direct echo" of that influence.[151]

> **Nowadays our people are not free** [writes Grujić in "The State of the Nation"] **either as far as foreign or as far as internal policies are concerned.** They are not free as far as foreign policy is concerned because they pay taxes to the Turks.... They are not free as far as internal [policy] is concerned because they do not have...they do not know - and they are almost forbidden to know - any of their rights. They are simply an instrument used now by one, now by

> another, in order to achieve their goals..... **Our people do not have their own opinion, but not because they would not be capable at all** [of having one].... Thus, they do not live in prosperity, but rather in adversity. Our state (rather its leaders), therefore, has not fulfilled its [their] task.[152]

He advocated the development of education, pointing out that it was the chief means by which Serbian people could "free themselves from its yokes." That they might achieve freedom faster and take a path of progress, Grujić made two suggestions - one for foreign and the other for internal liberation.

> 1. **In order to free themselves from foreign obligations** [taxes to the Turks] **they had to be made conscious of Serbia's greatness - conscious of her former Empire - and conscious of their bright future. - In addition, they should be better acquainted and more closely tied with all branches of the Slavs.**

> 2. **In order to achieve their internal freedom, our people have to be taught what they are as nation and what rights they should have. - What the government is, what its purpose should be, who formed it, and what are the limitations of its power. In other words they should be told exactly what it means to be a people who live in a state, and [we should] call upon them to live in that way.**[153]

Grujic's article "The State of the Nation" had great influence in the liberal stratum of Serbian society at the time of its publication as well as later. We completely agree with Jovan Skerlić, the well-known Serbian literary critic, historian, and political activist at the end of the nineteenth and the beginning of the twentieth centuries, who wrote that "The State of the Nation" may be considered "the first declaration of liberalism in Serbia, the first step into life of the first liberal party, and the germ of a program of the United Serbian Youth," which was established in 1866.[154]

The Serbian government thought that the Society of Serbian Youth took too much freedom in its activities, and that it did not observe the rules prescribed in 1847. When the Revolutions of 1848-49 were put down, thus eliminating a potential danger to the Serbian government, the tolerance enjoyed by the Society came to an end. On November 1/13, 1849, the Ministry of Education informed the rector of the Lyceum by letter, that "last year, the Society's members deviated from their prescribed rules because they took part in activities which are neither appropriate for their occupation, nor useful for their organization" and required from him to take care "that in the future the Society of Lyceum Serbian Youth strictly observer their rules so that it would advance in its task honorably and praiseworthily."[155] After 1849, partly because of more strict state control, partly because of dissension among its members, the importance of the Society of Serbian Youth began gradually to decline. From the very beginning, the Society had to cope with dissension which negatively affected its activities and several time even threatened its existence. In spite of that, it achieved rather good results due mostly to its leaders, who used various means to preserve the group's unity. They partially succeeded in their efforts. However, that unity was only on the surface, while a worm of dissension ate at the Society from within, weakening its activities and thus its importance. The Society's president, Jevrem Grujić, often warned about unhealthy relations within the Society. For example, during a meeting held on September 4/14, 1849, he said:

> Brothers, who among us here is unable to say what
> kind of worm came among us. During the two
> years of the Society's existence, there has not been
> one day when **dissension** did not tear it up. Many
> times it was near the end. Although it has looked
> strong from outside, it has not had any hardness
> inside. Now, we can see that the Society did not
> fulfill its task.[156]

Despite the fact that, after 1849, strict supervision made the execution of its activities more difficult, the Society of Serbian Youth continued to exist until the spring of 1851. On St. Vitus Day (June 15/27) of the same year, as in previous years, the Society held its annual meeting in the reading room of the Belgrade Reading Club. Besides regular and honorary members, such eminent persons of Serbian political and cultural life as the *Soviet* president, Stefan Stefanović-Tenka, Toma Vučić-Perišić, a member of the *Soviet*, and Metropolitan Petar Jovanović also attended.[157] On that occasion, Stevan Pavlović, Petar Protić-Sokoljanin, Stevan Ćirić, and Andrija Stamenković made speeches.[158] They sharply criticized some aspects of the Constitutionalists' regime and pointed out the need for the liberation of all Serbs from Turkish rule, and of those Slavs who were under Austrian rule. For example, Stevan Ćirić, a beginning civil service employee in the *Soviet*, began his speech with the following words: "Shall we, or shall we not, dare we go to Kosovo?"[159]

As the Society continued to carry out its non-literary activities in spite of warnings, the government abolished it on June 21/July 3, 1851.[160] In addition, the government decided to punish its officers, Andrija Stamenković and Stevan Ćirić, and also to transfer the liberal Lyceum professors, honorary members of the Society, to positions from which they would not have the opportunity for any close contact with the Lyceum students. On July 3/15 of the same year, Andrija Stamenković was transferred to the District Court in Čačak,[161] and Stevan Ćirić again lost his post.[162] Then Stefan Stefanović-Tenka said to Ćirić: "You, Ćirić, go to Kosovo and when you come back, you will get a job."[163] Of the professors, as was already indicated, Konstantin Cukić and Dimitrije Matić, were transferred.

During its short existence, the Society of Serbian Youth partially awakened the heretofore apolitical Serbian students and acquainted them with young Serbs outside of Serbia. It adopted and propagated modern liberal ideas in the execution of which it saw the progress of the Serbian state. True, during its activity, the results of its propaganda were insignificant, but the torch of liberalism which it lighted was not extinguished with its abolition in 1851. In the 1860s, when the situation for political activity in Serbia became more favorable, former members of the Society of Serbian Youth, now experienced champions of liberalism, such as Jevrem Grujić, Jovan Ristić, Milovan Janković, Vladimir Jovanović, and others, began to carry out liberal ideas more successfully. In addition, with the establishment of the Society of Serbian Youth, the first group of future native intellectuals appeared on the Serbian political scene. Their presence could not be ignored, and they at first indirectly, and later directly, influenced the making of Serbia's internal and foreign policy. Thus, it was that by spreading education and improving teaching, the Constitutionalists did not only create needed cadres but at the same time, they also created the men who directed their own downfall in 1858.

The makers of educational policy in the Constitutionalist period paid rather careful attention to teaching aids for the Lyceum. By the "Organization" of 1853, the government allocated an annual sum of 500 talers for that purpose.[164] However, from time to time supplementary sums were granted. Thus, for example, in 1855 in addition to the regular budget for teaching aids, the Lyceum was allotted an additional sum of 6,200 Austrian florins.[165]

At the beginning of 1845, the Lyceum officially received its library, which then had 319 books in 551 volumes, one manuscript, 119 letters and documents, and one portrait ("*1 živopisnij obraz*").[166] It gradually grew, and as early as 1850 it had 558 books in 927 volumes, numerous manuscripts, maps, plans, pictures, old coins, and the like.[167] The Lyceum library was enriched in various ways - by purchasing books, by gifts from the nation and from abroad, and by receiving free samples of all books published in Serbia. After 1850, the number of books was rapidly increased, especially by gifts. For example, in 1853, Professor Zelenecki from Russia gave to the library 23 books in 29 volumes;[168] in 1855, it received a gift of 270 books from Jovan Riznić, a respectable merchant, a Serb who was born in Trieste and lived in Gopchitse near Odessa;[169] in 1857, the Russian Imperial Academy of Science sent 17 books to the library, and so on.[170] The library was managed by one of the Lyceum professors who received a sum of 50 talers per year as a supplement to his regular salary.[171]

The makers of government educational policy during the Constitutionalist period were aware of the fact that without quality textbooks they could not expect any significant results from the students of their highest school. Therefore, various measures were used to publish them as soon as possible. "The Organization of Public School Education" of 1844 required the Lyceum professors to write textbooks for their courses. A professor's obligation was, it was emphasized in that part of the "Organization" which refers to the Lyceum, "to write a book himself for his subject if it does not already exist, so that after it is approved by the Ministry of Education, it can be published in order to make students' learning easier."[172] That this requirement would indeed be carried out, the Ministry of Education reminded professors from time to time about their obligations through the Lyceum rector.[173] Additionally, in order to stimulate professors to write better textbooks, the Ministry rewarded the best authors with monetary rewards.[174] These and other measures brought positive results, and by the end of the Constitutionalists' regime, the Belgrade Lyceum had textbooks for almost all subjects. The Educational Committee and the School Commission made significant contributions to the publication of the Lyceum textbooks.

Unlike the case with the textbooks for elementary, secondary, professional, and vocational schools among whose authors there were only a few native Serbs, among the authors of the Lyceum textbooks, the number of native scholars was considerably larger and their textbooks were among the best and most original books for Serbian schools of the Constitutionalist period. The best known among them were Dimitrije Matić, Konstantin

Cukić, and Rajko Lešjanin. How many textbooks and reference books for Lyceum students' needs were published before 1858 is difficult to determine precisely. According to Stojan Novaković's *Bibliography*, which may be taken as a rather reliable, though incomplete source, in Serbia during the Constitutionalist period, about 30 textbooks and reference books for Lyceum students were published.[175] *Osnovno mudroslovlje* (Elementary Philosophy) and *Misloslovlje ili logika* (Logic) by Konstantin Branković, *Javno pravo Knjažestva Srbije* (Public Law of the Serbian Principality), *Objasnenije Gradjanskog zakonika za Knjažestvo Srbsko* (Explanation of the Serbian Principality Civil Code), and *Načela umnog državnog prava* (Principles of Public Law) by Dimitrije Matić, and *Državna ekonomija* (The State Economy) by Konstantin Cukić were among the most important. Both of Brankovićs textbooks lack originality. They are more or less translations of works by Wilhelm Traugott Krug (1770-1842), a respected German Professor of Philosophy and a follower of Immanuel Kant. Branković wrote his *Elementary Philosophy*, which was published in 1848, according to Krug's book *Fundamentalphilosophie*, and his *Logic*, which was published in 1851, according to Krug's work *Denklehre oder Logik*.[176] Despite the fact that both of Branković's books lacked originality, they were very important books for the first generation of native intellectuals in Serbia. Through *Elementary Philosophy*, Branković convey to Serbia Krug's theoretical or speculative philosophy, which Krug himself called "transcendental synthetism," and which was for almost three decades "an important meditative preoccupation for a number of intellectuals."[177] It was precisely this book on speculative German metaphysics that "**marked the beginning steps in the Serbian school of philosophy.**"[178] *Logic* was the first textbook of its kind in Serbia written exclusively for Lyceum students, and it was used until 1871, when it was replaced with *Logika* (Logic) by Alimpije Vasiljević.[179] In writing it, Branković wanted to be as original as possible, but he did not succeed in his effort. Again, he relied heavily on Krug, and his *Logic* is nothing but Krug's *Denklehre oder Logik* slightly altered. Branković was original only in so far as he used his own examples for the illustration of logical principles, and most of those were taken from Serbian history.[180]

One of the most important contributions of Konstantin Branković as far as his textbooks were concerned was that he made one of the first and "partly successful attempts to create a **Serbian terminology** for the most important philosophical terms." Sometimes, however, he went too far and attempted to render entirely untranslatable terms into Serbian.[181] In addition, with these and others of his philosophical works, he was the first man to awaken an interest in scientific philosophy among a broad segment of Serbian society, and almost all of the first Serbian philosophers "received something from him - if nothing else at least a stimulus for philosophical speculation."[182]

The textbooks by Dimitrije Matić and Konstantin Cukić were much more original and permeated with liberalism. For example, in his *Principles of Public Law*, Matić advocated suffrage, equality before the law, the introduction of laws by which everybody would have the right "to defend himself on the basis of the constitution from every injustice and every attack."[183] He discusses in it a part of the French Constitution of 1791 regarding the rights of citizens and the well-known work *Du contrat social* by Jean Jacques Rousseau. He warns of the dangers of a police state, emphasizes that **"a state should be a guarantee for, and not a destroyer, or someone's liberty,"** and so forth.[184]

Cukić's liberalism was even stronger. Unlike Matić, whose presentation was theoretical and abstract, Cukić touched upon the state organization in Serbia and discreetly expressed his dissatisfaction. For instance, in the third volume of his book *The State Economy*, he argued that state officials have to be subjected to the tax obligation like all other citizens. "A state official," he wrote, "should be equal in his rights and obligations toward the state like any other citizen, because he is paid for his service to the state."[185] A comparison of the various institutions of Serbia with similar ones in the developed European countries such as Bavaria, France, and England, was one of the greatest values of Cukić's textbooks. He cited so much statistical data that almost every reader could draw his own conclusion about the conditions, especially economic, in Serbia, the operation of her social institutions, and about the state apparatus as a whole. It can be freely said that the textbooks of these native professors were superior to the standard textbooks of that time, and that they represent the first truly scholarly attempts in the fields of law, economy, and political science in Serbia.

Like the textbooks for elementary and secondary schools, a large number of Lyceum textbooks were more or less adaptations or translations of the well-known Austrian and German textbooks. Most often they were poorly written. Thus, for example, an anonymous critic of the book *Načelni osnovi umnopravoslovne polažitelne policie* (The Theoretical Foundations of Rhetoric: Elementary Principles) by Jovan Raić wrote: "Do not pay any attention to the [Serbian] language, grammar, and orthography; until now, thank God, no Serb knows them well."[186] Young native professors who began to write textbooks had to cope with many problems because, as Matić wrote, the "field was unprepared" and their works "cut almost the first furrows."[187] In spite of all the many deficiencies, of which in many cases the authors were aware themselves, the "first furrows" were plowed and each field was partially prepared for sowing.

The Constitutionalists paid great attention to higher education and achieved notable results. When they took power in 1838, the Lyceum was in a formative phase and did not significantly differ from the Gymnasium. Twenty years later, in 1858, when their reign came to an end, the Lyceum was a semi-university with three departments, numerous courses, and a solid teaching staff. However, in spite of all the improvements, the number of its students was only slightly increased. According to Konstantin Branković, one of its first professors, in the twenty years of the Constitutionalists' regime, only 165 young men graduated from the highest school in Serbia, or an average of eight students per year.[188] In spite of that, their presence was to be felt in almost every field of Serbian life.

CHAPTER V

THE EDUCATION OF SERBIA'S YOUTH ABROAD

*I, for one, know of no sweeter sight for
a man's eyes than his own country.*

Homer

The need for educating young Serbs abroad was already felt during Prince Miloš's first reign. He made the first steps in that direction and sent a number of young men to be educated outside of Serbia's borders at state expense. This action, however, was not the result of a defined educational policy of Serbia, but most often it was caused by the immediate needs of the state, or by the personal needs of the Prince himself. From 1838, when the Constitutionalists came to power, the education of young men abroad became part of their educational policy. In the same year, partly because of the Constitutionalists' need for specialists, partly because of their desire to increase their popularity, they issued the first decrees for the state scholarship holders abroad or *blagodejanci*, as they were officially called, and by doing so, the Constitutionalists opened a new and one of the most important pages in the history of Serbian education.

On September 14/26, 1839, the Regency, in agreement with the *Soviet*, informed the Ministry of Education of its decision to send several young men to be educated abroad and that it had allocated a sum of 2,000 talers per year for that purpose. At the same time, the Regency asked the Ministry to select candidates and to take care "that those who can support themselves not be accepted, but only those who are poor and cannot support themselves, and that it take into consideration their [the candidates'] ability and behavior so that as much as possible the most capable would be chosen. Then, their fields of specialization will be determined on the basis of their interests and they will be sent abroad."[1] By the same act the Regency asked the Ministry of Education to be sure to take into consideration the following: Filip Hristić, chief of personnel in the Ministry of Education; Stojan Jovanović, registrar in the Department of Health Care at the Ministry of Internal Affairs; Konstantin Magazinović, junior adjutant at the General Military Headquarters; and Manojlo Todorović, a type-foundry student. Several days later, the Ministry of Education informed the Regency that in addition to the young men recommended (except Manojlo Todorović who was chosen to be sent to Russia in the beginning of 1840), it selected eight more: Dimitrije Crnobarac, Danilo Danić, Dimitrije Tomić, Stefan Gruborović, Ivan Matić, N. Pavlović, Vasilije Božić, and Djordje

Branković.[2] Of the eleven selected candidates, seven had graduated from the gymnasium in Kragujevac, N. Pavlović graduated from the gymnasium in Sremski Karlovci, and Magazinović, Božić, and Branković had only elementary education. They were between nineteen and twenty-two years old, and most of them held government jobs. The list of candidates shows that the Ministry of Education strictly observed the Regency's instructions because eight of them were poor and without one or both parents. The other three - Magazinović, Pavlović, and Božić - were from middle-class families.[3]

According to the Ministry of Education's written suggestion, four candidates had to be sent to the Schemnitz Mining Academy (Banská Štiavnica, Slovakia) where two of them "could learn in the time prescribed the skills of mining, and the other two forestry (which our fatherland desperately needed)." For the studies in the Schemnitz Academy, the following were chosen: Ivan Matić, Vasilije Božić, N. Pavlović, and Djordje Branković.[4] On October 10/22, 1839, the Ministry of Education also informed the Ministry of Foreign Affairs of those students, and asked it "to be so kind as to ask the Austrian consul to recommend our forenamed young men to the director of the aforementioned Schemnitz Mining Academy, and ask him to inform the Ministry of Foreign Affairs of their acceptance [arrival] and later of their behavior."[5] The other seven students, the Ministry of Education suggested to the Regency, were to be sent to Vienna where all of them (except Magazinović who knew German so well that he could begin his studies in the Artillery School) would study only the German and French languages for a year. After that, four of them (Tomić, Danić, Jovanović, and Gruborović) were to remain in Vienna and begin their education, first in a secondary school, and later in a polytechnical school, for a duration of five years. The Ministry of Education's suggestion reads that they should give special attention to algebra, surveying, architecture, coastal engineering, and fortification so that later, "on coming back to the fatherland, they could not only be usefully employed as capable engineers and architects but, if the need arises, they could as experienced professors teach these same disciplines to Serbian youths as well." The remaining two, Hristić and Crnobarac, after a year of studying German and French, were to be sent to Paris. There, first, they were to study philosophy and afterward law or medicine so that after their return to Serbia, they could be used either as "perfect lawyers" or as physicians. But if the need arose, the Ministry of Education's suggestion read, these two young men could "teach students in the schools of their fatherland."[6]

The Regency accepted the Ministry of Education's suggestion and, on October 15/27, 1839, the first group of the Serbian state scholarship holders went to Schemnitz and Vienna. In addition to the eleven selected young men, the group was joined by Konstantin Cukić, Sreten Popović, and Gliša Božić, who went to study abroad at their own expense.[7] Since most of them had not been abroad, and since they had difficulty with German, the government assigned a guide to them. This task was entrusted to Josif Milovuk, treasurer of the Ministry of Justice and Education.[8]

Before they left Serbia, the Ministry of Education issued a list of instructions entitled "Instructions to the Young Men who are Sent to Foreign Countries in Order to Study Various Useful Disciplines" whose author was Dimitrije Isailović, chief of personnel in the Ministry of Education. It advised students how to study and to conduct themselves in foreign countries. They were advised "to educate themselves as much as possible, to discipline and to ennoble their hearts and feelings, and to accustom their character and will to be correct in all actions and procedures." The "Instructions" paid special attention to their behavior abroad "since all knowledge, even if it is divine," it points out, "without good behavior can be not only useless but even destructive." In order to preserve their exemplary behavior, they were advised to keep constantly in mind "that the eyes of all Serbs are focused on them, the people who are spending their hard-earned substance for their education." The students were also advised to go to church regularly, to a Russian church if there was no Serbian one, and not to abandon their nationality but always to "carry and nuture it in their hearts and their minds."[9] These "Instructions" present a "very important document which contains a basic program, stated concisely and solicitously but setting up a rule to be followed during the course of their education, regarding the forming of the moral and national consciousness of the young intellectuals" of Serbia.[10]

The Serbian students selected to study abroad traveled together to Budapest. They separated there - one group departed to Schemnitz, and the other accompanied by Josif Milovuk to Vienna. After they arrived in Vienna, Milovuk helped them get settled and he hired the teachers of German and French who were to tutor them for a year and to prepare them to undertake regular study in both languages. A Serb from Vojvodina, Georgije Petrović, a second-year law student, was hired for German, and a Frenchman, Jean Bisail, for French. Each of them was paid 10 talers per month and they were obliged to tutor them for two hours per day.[11] Since there was not a classroom in which they could study these foreign languages, Josif Milovuk rented another large room and made of it a "school." It was officially opened in the presence of the students, their language teachers, and several guests. On that occasion Josif Milovuk made a short speech which was permeated with parental advice. He said, among other things:

> Here, where we are now, a path will be started and
> it will begin to lead you to your determined goal.
> Make and effort, study, take care of yourselves,
> and avoid everything that could cause trouble to
> you, and disgrace and insult to your fatherland.
>
> These two educated men are assigned to teach you,
> one in German and the other in French. Respect
> and obey them so that they will not only be your
> teachers but your friends as well.
>
> And you, highly educated gentlemen, accept these
> young Serbs whom I ... entrust to you and try as
> much as you can, each in your subject, to teach
> and tutor them exactly and faithfully.[12]

After Milovuk's return to Serbia, the Serbian students in Vienna were
not left without supervision for long. As early as February 8/20, 1841,
Prince Michael entrusted their supervision to Vuk Stefanović Karadžić. At
that time Karadžić lived in Vienna and received a pension from the Serbian
government. He was given an additional 100 talers per year for his supervising duties.[13] His obligations were to supervise the students' work and
behavior and to send reports to the Serbian government. As far as is known,
Karadžić was the only supervisor of Serbian students abroad who was
officially appointed and paid by the government during the Constitutionalist
period. It was almost impossible to appoint such supervisors later because
the students were educated at some ten university centers of Western
Europe, as well as in Russia, the Ottoman Empire, and Greece.

The first months in Vienna were very difficult for the young Serbs.
At that time, Vienna was one of the largest cultural centers in Europe, and
the Serbian "peasant boys" had difficulty getting accustomed to it and
fitting into a new society. As they walked through Vienna's streets in their
free time, their dress and behavior drew the attention of passersby. Their
memoirs show that they wanted to meet someone who would be close to
them in language and customs.

> It was there [Sreten Popović wrote later] that we
> heard and found out about some Lusatian Sorbs
> and we waited impatiently for the opportunity to
> see some of those Sorbs and to talk with them.
> And the opportunity occurred. There were two
> young men and we talked with them, but how?

> Although our words were similar neither they understood us, nor we understood them.... We liked to associate with the Turks who were at that time in Vienna studying military disciplines (for with the fez on their heads they were somewhat closer and more similar to us).[14]

The first Serbian scholarship holders abroad did not know how to behave in the company of highly educated people, and very often they were embarrassed. "If someone who was present wished to describe a welcoming party prepared for us[15] as it actually was," S. Popović also wrote, "he could report a great deal of stupidity on our part."[16]

The cultural life of Vienna could not please them, and they often dreamed about their backward but, to them, beautiful Serbia and recalled some pleasant events which they had experienced there. Their first contact with Vienna's famous opera house, about which they had heard so much since their arrival in Vienna, disappointed them. When they heard the opera for the first time, they covered their ears. "That opera singing," said one of them, "sounded to us so disharmonious. Then we remembered with sadness our bandmaster Schlesinger and realized that there is nothing without him."[17]

Karadžić's report to the Ministry of Education of August 26, 1841, shows that these students did not think that they did them a favor by sending them to be educated abroad; rather, they felt that by leaving their country and living abroad that they were "sacrificing themselves for the people." In addition, they complained that the government did not keep its promises given to them in the fatherland, and that they did not wish to be treated as "pupils or children who are told and ordered how to behave," since they "as former officials and gentlemen know this themselves." "With such an attitude...," writes Karadžić in his report, "they acted in everything like willful young gentlemen."[18]

The policy of sending students to be educated abroad was continued after 1839 and lasted during the entire Constitutionalist period. Due to the development of Serbian schools it became easier with every year to select candidates with a relatively solid educational background. On average, they were younger than the first scholarship holders and most often they had graduated from the Belgrade Lyceum or had studied there for some time before their departure abroad. For the first ten years, there was no regulation which defined how many students were to be sent each year. They were usually sent individually or in small groups, and their number depended upon the state's financial ability and upon its most important needs. Such a practice came to an end in May of 1849 when the government passed a resolution that only two students with an annual scholarship of 300 talers each were to be sent abroad every year to continue their education.[19] However, there were occasional deviations from this decision, either in the number of students or in the amount of the stipend, usually due to the illness or deaths of some students, increased needs for some specialists, or the rising cost of living. For example, in the middle of 1850, the Serbian government chose twenty students who were to attend an artillery school abroad for four to five years. But, at the request of the Ministry of Internal Affairs on July 5/17 of the same year, that number was increased to twenty-three, and the request was confirmed by Prince Alexander on July 20/August 1, 1850.[20]

The largest number of state scholarship holders abroad studied law. This is fully understandable because the young Serbian state needed not scholars, but officials. Next in number were cadets, seminarians, and students of engineering. The number of medical and philosophy students was insignificant.[21] Some young Serbs tried to get scholarships from the government for the study of music and other artistic disciplines abroad. Thus, for example, on May 30/June 11, 1857, Marko D. Šarčević, a beginning civil service employee at the District Court in Kragujevac, applied to the *Soviet* for a scholarship for the study of music abroad. "Like other disciplines," Šarčević wrote in his application, "the knowledge of music is necessary for the ennoblement of our souls. It has a broad effect on life itself and therefore the need for music has become almost indispensable to the developed European nations."[22] The *Soviet* rejected his request on July 5/17 of the same year with the remark that the "applicant's desire and longing for skill in this beautiful art is fine and praiseworthy," but that his request cannot be granted because the state still needs "more urgent knowledge and skills than music."[23]

With the desire to educate its scholarship holders as best as possible, the government sent a larger number of them to the leading Western European university centers, including Vienna, Paris, Berlin, Halle, Heidelberg, Prague, and others. A certain number of them were sent to Russia, mainly to the seminaries and the theological academy, some to Istanbul to study foreign languages, especially Turkish, and also medicine at the Galatasaray school. As far as is known, only one state scholarship holder was educated in Greece - Todor Tomić from Belgrade. He studied in Athens, what discipline we do not know, and had a scholarship of 120 talers per year.[24] It is worthy mentioning that on the invitation of Patriarch Cyril of Constantinople, the Serbian Metropolitan Petar, in agreement with the Ministry of Education, in 1856 sent Joanikij Popović to the advanced theological school on Halki Island near Istanbul.[25]

It is surprising that, despite the fact that education in Russia was much cheaper than in Western countries, the number of Serbian scholarship holders sent there was very small. It can safely be said that their number would have been even smaller had the Russian government not given a certain amount of help to the Serbian students, and if Serbia had not had need for a better prepared clergy, because the largest number of the Serbian scholarship holders in Russia studied theology, while only a few of them were prepared for other professions. Better education in the West was only one, and probably the most important reason, that the Serbian government decided to educate the bulk of its scholarship holders in the West. Besides, tense relations between Russia and the Constitutionalists, especially in the beginning of their reign, and increased Serbian orientation toward the West after Ilija Garašanin's *"Načertanije"* in 1844, undoubtedly contributed a great deal to the decision of the government. It is important to note that the Slavophile movement, which in the time of the Constitutionalists reached its high point in the social life of Russia, did not have any significant effect on Serbia. Besides, the Russian Slavophiles did almost nothing to attract Serbian students to Russian schools and universities. The first significant action was taken only in 1860, when one of the Russian Slavophiles, Alexis S. Khomiakov, a few months before his death issued the so-called "Epistle from Moscow to the Serbs" in which the Serbs were warned about the noxiousness of Western influence and advised to preserve the purity of their language and culture. This "Epistle," however, did not have the desired effect because it caused more dissatisfaction than enthusiasm among Serbian intellectuals.[26]

The Constitutionalist gave scholarships for studies abroad only to Serbian citizens. For example, by a letter of November 3/15, 1844, the Prince's representatives and the Minister of Foreign Affairs, Avram Petronijević, recommended to the *Soviet* that a scholarship be given to Stefan Djurdjević, who lived in Istanbul, was a good student, and wished to study foreign languages. This recommendation was not accepted because, it is said in Prince Alexander's decision, "a government scholarship cannot be given to a foreign citizen."[27] It seems that the Constitutionalists were persistent in this policy because, for instance, the application of Joseph Schlesinger, the only military bandmaster and the best musician in Serbia at that time, sent to the *Soviet* on February 18, 1842 (O.S.) in which he asked for a scholarship for his son Hermann, a medical student in Budapest, was also rejected.[28]

Until November, 1857, the selection of students to be educated abroad and the entire work concerning them was exclusively in the competence of the Ministry of Education. After that, however, every ministry was obliged to take care of those students whose fields of specialization were most closely related to their activities. According to the *Serbian Journal* of July, 1858, the Ministry of Internal Affairs had the largest number of students abroad, followed by the Ministry of Justice and Education and the Ministry of Finance.[29]

Serbian students abroad were faced with numerous problems among which three can be singled out as the biggest: difficulties with foreign languages, financial difficulties, and homesickness. Despite the fact that the Serbian schools paid increasing attention to foreign languages with every year, their students could not use their knowledge in the first months of their stay abroad. Therefore, almost all of them had to work on foreign languages for a certain time in order to be able to begin their regular education. As has been indicated, private language tutors were hired for the first groups of students; later, the older students who had already spent a few years abroad helped their younger colleagues. Thus, for example, Dimitrije Matić tutored in German a group of students who came to Berlin in October of 1846. "I took it on myself," he wrote in his 'Diary,' "to tutor them in the language until they get accustomed to it and are able to understand the Germans."[30] A letter by Mihailo Panić, a civil engineering student in Prague, sent to the Ministry of Education on May 3, 1847 (N.S.), nicely illustrates the beginning of their education abroad. "In spite of various difficulties which blocked my way," he wrote, "due to the alien nature of the country and especially my inability to understand its language, I enrolled myself in October in the Polytechnical School of this place and took course in algebra and geometry, which were taught in a language [probably German] which I had some knowledge. In spite of that and the fact that I spent a month here, I could scarcely understand every fifth word."[31]

Most Serbian students abroad paid great attention to foreign languages and achieved astonishing results. For example, Konstantin Magazinović, one of the first Serbian scholarship holders in Vienna, wrote later in his "Memoirs" that he "learned by heart 100 French and 300 German words per day from the dictionary."[32] And Petar Protić, who could not understand "one German word" on his arrival in Berlin in 1846, after only three months of studying German, translated from this language into Serbian a "light theatrical play," and after four months he already knew German so well that he was able to translate "Napoleon I's political testament together with the testament of Peter the Great."[33] True, this information has to be taken with a certain degree of skepticism because it was supplied by students who might have the intention of showing themselves in the best possible light. But, if we accept as a real fact only half of what they wrote, it should be admitted that they did indeed achieve a great success.

During the entire Constitutionalist period, the state scholarship holders had financial difficulties. The scholarships were relatively small and the students did not receive them regularly. Some students could not get accustomed to big city life and did not know how to distribute their scholarships, and therefore were forced to go into debt. A Yugoslav historian has pointed out that the students' squandering was one of the chief causes for their financial difficulties.[34] Thus, squandering existed, but in isolated cases, and therefore it is incorrect to draw a general conclusion on the basis of several instances. Numerous individual letters and students' joint applications to different branches of the government show that their scholarships were so small that these were not sufficient to cover their basic living expenses. The government granted many requests and from time to time, increased some scholarships, but these increases were slight and only partly alleviated the students' material problems. Since the occasional increases of scholarships burdened the already poor state treasury, at the end of his reign Prince Alexander issued a decree with the intention of stopping the growth of stipends to the state scholarship holders abroad. On September 25/October 7, 1858, he informed all ministries that he had decided "that all state scholarship holders abroad have to be informed that they have to make ends meet with the scholarships granted, not only for living expenses, but also for all expenses regarding their studies, as for instance, the paying of a language teacher, tuition, buying of books, etc."[35]

Irregular sending of scholarships was common and often put students in unpleasant conditions. The first group of them was already faced with this problem after spending only a short time in Vienna. Their letter, sent to Prince Michael on January 29, 1840, shows they had to borrow money from Lazar Grčki, a Serb from Vojvodina who lived in Vienna, because they did not receive their scholarships on time. "If we had been deprived of this salvation, too," they wrote to the Prince, "we do not know what we would have done in this foreign city and among unknown people who do not want to do anything that may not be advantageous to them; we would have even suffered from worse poverty and greater misery until we received the sum for our support from there [Serbia]."[36] Borrowing money by the students was common, and if the students could justify their debts, these were paid by the state and the students were not obliged to repay them to the state. If, however, the students' debts could not be justified, the students were obliged to repay them after they returned to Serbia and began to work. Thus, for example, on April 26/May 8, 1858, the Ministry of Interior asked for a credit of 3,500 talers to pay off the debts of twenty-four military science students. The *Soviet* granted that request on the condition "that when the students return to their fatherland, the sum will be repaid by deduction from their salaries."[37]

Homesickness was undoubtedly the greatest difficulty that almost all Serbian students went through, especially in the first months of their stay abroad. About their spiritual anguish in foreign countries, several valuable records are preserved.

> Be quiet my wavering soul [Dimitrije Matić wrote in his "Diary"], you will never be able to forget for a moment the Serbian nation and her much-desired progress. Be calm, neither any distance, nor any absence will make you indifferent toward that which has been dearest to you since you began to know for yourself.[38]

The next citation from Matić's diary illustrates still better the difficulties that this young man went through.

> In the very moment when I put down the book from my hands, pacing the room [he wrote], my homeland and all my acquaintances and friends who live in her come to my mind.... Sometimes the song "Dear Serbia, you are full of happiness" can be heard in my room but it passes as fast as lightning so that I do not know myself when faster I became silent and became engrossed in my thoughts.[39]

In moments of homesickness, the young Serbs dreamed first about Serbia, whereas memories of their parents, relatives, friends, and pleasant moments experienced in their homeland had more or less a secondary importance. Thus, for example, Jevrem Grujić wrote in his *Notes*:

> I woke up early, but I did not want to go to downtown. The first thing that I thought about was that today is **St. Vitus' Day**. In my thoughts I was more in Kosovo than in my room. It made me sad. I could do almost nothing. Around twilight I wrote a letter to my mother and then I remembered how I used to drive lambs with her from meadow to water at dusk.[40]

In time their homesickness became weaker and weaker and the Serbian scholarship holders felt happy and proud to have the opportunity to be educated at well-known schools and universities. Dimitrije Matić, for instance, who constantly dreamed about Serbia, after spending only a few months at the University of Berlin wrote in his "Diary":

> I am so lucky to have such an excellent opportunity for education that I am unable to express my present satisfaction. I would not change this opportunity for anything because only by improving myself in this way I will be able to advance in my profession.[41]

Young Serbs were aware that they would be confronted with many problems and would have to sacrifice many things, but they were also aware that sufferings were unavoidable if they wanted to help their homeland which cried out for educated people. When they came to the modern European cities from backward Serbia, they were impressed and saw her progress in closer contact with the more developed European countries. When, for instance, Jovan Ilić, later a well-known Serbian poet, saw Budapest on his way to Prešov (Eastern Slovakia) in 1844, he shouted: "Into the world, into the world, if we want to be useful to ourselves and to other!"[42]

Despite the fact that Serbian students began their education abroad with a very poor educational background, they still achieved noticeable results, due mostly to their diligent work and persistence. Almost all of them successfully completed their education, and a rather large number of them received their doctorates, mainly in philosophy and law.

Serbian students, especially at the West European universities, had the opportunity to take courses with famous professors of that time, among whom Friedrich Wilhelm Schelling and Carl Ludwig Michelet were the best known. Michelet, a follower of Hegel's philosophy, was one of the most popular professors in Germany in the 1840s. Dimitrije Matić, who left the most detailed and the most valuable information about life and work of the Serbian students abroad, was so enthusiastic about Michelet's lectures that he wrote in his "Diary":

> My soul is melting in delight listening to the excellent lectures of famous scholars, especially Michelet's, a very capable and spiritually-gifted Professor of Philosophy and Natural Law.... I am unable to describe the excellence of his lecturing

and I have already written to my friends in
Belgrade about it....[43]

Hegel's ideas did not fill with enthusiasm only those Serbian students abroad who studied philosophy, but the students in other fields as well. They wanted to transmit these ideas to their younger colleagues in Serbia and they partly succeeded in this. It should be indicated that the works of the famous English economist, Adam Smith, also had a significant influence on a certain number of them.

Besides learning, the Serbian students abroad, especially in Western Europe, were engaged in other activities. One of the most active was Ljubomir Nenadović who sent accounts of his travels to the *Serbian News*. Jovan Ristić, later known as a statesman, examined old Serbian manuscripts in the "Paris Imperial Library" at the request of the Serbian Literary Society.[44] Milovan Janković sent some advice of an economic nature to the Constitutionalists' leaders, and the like.[45]

Western Europe at that time knew very little about Serbia and what was known was written by foreigners who did not present her in the best light. With the desire of acquainting numerous European countries with Serbia, Milovan Janković and Jevrem Grujić, government scholarship holders in Paris, wrote a book in French about Serbia.

Because we noticed among Frenchmen [Grujić
wrote] that these people here know almost nothing
about us. If someone heard and learned something
about us, most often they heard it from the mouths
of our enemies and slanderers who call us bandits
and bad people....[46]

Their book was published in Paris in 1853 under the title *Slaves du sud ou le peuple Serbe avec les Croates et les Bulgares*. The glorification of the Serbian people, their past, and their social relations were the basic characteristics of this work. Great attention was devoted to Serbian villages and to social institutions. In the glorification of Serbia, these two young men went so far that they wrote: "*Si Thomas Morus, Fourier et les autres socialistes et communistes connaissaient notre pays, ils n'auraient pas créé des utopies imaginaries.*"[47] They were critical about the Constitutionalist government, condemned some actions of its leading members (Toma Vučić-Perišić, Stojan Simić, Aleksa Simić, to mention just a few), mentioned the notorious prison in Gurgusovac, and negatively characterized the Ottoman Empire and Austria.

Janković and Grujić sent their book to many monasteries, Serbian ministers, gymnasium and lyceum professors, and to all "writers who were interested in the Eastern question." It did not remain unnoticed in Serbia and abroad. For example, the official French newspaper *Moniteur* in its issue of April 9, 1853 (N.S.), published an excerpt from it, and the papers *Journal des Debats* and *Revue des deux mondes* reviewed it.[48] Janković's and Grujić's book was well accepted abroad. In Serbia, however, it caused dissatisfaction in the government because the censor was of the opinion that it was directed against some of its members. It seems that Janković's and Grujić's opinion about the Minister of Interior, Aleksa Simić, upset the officials most. Writing about him they pointed out that "activity was his good characteristic, and, a bad one was his interfering in the field of literature about which he did not know anything."[49] The government prohibited distribution of the book. In addition, at the request of the Minister of Education, the *Soviet* decided to cancel the scholarship of Jevrem Grujić. This decision was approved by Prince Alexander on July 6/18, 1853.[50] Milovan Janković had lost his scholarship before the book was published for criticizing government policy. On July 7/19 of the same year, the Ministry of Education sent a letter to Jevrem Grujić ordering him to return immediately to Serbia with the request to convey the same order to Milovan Janković "if he is still in Paris."[51]

Janković's and Grujić's book *Slaves du Sud* is not worthy of any special attention either as history or as a literary work. It was simply a work to publicize Serbia and criticize her government by young men inspired with the ideas of nationalism and liberalism. In spite of all its deficiencies, this first book by Serbian scholarship holders drew the attention of the European public, which thereby got a little clearer picture of small and backwards Serbia. When one reads that book today, one wonders how those Serbian "peasant boys" were able to write a book in French, regardless of how poor it was, after spending only a few years abroad.

In selecting students to go abroad, the Serbian government paid great attention to their health and physical condition. Despite these precautionary measures, some sickly students were still sent abroad. Most often they became ill, and a certain number of them died. The sick ones received special attention from their colleagues and in moments of sickness and personal tragedy, the young Serbs abroad demonstrated their closeness, friendship, and devotion. Since physicians and medicines were expensive, the students were forced to borrow money for their treatments or for the funerals of their colleagues. They usually borrowed from the Vojvodina Serbs who were merchants in the important commercial centers. Debts of this kind were paid by the state with almost no difficulty. Thus, for example, when Gavril Milićević, a state scholarship holder, died in Kiev in

August of 1848, Prince Alexander decided on September 27/October 9 of the same year, on the suggestion of Metropolitan Petar, that all his medical and funeral expenses be paid from the state treasury.[52] The Prince made a similar decision after the death of Andrija Stefanović, an engineering student in Vienna, who died in April, 1856. The only difference was that for Stefanović an additional sum of 240 *grošes* for the "erection of a marble cross with an appropriate epitaph on the deceased's grave" was allocated.[53] The Serbian government also paid rather great attention to the health of its students during their study abroad. For instance, Filip Hristić, a philosophy and law student in Paris, had his scholarship extended for six months because his physician "forbade him most strictly intellectual work for several months."[54]

Besides regular scholarships and expenses for medical treatments and funerals, the state budget of Serbia was burdened with other numerous expenditures for the students abroad. Among the most important was the purchase of clothing and shoes for the poor students before their departure abroad, the sending of books and newspapers published in Serbia, additional expenditures for those students who wished to continue their education and work for their doctorates, expenses of those students who were required after their graduation to visit several of the most important European countries in order to get acquainted with various customs, cultures, political and social institutions, and so forth, and expenditures for the purchase of gifts to some foreign professors who showed great interest in the progress of the Serbian students.

As most state scholarship holders were from poor families and their parents could not dress them properly, the government provided clothes and shoes for them so they would not disgrace the Serbian state. "The honor of the government requires," wrote Metropolitan Petar to the Ministry of Education on May 23/June 5, 1850, "that its scholarship holders be decently dressed when introduced to the Metropolitan of Kiev and to the city mayor and his officials."[55] They were mainly modestly dressed. For example, the students who were sent to the Kiev Seminary in the spring of 1846 received: coat, trousers, vest, boots, and three shirts.[56]

Josif Milovuk was the first to suggest to the Ministry of Education that all Serbian newspapers be sent regularly to the Serbian students abroad so "that they can also be informed about progress and circumstances in their fatherland and be proud of it."[57] The Ministry received a similar suggestion from Georgije Petrović, the German language tutor of the Serbian scholarship holders in Vienna, on February 13, 1840. In addition to the newspapers, he recommended sending Serbian books so that "the spirit of love for the fatherland in the scholarship holders" would be preserved.[58]

There is no reliable information as to whether those suggestions were fully accepted. There are only some indications that Serbian newspapers were sent periodically, not to all students abroad, but only to the group who studied in Vienna. It should be said that those periodical consignments could not satisfy them because not only did they receive them intermittently, but they received them after long delays, mostly due to slow and ineffective postal and shipping services.

The extension of scholarships was not rare, but the students who enjoyed it were usually obliged to repay gradually part of their scholarships after their graduation.[59] Some students, however, usually the outstanding ones, were exempted from that obligation. Such a one was Miloje Janković, who graduated from the Kiev Seminary in 1849. By Prince Alexander's decision of April 7/19/, 1849, he was allowed to continue his education at the Theological Academy and was promised that the Serbian government would continue to send his previous scholarship of 100 talers per year on the condition that the Russian government also continue to send its support.[60] There were some cases, although not many, in which the Serbian government, because of financial difficulties, was forced to withdraw some of its students from their studies abroad. Such was Stojan Nikolić's case, who was withdrawn from Heidelberg in 1847.[61]

It was almost a custom to require from the Serbian graduates abroad that they visit some places or states in order to enrich their knowledge and experience before their return to the state. For example, in the spring of 1845, the Serbian government ordered three students who graduated in mining from the Schemnitz Academy "to visit various mines in Europe in order to get practical experience."[62] There were some instances when the teaching vacancies in vocational schools could not be filled with foreigners and Serbian graduates educated abroad had to be hired. But before they were appointed, the government sent them abroad to get acquainted with the latest achievements in their fields of specialization. These were usually isolated cases. Such a one was the case of Petar Protić who, in 1852, was sent for eight months to France and England "in order to observe and compare the artillery systems of these countries" and he was given a sum of 250 talers for his traveling expenses. Upon his return, he was appointed professor of artillery in the Artillery School in Belgrade.[63]

In several cases, the Serbian government sent gifts to some professors or principals of the schools abroad where its students were educated. Thus, for example, on the Ministry of Education's suggestion of January 12/24, 1852, Prince Alexander decided "as a sign of appreciation and deserved generosity" to send a signet-ring to the director of the Artillery School in Berlin on behalf of the students who were to be sent there because "he has been taking care of the Serbian students and by it obliged the Serbian government." The ring was edged with diamonds, and in the middle decorated with the Prince's initials.[64]

In the beginning of their reign, the Constitutionalists set aside a modest sum from the state budget for the education of native young men abroad. As already indicated, that sum for 1839 was only 2,000 talers. Because of the rise in educational costs and the growth in numbers of students abroad, the sum for their support was increased from year to year. For example, after ten years, that is in the academic year 1849-50, it already amounted to 5,040 talers,[65] and in 1857-58, it was increased even more to 13,550 talers inclusive of the scholarships of the military school students, or 8,550 talers without those scholarships.[66]

The changing of educational institutions or the changing of fields of specialization without the knowledge or permission of the educational authorities in Serbia was often a practice of the Serbian students abroad. Those students most often lost their scholarships, though it was not rare that after a certain time, some of them were not only renewed but even increased for the field of specialization of their choice. Among numerous examples, the case of Konstantin Magazinović is illustrative. He was sent to Vienna in 1839 to study military disciplines with an annual scholarship of 200 talers.[67] After spending a short time in Vienna, he went to Russia to continue his education without permission from the Serbian government and thereby lost his scholarship. Since he was not accepted by Russia's universities, he went to Leipzig and began to study philosophy. After this, he went to Paris and began to study law. As a law student in Paris, he again became a state scholarship holder with an annual stipend of 300 talers, confirmed by the Prince on April 10/22, 1844.[68] In the desire to end this practice which might jeopardize the quality of education and increase the expenses of the state, Prince Alexander issued an order on October 5/17, 1856, that in the future "requests from the government scholarship holders who wish to change their fields of specialization cannot be granted, but everyone has to complete his degree in those disciplines to which he was assigned by the government."[69]

After completing their education abroad, the scholarship holders returned to Serbia. As far as is known, only one of them refused to return to Serbia during the entire Constitutionalist period. That was Dimitrije Dimitrijević who, in 1849, was sent to France to study the French language and literature. He was given a scholarship of 400 talers per year as was to be prepared for a professorship in the Belgrade Lyceum.[70] The Serbian government was not easily reconciled to the loss of the young man in whose education a rather large sum of money was invested and tried to bring him back. For example, in its letter to Jevrem Grujić of July 7/19, 1853, the

Ministry of Education required from him to bring Dimitrijević back to Serbia "by all possible means."[71] We could not find any document which would reveal the end of Dimitrijević's case, but since his name does not appear among the names of the Lyceum professors or among any other state officials, it may be assumed that all government attempts failed and that he remained abroad.

During their education abroad, the students admired the splendor, luxury, and riches of Vienna, Paris, Berlin, and other European metropolitan centers, but they could not forget Serbia. They were abroad only physically whereas in their thoughts they were tied to their homeland and impatiently counted the days until their return. On his way to Serbia, Dimitrije Matić visited several cities among which was Paris. After leaving this beautiful city and also Versailles, both of which impressed him, he wrote in his "Diary":

> These are the last words I am writing in Paris and
> by all means and forever last because I do not
> want to leave our parts any more; to live there, to
> die there, a life without the Serbian people would
> be worse for me than death.[72]

After returning to Serbia, these young men received high administrative positions and were very respected. Together with the young men who graduated from the Belgrade Lyceum, they formed the first group of native intellectuals and greatly influenced the "creation of their social and ideological-political profile."[73] There is no information about their relation to the common people. It is only known that a large number of them were mainly interested in the making of a civil service career and high salaries. Thus, for example, Dimitrije Crnobarac, one of the first students sent abroad, after returning to Serbia used to say that "a man begins to be a man only with a salary of 1,000 talers [per year]."[74]

The emergence of native intellectuals caused a split within Serbian society between the old, uneducated and the young, educated generations - between fathers and sons. In the second half of the Constitutionalist period, it was a common phenomenon that, for instance, a minister or chief of personnel of some department had only an elementary school education whereas their secretaries had doctorates in philosophy or law from the best-known European universities. The older generation was more or less satisfied with its political achievements and with limited autonomy. The younger generation, however, wanted much more. It wanted full independence for the Serbian state and advocated numerous liberal reforms by means of which Serbian society would move faster along the path of progress, modernization, and political freedom. The older generation was aware of its deficiencies and limitations as well as the potential power of the small number of young intellectuals, and during the entire period of the Constitutionalists' regime was tolerant toward them. For example, when the state scholarship holder Alimpije Vasiljević came to the *Soviet* to express his appreciation for the opportunity given him to be educated abroad, Jevrem Nenadović, vice-president of the *Soviet* and father-in-law of Prince Alexander, told him "that younger educated people should not become conceited and should not despise their elders who are less educated."[75]

The conceited attitude of some intellectuals educated abroad and their request to be given the highest positions in the civil service cause a reaction among some Serbian intellectuals who did not have the opportunity to be educated outside of the Serbian borders. One of the most vociferous critics of the conceited behavior of the returnees was Stojan Bošković. In August of 1857 he wrote in the *Serbian Journal*:

> Let us ask now: Why does the government promote often and in a surprisingly short time those who spent several years abroad at state expense regardless of whether they are knowledgeable or not? They fly up to high and important positions out of turn and regardless of whether they deserve it or not. All honor and respect to those who are what they claim to be, who are in the true sense educated and capable, but of those there are not many. The rest of them are mostly only empty arrogance and behind their educated looks, ignorance, laziness, and corruption are hidden.[76]

Many other sources confirm that Bošković's criticism was justified because not only a large number of the first intellectuals educated abroad, but also a large number of those educated in the Belgrade Lyceum, had limited professional knowledge, and the latter did not show any greater enthusiasm for the jobs which they performed. Their greatest preoccupation was climbing up the ladder of the bureaucratic hierarchy, which brought great social reputations and large incomes.

> Look at our lawyer two or three years after his graduation [wrote Svetozar Marković]. What is it that distinguished him from that bureaucrat who did not graduate in law? Absolutely nothing.

> Except that he looks more curly, more
> distinguished, a twisted and stupid paragraph sign
> [a common Serbian expression for someone who
> act unnaturally].... The difference is that he knows
> how to find more quickly and easily a paragraph
> which contains needed information, that he knows
> how to write a verdict so that a peasant, when it is
> read to him, asks "What does he say, for God's
> sake?", that they advance faster, and that they
> marry into richer families.[77]

Besides a positive influence, the returnees educated abroad had also a negative influence on Serbian society. Under their influence, especially of those who studied at Western European universities, there emerged a group of citizen who tried in almost everything to imitate foreigners, who despised and abandoned their native customs, culture, and even language as something backward and unworthy of their attention.

> It has gone so far [wrote Vladimir
> Jovanović in 1864] that some people scold
> shamelessly as "vulgar" [*prostačko*], "rustic"
> [*gejačko*], "boorish" [*paorsko*], "plebeian"
> [*grmaljsko*], "*Šumadian* (provincial)" [*Šuma-
> dinsko*], in short as bad "everything that is ours"
> and to glorify as "noble" [*nobl*], "fine" [*fajin*],
> "distinguished and gentlemanly" everything that is
> not ours. So a new circle has been created in our
> private and public lives, the circle of the "nobles"
> in contrast to the "common people."
>
> In their way of life the common people
> have remained faithful to the Serbian customs and
> they are always proud of the name "genuine Serb"
> [*Srbenda*]. The "nobles" joined the wheel of
> "foreign circumstances" and they are called now
> "Tsarigradians" [*Carigradlije*], now "Russomans"
> [*Rusomani*], now "Swabians" [*Švabe*], now
> "Parisians" [*Parizlije*], or by the general name
> "parasites" [*gotovani*], who are waiting for
> everything to come ready-made from abroad.[78]

This practice of accepting foreign customs and ways of life was even more noticeable in Serbian society at the end of the nineteenth century.

It is not exactly known how many young Serbs were educated abroad during the Constitutionalist period. That is almost impossible to establish because some died during the time of their education, some did not complete their studies, some returned to Serbia after spending a short time abroad (mostly due to the financial difficulties of the state), some were educated at their own expense, and so on. According to the estimate of Slobodan Jovanović, one of the best experts in Serbian history of the nineteenth century, by 1855, about fifty young Serbs were educated abroad.[79] Since the Constitutionalists' reign lasted until 1858, their number was probably somewhat larger and it could amount to around seventy or eighty young men. Although that number was rather small, their influence could be noticed in all fields of social, cultural, economic, and political life of the still young and undeveloped Serbian state. They were the first who tried to, and partially succeeded in, drawing Serbia closer to the developed Western European countries - this was their greatest contribution to the modernization of their fatherland.

CHAPTER VI

CULTURAL INSTITUTIONS
AND SOCIETIES

*Kultur kann nur aus dem Leben
hervorwachsen und herausblühen.*

Friedrich Nietzsche

1.

In the educational development of every country, cultural institutions have a special place because they are bastions of learning and kaleidoscopes of human thought. Their development in Serbia was slow and they had, especially in the first days of their existence, more of a political than a cultural character. The establishment of public institutions in which domestic and foreign newspapers, as well as books, were available to the educated stratum of Serbian society and in which Serbian citizens could exchange their opinions and ideas occurred in the 1840s. The first suggestion for the establishment of such an institution in Serbia came from a group of Belgrade citizens in December, 1840, but it is uncertain whether one was ever established.[1] Serbia had to wait for a full three years before the question of establishing a public reading place, or *"kasina,"* as it was officially called, became one of the main issues. Some changes in the internal life of the state led to this question being raised again. In particular, at the end of 1843 a new building, the so-called *"Zdanije kod Jelena"* (Building by the Deer - a statue) was completed in Belgrade. It was the most beautiful building of that time in Serbia and belonged to ex-Prince Michael Obrenović. In November of 1843, the *Serbian News* reprinted an article from *The London Times* in which *"Zdanije kod Jelena"* was mentioned. The article pointed out that in the winter of 1843 a public reading places as a "place for entertainment and rest" would be opened in this building.[2] Miloš Popović, the editor of the *Serbian News*, who wrote remarks below the reprinted text, emphasized "that it would be very useful to have a place where a large number of newspapers, without which every man in the world is fatal to political life, and various books would be available."[3] Despite the need for a public reading place, Popović's suggestion was not immediately accepted and Serbia had to wait for its opening until October 26/November 7, 1845.[4] The members of a secret democratic Panslavic club[5] in Belgrade, headed by Stefan Hrkalović, former director of the Military Academy during Prince Miloš's first reign and at that time a state official, established the first reading club.[6] It was opened in *"Zdanije kod Jelena"* and was officially called *"Kasina"* (from the Italian *casino*), but since its members were mainly supporters of the Illyrian movement in Croatia, it is also known under the name *"Ilirska kasina."*[7]

Kasina kept domestic and foreign newspapers and it was visited mostly by the members of a secret Panslavic club who discussed the latest news there. Moreover, from the very beginning of its operation, it offered free instruction in French, and it planned to provide tutoring in the Slavic languages.[8]

Since its founders and a large number of its members were supporters of the Illyrian movement, from its very beginning it aroused suspicion among many of the educated Belgrade citizens who opposed the spread of Illyrian ideas in Serbia, ideas which were "something foreign, something unacceptable."[9] As early as the beginning of 1846, with the aim of stopping the spread of these notions through the *Kasina*, its opponents began to work actively to establish a reading place which would indeed be public and which would reduce the importance of *Kasina. Kasina* did not succeed in increasing its membership significantly or in becoming a public reading place in the true sense. The reason for this was not only a strong anti-Illyrian opposition, but also the fact that *Kasina* was not accessible to everyone.[10] It is not known for certain when *Kasina* stopped operating. It is only known that after 1848, it was no longer mentioned in the archival documents and newspapers, and it may be assumed that it discontinued its operations in late 1846 or early 1847, because in 1846 the *Serbian News* still periodically reported its activities.[11]

Kasina operated for but a short time and did not play any significant role in the cultural and educational development of Serbia. Its greatest contribution was that its Illyrian policy prompted a large number of educated and prominent Belgrade citizens, opponents of the Illyrian movement, to establish a public reading place which would be accessible to everyone and which would be in accordance with the cultural needs of the country.

With the opening of new schools, especially the Lyceum, the growth in numbers of educated people, the economic development of the country and its more frequent contacts with foreign countries, the need for a public reading place had been felt long before the opening of *Kasina*. But with that event, the need became even greater, more for political than for cultural and educational reasons, because in the opening of a popular public reading place, its opponents saw a gradual reduction of their influence in the political life of the country and so their end.

Jelisej Vukajlović, a secretary in the administration of the city of Belgrade, was the initiator of a reading club which would be open to everybody.[12] His initiative was supported by distinguished and influential citizens of that time, such as Miša Anastasijević, one of the richest and most powerful people in Serbia, Radovan P. Damjanović, Assistant Minister of Interior, Maksim Simonović, Lyceum professor, Petar Radovanović, director of elementary schools, and others.[13] They formed the "Committee for the Opening of a Reading Club" at the end of 1845, and on December 30, 1845/January 11, 1846, issued a statute for it.[14] Two days later, on January 1/13, 1846, the Committee applied to the Ministry of Interior to be allowed to establish a Serbian Reading Club in Belgrade, and on January 2/14 of the same year, they submitted its by-laws for approval.[15] Their request was granted on January 17/29, and on February 24, 1846 (O.S.) *"Srbsko čitalište u Beogradu"* (The Serbian Reading Club in Belgrade), as it was officially called, was solemnly opened "in the presence of all its members and our [Serbian] distinguished gentlemen and the foreign consuls who are here."[16] On that occasion as special religious service was held, followed by several speeches. The main speakers were Radovan P. Damjanović, president of the Committee, and Maksim Simonović, who besides his professorship was the editor of the newspaper *Srbskij ulak-Serbischen Courrier* during 1843 and 1844. He said, among other things:

> So, thus, we now have one more institution useful
> for the people, in our circle, We have made one
> step more toward European education. Thanks to
> those persons who initiated this beneficial sugges-
> tion! ... Thanks and honor to those patriots who
> made possible the establishment of this very
> important institution and who regularly support it
> today! Thanks to [its] creators![17]

The Belgrade Reading Club operated in a communal building across the street from *"Zdanije kod Jelena"* where *Kasina* had its reading room.[18] It had several large rooms "spacious as saloons." Its reading room was nicely arranged, and in the room "where discussions were held there were sofas [*minderluci*] all around where people sat and talked."[19]

The Reading Club did not receive any financial help from the state, and all of its expenses were paid from membership fees and donations. Each of its members was obliged to pay the membership fee which was "at least one *cvancig* per month" and this had to be paid for at least three months in advance.[20] There were, however, a rather large number of its members who gave much more than its regulations defined. For example, Metropolitan Petar Jovanović and the Simić brothers gave more than 40 *cvancigs* per year each.[21] Prince Alexander and Miša Anastasijević, who was elected the first president of the Reading Club in 1846 and performed this duty until his death in 1885, gave the largest contributions to the Club. It is known, for instance, that Anastasijević's contribution was 300 *cvancigs* per year.[22] The Lyceum students were exempted from the membership fee and could visit the Reading Club as guest when they got permission from their superiors.[23] In addition, guests of the Reading Club members could visit it without any contribution, but not for longer than a month.[24] It is important to mention that Article 3 of the first "Rules for the Serbian Reading Club in Belgrade" of January 2/14, 1846, says that "every Serb regardless of whether he is an ecclesiastic, a military man, or an ordinary citizen can become a member of the society [club]."[25] This article, however, was not strictly observed because some of the members were not Serbs, such as Janko Šafařik, Paja Pavlović, and others.[26]

In the first year of its operation, the Belgrade Reading Club had 358 members[27] - not a large number for the city which had 14,371 inhabitants at that time.[28] However, that number gradually decreased so that even the further existence of the Reading Club came into question. As early as 1847, the number of members dropped by 50 to a total of 308.[29] Three years later, that is in 1850, it dropped to 227 members.[30] This rapid decrease in membership prompted its president, Miša Anastasijević, to publish an article in the *Serbian News* in which he warned citizens about the serious problem which the Club faces and called upon them to support its operation as much as possible.

> Instead of **progressing** - shall we go **back**? [he wrote] God save us from it! It would be shameful that this chief city of all Serbs be blamed for not wanting, or not knowing how to support such a useful institution.[31]

Anastasijević's appeal did not significantly alter the number of the Reading Club members. For example, in 1852, its number was 277; in 1856, it increased to 347; and in the last year of the Constitutionalists' regime, the number again dropped to only 276 members,[32] while the population of Belgrade had increased to 18,860.[33] The main cause for the small number of Reading Club members should be sought in the rapid increase of foreign newspapers in Serbia and in the absence of a reading habit among her population. In 1846 when the Reading Club was established, Serbia received only a few foreign newspapers, whereas by the end of the Constitutionalists' regime, that number was considerably enlarged. According to the *Serbian News*, in 1856 Serbia received 138 different foreign newspapers: 5 in Serbian (from Vojvodina), 1 in Bulgarian, 2 in Croatian, 4 in Russian, 1 in Czech, 3 in Polish, 3 in modern Greek, 84 in German, 7 in English, 21 in French, 4 in Italian, 2 in Hungarian, and 1 in Turkish, or 906 issues (copies): 600 in Serbian, 2 in Bulgarian, 4 in Croatian, 10 in Russian, 1 in Czech, 3 in Polish, 3 in modern Greek, 218 in German, 9 in English, 43 in French, 5 in Italian, 3 in Hungarian, and 5 in Turkish.[34] It should be noted that in the same year, Serbia received more copies of foreign newspapers than were printed at home because her two newspapers, the *Serbian News* and *Šumadinka* (literally "A Woman from Šumadija"), together printed only 900 copies.[35]

Despite the fact that the income of the Belgrade Reading Club was small, it had a large number of domestic and foreign newspapers and journals, books, geographic maps, a collection of old coins, etc. For example, in 1852, it kept forty different newspapers; nineteen were bought from its own budget, eighteen were received as a gift from the editor of the *Serbian News*, Miloš Popović, one was borrowed from the Ministry of Finance, and two were received from the *Soviet*.[36] With the desire of reducing its expenses for the acquisition of newspapers from abroad, the Reading Club management applied to the Ministry of Education on August 6/18, 1846, asking to be exempted from postage for foreign newspapers. The Ministry informed the *Soviet* and Prince Alexander of this request on August 13/25 of the same year with the recommendation that it should be granted because "the wide reading of newspapers positively affects the spread of education."[37] This request was granted and the Belgrade Reading Club was exempted from paying postage for foreign newspapers.[38]

The Belgrade Reading Club also had its own library. As far as is known, this was the first circulating library in Serbia. For example, in 1852, its members took out books and newspapers in 120 cases.[39] In the first year of its operation, the Reading Club had a small number of books. According to the report of its first librarian, Milovan Spasić, which he presented at the annual meeting of the Club held on January 26/February 7, 1847, at the end of 1847 the library had 329 books in 615 volumes, of which 194 books were in Serbian, Russian, and other Slavic languages, and 135 in German and other important Western European languages.[40] Spasić concluded his report full of hope that this library would be rapidly enriched and enlarged.

> It is indeed a nice collection for such a short time
> [he said], and if the number of its books continues
> to increase at the same [rate] and if it continues to
> receive donations, for which the supporters of
> public education are cordially asked and invited, it
> can be hoped that the Reading Club library will
> become one of the best known South Slavic
> libraries and it will be for our young fatherland
> what the Alexandrian Library would have been for
> the whole world if inhuman barbarians had not
> burnt it.[41]

Spasić's desire was not fulfilled. The Reading Club library never became either the Alexandrian Library of the South Slavs or one of significant Slavic libraries. Nevertheless, it should be pointed out that in spite of its great material difficulties, it was considerably enlarged in the period from its establishment in 1846 until the downfall of the Constitutionalists' reign in 1858. A certain number of books were bought from the Reading Club budget, and a large number of them were gifts from well-known writers, ordinary citizens, foreign cultural institutions, and from the State Printing Office. Among writers who gave to the Reading Club library of their own works, and very often other books were: Petar Petrović-Njegoš, sovereign of Montenegro, writer and philosopher; Vuk Stefanović Karadžić; Jovan Sterija Popović; Milan Dj. Milićević; Ljubomir Nenadović; and others.[42] On the request of its management, the library also received free copies of each book published in the State Printing Office. Namely, on March 2/14, 1847, Miša Anastasijević asked the Ministry of Education to rule that the "Printing Office of Principality be obliged to send a copy of every book printed to the library." This request was granted and on April 1/13 of the same year, the Ministry required that the "Printing Office had to give a copy of every book which it printed at its expense to the aforementioned library, except those which were expensive, as, for instance, church service books."[43] The number of books in the library of the Reading Club rapidly grew in the first three years of its operation, but later on the increase was insignificant. For example, in 1847, the number of its books grew from 329 to 1,787, and in 1848 to 2,200 titles.[44] After 1848, that increase was significantly reduced so that in the next ten years, the library was enriched by only 673 new works, or by 1,198 fewer books than in the first two years of its operation.[45] There were some years when the library holding were enlarged by only a few books. Thus, for example, from 1854 to 1855, it received only six new books and its total holdings enlarged from 2,849 to 2,855 titles.[46] The main reasons for this occurrence should be sought in the decrease of the Reading Club membership, in its financial difficulties, in a rather small number of published books in the State Printing Office, and in reduced donations. It should be indicated that as early as August 6/18, 1846, the Belgrade Reading Club asked the Ministry of Education to exempt it from custom duties on books as well as on other needed items. Prince Alexander declined this request with the explanation that its acceptance "would be harmful for the government" and on September 6/18, 1846, informed the Minister of Education of his decision.[47]

Merchants, bureaucrats, and Lyceum, Seminary, and Artillery School students were the most frequent visitors to the Belgrade Reading Club. As has been indicated, the Lyceum students were permitted free use of Reading Club facilities without charge from the very beginning of its operation. At the end of 1846, when the Club's rules were partially revised, the same permission was given to the third and fourth year Seminary students, and ten years later, that is, in 1856, these privileges were extended to the Artillery School students as well.[48] In addition, numerous guests from the interior of the country as well as from abroad were frequent visitors. For example, the register of visitors shows that in January of 1848, four hundred and eighty-six persons visited the Reading Club. Some of them were from as far away as Zagreb, Dubrovnik, Istanbul, Vienna, Berlin, Prague, Dresden, and Budapest.[49] The Reading Club was mainly a place where newspapers and books could be read. However, it also organized public lectures and tutoring in foreign languages. Its members translated foreign newspapers for those who could not read them. There were also political discussions which was, and still is, the most frequent and favorite pastime among the Serbs, as well as talks about the Serbian language, trade, and many other topics. It also organized various cultural and political manifestations, and so on.[50]

The Belgrade Reading Club was most active in the first years of its operation. A special committee made up of its members began publication of its own newspaper under the title *Novine Čitališta Beogradskog* (The Belgrade Reading Club News). Its first issue came out on January 3/15, 1847. From then until the end of 1848, when its publication was discontinued, it was published weekly, on Friday. Its first editor was Pavle A. Popović, a well-known cultural figure and former editor of the *Serbian News* from 1841 to 1842. He successfully performed his job for the entire year of 1847, but, for reasons unknown to us, he refused to be its editor in the following year, that is, in 1848. He was succeeded by Petar Radovanović, already mentioned several times, who edited it without salary and prolonged its life for only one year.

According to the first conception of the Reading Club Committee, the *Belgrade Reading Club News* should have had a large number of editors and correspondents. The editorship was to have been entrusted to four persons: Pavle A. Popović, Sergije Nikolić, Ilija Zaharijević, and Kornelije Popović. The number of its correspondents was to have been twenty and they were to have been sent to different countries and regions in order to become specialists for them. According to the same conception, the correspondents' work was to have been oriented toward the following regions and countries: "South, Central, and North America, Eastern and Western India, Africa and Algeria, Pyrenean Peninsula, Spain and Portugal, France, England, Switzerland, Belgium, Holland, Prussia, Austria, European Turkey, Greece, Lisbon, *Misir* (Egypt), Russia and the Caucasus region, the Scandinavian countries, and China."[51] After publication of this conception or plan regarding the *Belgrade Reading Club News*, one citizen asked the following questions in the *Serbian News*:

> Will this newspaper for the Serbs, published in Serbia, and intended for the Serbian public [a newspaper], for which so many Serbian patriots promised to work voluntarily, also report something about Serbia and the Serbian people? - It will write about all the people in the world, but will any Slavic people, at least the South Slavs, be discussed, or will that newspaper, in Serbia and among the Slavs, written by the Serbs-Slavs be silent about the Serbs and the Slavs?[52]

The editor of the *Serbian News* answered these questions. He pointed out that the Reading Club announcement clearly shows that the *Belgrade Reading Club News* will be a kind of middle-man "between foreign countries and our fatherland" and therefore the question raised was "unnecessary."[53]

The plan of the Belgrade Reading Club was too ambitious and unrealistic in view of its capabilities and it was never completely realized. Instead of four editors, it had to be satisfied with one, and instead of a large group of correspondents, it had to be satisfied with a considerably smaller number. In spite of that, the *Belgrade Reading Club News* was rather good and in demand, due mostly to Pavle A. Popović, who organized "a broad network of contributors to the paper, published original articles, and wrote about internal Serbian policy."[54]

The *Belgrade Reading Club News* was the first unofficial paper in Serbia and because of that, it was subjected to state censorship. It published news from Serbia and abroad, reports about the operation of the Belgrade Reading Club and of other reading clubs which were established throughout

Serbia, regularly published the names of contributors who financially supported the Club, and the like. Unlike the *Serbian News*, the official paper of Serbia, which had a relatively small number of readers, the *Belgrade Reading Club News* was very well accepted. For example, in 1847, the *Serbian News* was published in only 400 copies, and the *Belgrade Reading Club News* in 1,115 copies.[55] It is important to point out that with the popularity of the *Belgrade Reading Club News*, competition occurred for the first time in the Serbian press. Frightened by this popularity, the editor of the *Serbian News*, Miloš Popović, requested from the Ministry of Education and the Ministry of Internal Affairs that all of their news and reports be sent first to him because otherwise the "government newspaper [will be] dead and buried."[56] Although the *Belgrade Reading Club News* had been received well, it was short-lived. It ceased publication, as has been indicated, at the end of 1848. It is not known what was the chief reason for this. Despite the fact that it was the organ of the first public reading club in Serbia, the *Belgrade Reading Club News* was not cultural in character, but exclusively a political and informational newspaper. Its greatest contribution was that it was the competitor of the *Serbian News* and forced its editor to improve the quality of that oldest, and at that time, only official paper in Serbia, and thereby the quality of Serbian journalism as a whole.

In the second year of its operation, the Belgrade Reading Club began to work on the opening of a theater. In agreement with the Club management, actor Nikola Djurković, who had his theatrical group in Pančevo, applied on April 3/15, 1847, to the Ministry of Education for permission to perform with his group in Belgrade. Four days later, on April 7/19, the Club management also applied to the Ministry asking that a temporary theater be allowed to perform in the capital of Serbia.[57] Djurković's request, supported by the Reading Club leadership, which was composed of distinguished state officials, was granted with the stipulation that all theatrical plays were to be censored by the chief of personnel of the Ministry of Education before they could be included in their repertoire.[58] Djurković's group utilized some stage properties of a closed theater in Djumruk (a section of Belgrade), and that Princess Persida Karadjordjević gave 60 ducats for a building to be adapted into a theater hall.[59]

Nikola Djurković's group began its work in Belgrade on May 15/27, 1847, in the hall "*Kod Jelena*" ("By the Deer" - a statue) with the national-historic play *Miloš Obilić* by Jovan S. Popović. The work of this "theater" was not long-lived, for it was discontinued on March 9/21, 1848.[60] The repertoire of "*Pozorište kod Jelena*" (Theater by the Deer) included mainly works by the Serbs of Vojvodina, especially Jovan S. Popović, and those which especially treated the Serbian past. Among foreign playwrights, the following were represented: August Kotzebue, Molière, Voltaire, Schiller,

V. Hugo, and some Italian writers translated by Nikola Djurković himself.[61] Since it performed for a short time, *"Pozorište kod Jelena"* could not play any significant role in the cultural life of Serbia. Nevertheless, its importance should not be underestimated because the memory of it had a great effect when, a few years later, the educated people of Belgrade took more energetic measures for the building of a people's theater, a theater which would be the pride of the city and which would be able to satisfy the needs of its inhabitants.

During the Constitutionalist period, the Belgrade Reading Club also made a considerable contribution to the political life of the country, especially in the time of the Revolution of 1848-49 in Vojvodina. People of various occupations gathered in it, and the more knowledgeable among them explained the news, analyzed current events, and offered advice. Jovan Ristić, the well-known Serbian statesman in the second half of the nineteenth century and the first Serbian diplomatic historian, left a valuable account of such a political discussion held in the Reading Club in the time of the Revolution.

> In the Belgrade "Reading Club," the center of the capital city intelligentsia of that time [he writes] a group of its members indeed gathered to discuss "reforms" which should be introduced in Serbia. The president of this group asked in a serious tone: "What is a 'reform?'" .... The president took it on himself to consult the government and at the next meeting explained to those who advocated reforms that Serbia has been enjoying for a long time those freedoms for which Western Europe rose up. [He pointed out] that Serbia had her parliament in her People's Assembly, though it was not convoked for many years, that every Serb may carry arms at his belt, or in holsters, that he has his people's guard, and if someone knows how to write intelligently he will also find freedom of the press.[62]

The activities of the Belgrade Reading Club during the Revolution of 1848-49 did not consist only of discussions and propaganda, but numerous activities were undertaken to help the Serbs in Vojvodina. For example, in 1849, the Club collected contributions throughout Serbia and helped the Serbs who escaped from Vojvodina to Serbia.[63]

The Belgrade Reading Club enlarged its activities almost every year. Sometimes it engage in activities which did not have any relation to education or culture. For example, in the beginning of the 1850s, the first Belgrade stock exchange was opened in it. With the desire of making it possible for all interested persons to get needed information as soon as possible, especially exchange rates, the Club management acquired a blackboard which was placed in the corridor and an official copied the exchange statistics from various newspapers on it every day. However, this was not all. With the permission of the Ministry of Education granted on September 9/21, 1852, the Reading Club kept a thick notebook in which anyone could describe a product which he wanted to sell or to write down the name of a product which he wanted to buy. These advertisements were printed in the *Serbian News*. Everybody who wanted to advertise his products this way was obliged to pay to the Reading Club half of a *cvancig* per advertisement.[64]

Influenced by the Belgrade Reading Club, several other Serbian towns established similar clubs. There were some cases, though not many, in which even small towns began to open their own reading clubs. For example, on March 15/27, 1858, the *Serbian News* reported that a reading club with forty members and which kept five different newspapers had opened in the small town of Despotovac.[65] Their number was gradually increased so that at the end of the Constitutionalists' regime in 1858, Serbia had about ten reading clubs which were partially supported by the Belgrade Reading Club. This support consisted mostly of lending newspapers, gifts in books, advice on how to organize the clubs' operations, and the like. In addition, the Belgrade Reading Club published its rules in the *Serbian News* of May 31/June 12, 1846, so "that they could also be used as an example and stimulant in other places."[66]

The reading clubs in the interior of Serbia were largely supported and enriched by gifts and donations inasmuch as their membership fees could not cover all of their expenses. Since the Serbian people were not particularly generous, the *Serbian News* wrote many times about the need of helping these institutions. One of the most beautiful articles was published in the middle of 1858 when Platon Simonović gave 160 books and 7 geographic maps to the Reading Club in Užice.

> Thus, brother Serbs, wherever you are [it wrote]
> emulate Mr. Simonović's gracious example, who
> is an official and citizen of a foreign country, but
> yet in his soul a real Serb, and from your God-
> given possessions help those institutions every-
> where which were established for the intellectual

development and education of the Serbs; try eagerly that we, the Serbs, do not lag far behind the other educated nations; emulate the Greeks, the people who have the same religion as we have, who established their state not so long ago, but who have greatly outstripped in science and education some states which have been developing for many centuries [thanks to] her citizens' generous contributions; and finally, brother Serbs, let us take care of everything that leads toward the happiness of our people so that one day we shall be able to say boldly that "what is ours is not bad."[67]

It is questionable whether the Belgrade Reading Club can be considered a cultural institution. The answer can be yes or no, depending on how one views it. If it is taken into consideration that it was the only place, not just in Belgrade but in all of Serbia, where in addition to the domestic press, the best-known European newspapers could be read; that for Serbian conditions, it had available a rather rich library; that it organized theatrical presentations; that eminent foreigners could be met in it; that it offered numerous popular lectures; that various discussions were held in it; that it prompted the establishment of the reading clubs throughout Serbia; and so on, it can definitely be considered one of the first cultural institutions in Serbia. If we, however, compare it with today's cultural institutions, which would not be fair, it looks more like a club for entertainment than a cultural institution.

The educational role of the Belgrade Reading Club in Serbian cultural development was considerable, especially since it gave numerous secondary school and Lyceum students the opportunity to get acquainted with cultural progress and political events in Europe and to spend some time in the company of the most educated people in Serbia of that time.

In addition to the Lyceum, secondary schools, and reading clubs, the Serbian ministries also had their own libraries. They were enriched by purchasing books, sometimes complete libraries. Thus, for example, in the beginning of 1846, the Serbian government bought the library of Mihailo German, former agent of Prince Miloš. It was bought from his widow in Bucharest for the sum of 200 imperial ducats and became a part of the Ministry of Education library.[68] Two years later, on January 15/27, 1848, the Serbian Literary Society suggested that the government buy a collection of Russian books of the well-known Slavic writer, linguist, and librarian from Prague, Pavel Josef Šafařík, which had 92 works in 265 volumes and could be bought for the sum of 643 silver florins. This time, however, the government was not generous. In its answer to the Serbian Literary Society of March 4/16 of the same year, it said "that those books cannot be bought until the government erects a building and provides the rest of what is needed for a public library, and furthermore all available places are already filled with books."[69] The richest among the libraries was the Ministry of Education library, which, for instance, in the beginning of 1845 had 1,421 titles in 2,283 volumes.[70] At the same time, the libraries of other ministries were insignificant. In 1853, the *Soviet* had 78 titles in 562 volumes, the Ministry of Foreign Affairs had 41 titles in 205 volumes, the Ministry of Internal Affairs had 29 titles in 47 volumes, and the Ministry of Finance had 40 titles in 207 volumes.[71]

With the development of education and the opening of the first cultural institutions in Serbia, the question of the opening of a public library began to be raised. The Serbian Literary Society was one of the strongest supporters of such a library. Its member and well-known cultural figure, Atanasije Nikolić, suggested the opening of a public library at the third regular meeting of the Society held in Belgrade on July 11/23, 1842. It was his opinion that all libraries of the ministries should be joined to that library, for which a new building would be erected, and that it should have a regular librarian.[72] This suggestion was not accepted, and Serbia had to wait for a full twelve years for her first public library. Only with the decree of February 13/25, 1853, was it decided "that all books, old manuscripts, old coins, and other important valuable rarities possessed by various state offices be given to the Ministry of Education and that a librarian with an annual salary of 300 talers be appointed to whom the management of a library and of a museum at the same Ministry will be entrusted."[73] This decree was executed and in the spring of the same year, the libraries of all ministries were joined to the Ministry of Education library, and so the first public library in Serbia, known under the name *"Narodna Biblioteka"* (the National Library) was born in Belgrade. On the recommendation of Platon Simonović, the chief inspector of all schools in Serbia, Filip Nikolić, Business School professor, was appointed its first librarian by Prince Alexander's decree of December 16/28, 1853. He kept this position until January 13/25, 1856, when he resigned to devote himself to the monastic life.[74] In the two years of his library work, Nikolić was able to gather books and other library materials from all ministries and put them in some order. He was succeeded by Djuro Daničić, the well-known Serbo-Croatian philologist, who successfully performed his librarian's function to the end of 1859, when he was appointed professor of the Belgrade Lyceum to replace the deceased Aleksa Vukomanović.[75]

Despite the fact that the National Library received insignificant financial help from the government, its book holding grew rather fast. For example, at the end of 1856, it had 3,360 titles and two years later, in 1858, that number was increased to 4,763 titles.[76] Most books were bought from a regular library fund and with donations, while some were gifts to the library. One must remember that at that time, Serbia did not yet have a large reading public. For example, in 1858, the National Library had only 74 readers whereas Belgrade had 18,860 inhabitants, and the population of all of Serbia numbered 1,078,281.[77] Such a small number of readers was the result of illiteracy and indifference. A larger number could not be expected because the creation of a wider reading public was still in the future. With the opening of the National Library, a significant step in that direction was made.

2.

Theaters also played an educational role in modern Serbia's cultural development. After the closing of Vujić's theater in Kragujevac in 1836, theatrical life in Serbia did not stop. During the entire Constitutionalist period theatrical shows were performed not only in cities such as Belgrade, Kragujevac, and Šabac, but in small towns as well. Thus, for example, in the beginning of 1850, the *Serbian News* reported the founding of a theater in Loznica.[78] However, these were amateur theaters, poorly equipped, and most often housed in abandoned warehouses or in sheds. True, there were some attempts to open a permanent professional theater in Belgrade, but they were not realized until October 30/November 11, 1869, when the National Theater was officially opened. The first significant attempt to found a professional theater in Serbia was made on December 4/16, 1841, with the opening of a theater, which was called *"Pozorište na Djumruku"* (the Theater at the Customs House) because it was housed in the old Customs warehouse at the Sava River. However, it was not long-lived. It discontinued its work on August 26/September 7, 1842, apparently because of the revolt led by Toma Vučić-Perišić and the change of dynasties.[79] It is important to point out that as early as December 20, 1841/ January 11, 1842, the management of this theater placed an advertisement for professional actors and actresses, original theatrical plays, and translations of foreign plays in the *Serbian News*. It was the first notice of this kind published in the Serbian press. The future actors and actresses were offered a monthly salary of between 12 and 25 talers, a very small sum; the playwrights were offered from 6 to 15 imperial ducats per play, while the translators of foreign plays were to receive from 4 to 8 imperial ducats per play.[80]

After the closing down of the Customs House Theater, various individuals and the press in Serbia as well as in Vojvodina pointed out the need for the founding of a professional theater in Belgrade. On June 29/July 11, 1851, one further step toward it was made by the creation of a committee for the building of a theater house. It consisted of distinguished cultural figures such as Atanasije Nikolić, Djordje Maletić, Matija Ban, Petar Radovanović, and others, and in the beginning of 1852, it began to collect donations.[81] This project, like almost all projects in the cultural-educational field, was supported by the *Serbian News*. In mid-July, 1851, it published an article entitled "The Theater is a School of Human Life."

> There is no larger city in enlightened Europe [it wrote] where a theater does not exist. Only our Belgrade is retrograde in this, Belgrade which is considered to be the hearth of the Serbian nationality, whose progress in culture and education has so beneficial an influence on the Serbian people. Indeed, it is already high time to put an end to this deficiency of ours.[82]

Donations flew into the fund for a new theater from all sides and from all strata of Serbian society. The government of Serbia, Prince Alexander, and Miša Anastasijević contributed most. The government gave the land on which the building was to be erected and 2,000 ducats, Prince Alexander 1,000 ducats, and Miša Anastasijević 500 ducats.[83] The new theater began to be built as early as September, 1852, but because of the swampy terrain, the building had to be discontinued in the middle of the following year, and it was not resumed, although some attempts to do so were made, during the remainder of the Constitutionalists' regime.

Even so, theatrical life in Belgrade was not stopped. In the middle of 1857, the Youth Amateur Theater, under the leadership of attorney Lazar Praporčetović, was founded. It gave its performances in the Prince's own brewery until October of 1858, when it had to discontinue its activity because St. Andrew's Assembly began its work in the brewery's hall.[84] The repertoire of this theater was very rich. In the short time of its activity, it showed more than fifty plays exclusively by Serbian authors, especially the Serbs from Vojvodina.[85]

During the Constitutionalist period, the theater was in a formative phase and its contribution to Serbian cultural development was very slight. However, its contribution to the awakening and inflaming of national consciousness, especially among the youth, was great. It seems that this was the chief aim of its founders because it presented most often the works of

Serbian writers which treated and sometimes glorified the past of the medieval Serbian state.

In the period of forming her national theater, Serbia had a small and theatrically uneducated public which most often consisted of officials, merchants, and the Lyceum students. Many of them not only did not know how to watch theatrical shows, but were also ignorant of how to behave during their performance. The first theater critics pointed out this deficiency in their occasional reviews published in the *Serbian News*. Thus, for example, Vladislav Stojadinović, chief of personnel in the Ministry of Education and one of the best theater critics of that time, wrote:

> As far as the viewers are concerned we have those who come only to enlarge the audience. They usually hardly watch the performance but they talk [among themselves] and with their conversations disturb the others, and so without following what is happening there [on the stage] they shout *"fora"* [probably "go ahead"] or *"pravo"* ["true"] at inappropriate times. They indeed would not do so if they wanted to **learn a lesson** and get **directions** for their future life from the theatrical performances.[86]

Occasional theatrical performances by amateur groups was not the only form of cultural activity in Serbia during the Constitutionalists' regime. The amateur vocal groups, which had been established in Kragujevac during Prince Miloš's reign continued with their activities, and in larger places several new ones were established. The First Choral Society of Belgrade was one of the best known and it had in its repertoire the songs of "all the more educated European nations."[87] In addition, the first concerts were held and even an opera was performed. The so-called *"Knjažeska Banda"* (the Prince's Band), the only orchestra in Serbia, gave all concerts. The first opera in Serbia, if it can be called so, was performed in Kragujevac on November 8/20, 1840. It was a melodrama by Atanasije Nikolić, for which Joseph Schlesinger, military bandmaster, wrote the music, and it was performed by amateurs who had never before sung on the stage.[88]

In writing about the cultural activities in Serbia during the Constitutionalists' regime, it should be mentioned that the first dancing school in Serbia was opened in the building *"Kod Jelena"* in Belgrade in the middle of 1844. Its first teacher was Friedrich Goldhamm, a professional dancer from Austria.[89]

Obviously, the cultural life of Serbia was on a very low level. Attempts to elevate it were more or less isolated and occurred mainly in larger places, especially in Belgrade and Kragujevac. The chief promoters of cultural life in Serbia until 1858 were not native Serbs, but the Serbs from Vojvodina, with Atanasije Nikolić and Djordje Maletić at the head. The principal reasons for the poor cultural life of Serbia during the Constitutionalist period should not be sought only in the government's cultural policy and the financial difficulties of the state, but also in the passivity of a Serbian society which did not yet feel the need for a rich and varied cultural life. It may be freely said that Serbia's cultural life would have been considerably poorer had it not been permeated with nationalism which became more and more marked. In spite of its poverty, cultural life under the Constitutionalists' regime should not be underestimated because it did influence, to some degree, the forming of the personalities of the young people, the people who would later be the first native promoters and bearers of cultural life in Serbia.

3.

Some Serbs from Vojvodina suggested the establishment of a learned society in Serbia in the first years of her autonomy, in a time when the educated man was a rarity in Serbia and when she had neither the need nor the cadre for such a society. Only several years after Serbia received her autonomy, a Serb from Budapest wrote:

> God grant that a learned society will also be established! If it emerges, let us, brothers, greet it, bow to it, embrace it, cherish it, love it, or at least let us not hate it and not reject it. So we shall come closer to the other nations and we shall be also happy, and our descendants blessed, famous, and beneficial.[90]

Similar suggestions were also made in Serbia. For example, in the beginning of 1833, Dimitrije Tirol, an educated Serb from Vojvodina who came to Serbia in 1830 and was the teacher to the children of the Prince's brother, Jevrem Obrenović, suggested the establishment of a learned society. He made a plan for its operation under the title "The Plan for the Constitution of a Learned Society" and sent it to the State Printing House to be published. This suggestion, however, was not accepted, and the plan was not printed. Prince Miloš informed the censor who recommended Tirol's plan that "he cannot allow the establishment of a learned society now because our fatherland has a small number of such persons who could with their intellectual abilities help it and carry out its activities."[91] Miloš was probably right, because to create a learned society in a state which did not yet have many educated people would have been an absurdity.

With the development of education and the opening of higher schools, the question of the establishment of a learned society in Serbia arose again in late 1840 and early 1841. This time, the initiators of its establishment were two professors of the Lyceum, Jovan S. Popović and Atanasije Nikolić. They wrote a plan for the establishment of such a society and enclosed it with their application to the Ministry of Education on September 28/October 10, 1841. They explained the importance of such a society for the further cultural development of Serbia and emphasized that its principal task would be to establish a uniform terminology for the Serbian language.[92] Prince Michael approved this plan on November 7/19, 1841.[93] But, because of the political tension and long preparations, the first learned society in Serbia or *Družstvo Srbske Slovesnosti* (The Serbian Literary Society), as it was officially called, began its operation only with the session held on May 31/June 12, 1842. On June 8/20 of the same year, a formal session was held, which was attended by Prince Michael as well as other guests.[94] On that occasion, the Prince, Stefan Radićević, Minister of Education and the first president of the Serbian Literary Society, and the secretary of the Society, Atanasije Nikolić, all made speeches. Nikolić pointed out that the Society would be faced with many difficulties, but that with mutual work and a great desire for the progress of the Serbian people, they would be overcome.

> What difficulties? There are no difficulties where [the people] work in harmony for the common good. A patriot scorns problems, does not consider obstacles, walks boldly because it concerns the glory of his people. So this society, too, regardless of its seeming weakness, must walk boldly toward the determined goal bearing constantly in mind the glory of the Serbs, if it would encourage unity and close relations among the Slavs.[95]

The principal tasks of the society were prescribed in its first Constitution of November 7/19, 1841. "The aim of the Serbian Literary Society is to spread education in the language of the Serbian people," the first article of the Constitution reads.[96] Additionally, the Constitution prescribed that the Minister of Education was always to be the president of the Society, while the vice-president and the secretary were to be chosen from among the Society's members. They were to be confirmed by the Prince. The first members of the Society were appointed by Prince Michael on the recommendation of the Minister of Education, and its future members were to be chosen by the Society itself. The fourth article of the Constitution emphasized that the regular members of the Serbian Literary Society could be "all those, regardless of their religion or tongue, who are able to give their contribution to this important aim."[97] In practice, however, the Society did not strictly observe this part of the Constitution because although most of its members were persons with a university education, only a few had distinguished themselves with their scholarly work. Well-known persons outside of the Serbian borders could also be corresponding or honorary members of the Society. For example, Dimitrije Milaković from Montenegro was elected its corresponding member on June 11/23, 1842, because of "his significant works in philology and in Serbian literature," and Petar Petrović Njegoš its honorary member "for his contribution to literature and to the education of the Serbian people."[98] It is interesting that although the Serbian Literary Society was a **Serbian** learned society in Serbia, none of its original members were native Serbs. Seven were Serbs from Vojvodina, and one, the poet, Sima Milutinović-Sarajlija, was a Serb from Bosnia.[99] By the end of the 1840s, when the first Serbs educated abroad began to return to Serbia, the Society began to enlarge its membership with native intellectuals.

The first period of the Serbian Literary Society was very short and, except that several sessions were held, nothing significant was done. It had to end its activity in August of 1842 because of the unrest in the country caused by the revolt led by Toma Vučić-Perišić, and the changing of dynasties.

When political life in Serbia had been stabilized and Prince Alexander had consolidated his power, the Ministry of Education raised the question of restoration of the Serbian Literary Society. The Ministry applied for the permission to the Prince on July 10/22, 1844. Its request was granted on July 18/30, and the first session of the former Society was scheduled for August 1/13 of the same year.[100] The Serbian Literary Society resumed its activity under its old Constitution of 1841. A new constitution was passed on May 8/20, 1847, but it did not essentially differ from the old one. The only significant differences were that the new constitution did not prescribe that the vice-president and the secretary of the Society had to be confirmed by the Prince, and it stipulated that the secretary was to receive from the state treasure and annual salary of 100 talers.[101]

The Serbian Literary Society began to work actively. It cooperated closely with the Belgrade Lyceum, most of whose professors were members. The exclusion of foreign words from the Serbian language and the introduction of a uniform terminology was one of the Society's first and basic tasks. The Society emphasized this need in its report of February 2/14, 1845, with the observation that the "Society indeed does not wish to tyrannize the language but only to help it as much as possible by increasing its terminology and excluding foreign words, especially barbarian, from it as much as is now possible."[102]

The terminology of some disciplines, such as law, philosophy, logic, and so on, caused difficulties for the Lyceum professors and confused their students. Since the Serbian language lacked the needed terminology, the professors who usually did not know Serbian well, translated freely, and sometimes the students could hear several different Serbian equivalents for the same term or foreign word, which made it more difficult for them to study and to completely understand new subjects. The student could hear that one professor, for the Latin word *praescriptio* (in law: an exception, objection, demurrer) used the Serbian word *zaostalost* (backwardness), whereas another professor, for the same word, used the Serbian word *prevremenost* (prematurity). Or, for instance, for criminal law, several names were used: *krivično pravo, kaznatelno pravo, kaznislovno pravo*, and *kriminalno pravo*.[103]

The various translations of the same terms and frequent usage of foreign words in the Serbian language caused confusion among ordinary people, too. Jovan S. Popović cited such an example.

> When XB, resident of this area [he writes] had to go to Kragujevac, he carried with him a letter from a higher office by which he had been informed that he was the curator of real estate I. When this letter was read to him in which this word [curator] was repeated several times, XB said discontentedly: Gentleman, I was always an honest man; why do you now in my old age disgrace me by calling me a *kurator* (curator)?[104]

Resident XB did not understand the Latin word "curator" (*curator,-oris*) and probably confused it with the Serbian slang *kurvar*, which means a lecher.

The work on the creation of a Serbian terminology was carried out in a rather simple fashion. Some members of the Society were assigned to make lists of terms for the disciplines which they knew. When such lists were completed, the regular members discussed them at their sessions. The accepted words or terms were to be published in *Dodatak k srbskim novinama* (The Supplement to the Serbian News) and in the literary paper *Podunavka* in order to acquaint the general public with them so that they could express their opinion. The members of the Society who were assigned to create a uniform Serbian terminology most often simply translated words from German and Latin dictionaries.[105] In addition, the Serbian Literary Society reviewed the manuscripts of the new textbooks until July, 1845, when the Educational Committee was established and took over that function.

After several years of existence, the Serbian Literary Society extended the scope of its activities. In addition to its work on the terminology and improvement of the Serbian language, to which it devoted most attention, the Society worked on history, geography, biology, statistics, etc. Its activities were extended still further after the middle of 1847 when the Society began to publish its journal entitled *Glasnik Družstva Srbske Slovesnosti* (The Herald of the Serbian Literary Society). It was published once a year, and the regular and corresponding members of the Society were its contributors. They wrote on various subjects such as statistics, economics, history, and the like. Additionally, the *Herald* published reports of the Society's activity and lists of newly published books in Serbian as well as in foreign languages.[106]

Like other institutions in Serbia, the Serbian Literary Society was also confronted with financial difficulties which limited its activity. State support was not large, but it was nevertheless very useful. It is hard to believe that the Society would have been able to publish its journal and other publications without it. In addition to its regular financial support, the state paid a large part of the expenses related to the Society's publications. For example, on July 17/29, 1847, Prince Alexander ordered that *The Herald of the Serbian Literary Society* was to be published gratis by the State Publishing House, and for other books which the Society published as its own, it was to pay only for the paper and other material needed for their printing.[107] State financial support for 1845 and for 1849 was only 100 talers,[108] for 1857 and 1858 five hundred and twenty talers,[109] and 340 talers for the other years of the Constitutionalists' regime.[110] It is not known, however, whether the Society had to pay its secretary from these sums because, as has been indicated, according to the Society's constitution of 1847, he was to be paid from the state budget. It can be assumed that his salary was included in these sums because it does not appear in the lists of the state annual budget.

The Serbian Literary Society was very useful in the educational development of Serbia during the Constitutionalist period because it was the only learned society in Serbia where the best educated native people, as well as foreigners, gathered. It initiated many projects which were to bring a cultural prosperity to the state, a prosperity which positively affected her entire life. Its *Herald* had a special importance because it published works by distinguished scholars, works which dealt with various subjects and were much more valuable and critical than any other works published in the other Serbian journals or newspapers. It can rightly be said that the Serbian Literary Society was indeed the first cultural institution in the true sense in Serbia and, as such, the forerunner of the Serbian Academy of Sciences and Arts which was established in 1886.

Serbian cultural institutions and societies were only in their formative stage in the Constitutionalist period. They were established more on the initiative of individuals than as a result of any policy planned by the government. The Constitutionalists, who invested a rather large sum of money in schools taking into consideration the state national income, were not so generous toward cultural institutions and societies. This was partially the result of finances, partially of skepticism, especially toward the societies, partially of ignorance of how much various institutions and societies could influence the cultural development of a state, and partially of lukewarm interest on the part of a large segment of the population. Regardless of how poor the cultural life of Serbia was, it was still a significant supplement to her planned educational development and positively affected the creation of her first native educated class, the awakening of the national consciousness, and the enlightenment of her society in general.

CONCLUSION

The Constitutionalist reign marked a new period in Serbian cultural history. The education of the young was not left to a spontaneous development, but educational policy was defined and the government took needed measures to put it into effect. For the first time, a uniform curriculum for all schools was introduced, the state determined annual budgets for education and cultural activities, a school fund was established, and so on. True, educational policy was occasionally altered and adapted to the country's needs, but basically it remained unchanged.

The education of promising young Serbs abroad was the brightest point in the Constitutionalists' educational policy. These young men were Serbia's hope and the pillar of her modernization. They were among the first who saw the prosperity of Serbia in closer relations with the advanced Western European states. After returning to Serbia, they tried by various means to realize their dreams regarding the prosperity of their homeland. They partially succeeded in this because, as the most educated people of their time, they began gradually to hold the key positions in the state which made it possible for them to influence the making of its foreign and internal policies.

To entrust the education of its youth to foreigners, who did not know Serbian well, who were not sufficiently acquainted with the state's needs, who did not know the students' abilities or the mentality of the people, was not easy for a state trying to establish its identity and in which the awakening of a national consciousness was more and more marked. But Serbia did not have any choice because she did not have her own educated people to whom she could entrust that delicate and responsible function. She was fortunate that so many of her first educators and cultural figures were mainly Serbs from Vojvodina who knew the Serbian language and were able, immediately after their arrival in Serbia, to take on their functions in the educational field and in cultural life. Without their contributions, the process of Serbia's educational and cultural development would have been considerably slower and the quality of education probably poorer.

The educational and cultural development of Serbia in the Constitutionalists' time was concentrated in Belgrade, Kragujevac, and several towns. In a large part of Serbia, little was done. True, elementary schools were opened, but this was more the result of initiative by individuals and communes and their financing than the result of the state's educational policy. The government was mainly interested in secondary and higher schools because they prepared the cadres which the state needed most.

During the Constitutionalists' regime, the first group of native education people emerged in Serbia. Although they numbered only several hundreds, including the gymnasium graduates, what was relatively a small number for the Serbian society which at that time had over a million people, their influence was felt in all fields. They gradually replaced foreigners in leading positions, and were the sharpest critics of the regime, propagators of new ideas, and initiators of numerous reforms. Only thanks to their diligent and devoted work did Serbia begin to free herself from her centuries-old backwardness and begin to move along the way of progress.

The Constitutionalist period was, undoubtedly, a vital period in the educational and cultural development of modern Serbia. In this time solid foundations were laid, especially in education, foundations on which the future development and modernization of the Serbian state were to rest.

NOTES

CHAPTER I: THE FIRST STEPS IN EDUCATION

1. Mateja Nenadović, *Memoari* (Beograd, 1966), p. 50. During the Austro-Turkish War (1788-1791), the volunteers from Serbia played a noticeable role in the Austrian army. They fought in the volunteer detachments, the so-called *Freicorps*, under the leadership of the Serb major Mihailo Mihaljević who was a professional officer of the Austrian army. Among numerous Serbian volunteers was also Aleksa Nenadović, a distinguished local leader in Serbia, who indignantly left the Austrian army after the Peace of Svishtov in 1791, when all of Serbia came again under Turkish rule.

2. Vuk Stefanović Karadžić, *Srpski rječnik istumačen njemačkijem i latinskijem riječima* (Beograd, 1898), pp. 870-871.

3. *Ibid.*, p. 871.

4. Tihomir R. Djordjević, *Srbija pre sto godina* (Beograd, 1946), p. 89.

5. *Ibid.*, p. 87.

6. V.S. Karadžić, *op. cit.*, p. 871.

7. *Nahija* - an administrative unit in the Turkish Empire.

8. Milan Dj. Milićević , "Škole u Srbiji," *Glasnik* SUD, KNJ.VII, No. 24 (Beograd, 1868), pp. 3-4.

9. *Ibid.*, p. 4.

10. T.R. Djordjević, *op. cit.*, p. 89.

11. V.S. Karadžić, *Izabrana dela* (Beograd, 1964), p. 349.

12. T.R. Djordjević, *op. cit.*, pp. 90-91.

13. Barthelemy S. Cunibert, *Srpski ustanak i prva vladavina Miloša Obrenovića 1805-1850*, Translated from French by M.R. Vesnić (Beograd, 1901), p. 28.

14. *Zadruga* - the communal joint-family which existed in Serbia for several centuries. The number of its members varied. It was not rare that the *zadruga* had one hundred members and sometimes even more.

15. M.Dj. Milićević, *Pomenik znamenitih ljudi u srpskog naroda* (Beograd, 1959), p. 384.

16. V.S. Karadžić, *Srpski rječnik, op. cit.*, p. 871.

17. Cited by M.Dj. Milićević, "Škole u Srbiji," *op. cit.*, pp. 4-5.

18. *Ibid.*, p. 5.

19. Srećko Ćunković, *Školstvo i prosveta u Srbiji u XIX veku* (Beograd, 1970), p. 6.

20. Cited by Ćunković, *op. cit.*, p. 7.

21. *Ibid.*

22. The real name of Ivan Jugović was Jovan Savić. He changed his name in 1805 when he came to Serbia. The reason for that is not known.

23. Andrija B. Stojković, "Misaoni razvitak Vuka Karadžića u odnosu prema Dositejevom," *Filozofija*, No. 4 (Beograd, 1965), p. 502.

24. T.R. Djordjević, *op. cit.*, p. 11.

25. Cited by Radmila Petrović-Popović and Vukoman Šalipurović, *Srpske škole i prosveta u zapadnim krajevima stare Srbije u XIX veku* (Beograd, 1970), p. 30.

26. V.S. Karadžić, *Izabrana dela, op. cit.*, p. 352; M.Dj. Milićević, *Pomenik, op. cit.*, p. 131.

27. Cited by Ćunković, *op. cit.*, p. 11.

28. *Ibid.*, p. 12.

29. Petar Despotović, *Istoriska pedagogika* (Beograd, 1902), p. 389.

30. *Ibid.*

31. V.S. Karadžić, *Izabrana dela, op. cit.*, p. 352.

32. *Ibid.*, p. 353.

33. S. Ćunković, *op. cit.*, p. 12.

34. Andra Gavrilović, *Beogradska Velika škola, 1808-1813* (Beograd, 1902), p. 106.

35. Lazar B. Arsenijević, *Istorija srpskog ustanka*, Vol. 1 (Beograd, 1898), pp. 406-407.

Since Serbia did not have her own currency until 1873, numerous foreign currencies, especially the Austrian Taler (in Serbian *talir*), Groschen (in Serbian *groš*), Zwanzig (in Serbian *cvancig*), were in circulation.

36. According to Dušan Petrović, it worked until the fall of 1813. See Dušan K. Petrović, "Spomenica Beogradske bogoslovije, 1836-1936." (Manuscript, Bogoslovija "Sv. Savo," Beograd), p. 9.

37. See L.B. Arsenijević, *op. cit.*, p. 407 and D.K. Petrović, *op. cit.*, pp. 8-9.

38. D.K. Petrović, *op. cit.*, p. 9.

39. Miloš B. Janković, *Pedagoške rasprave i članci* (Beograd, 1967), p. 21.

40. Vladimir Stojančević, *Miloš Obrenović i njegovo doba* (Beograd, 1966), pp. 299-300. See M.B. Janković, *op. cit.*, p. 28.

41. Milovan Spasić, "Neki podaci o osnovnim školama u Srbiji od 1845. do 1861. god.," *Glasnik* SUD, No. 73 (Beograd, 1892), p. 190.

42. M.B. Janković, *op. cit.*, p. 27.

43. *Ibid.*, p. 28.

44. T.R. Djordjević, "Školske prilike u Srbiji za vreme prve vlade kneza Miloša Obrenovića, 1815-1839," *Prosvetni glasnik*, No. 5 (Beograd, 1920), p. 274.

45. *Hatt-i Şerif*: the name for the sultan's solemn decree which had to be implemented immediately.

46. B.S. Cunibert, *op. cit.*, pp. 259-260.

47. V.S. Karadžić, *Izabrana dela, op. cit.*, pp. 261-262; T.R. Djordjević, "Školske prilike u Srbiji," *op. cit.*, p. 332.

48. V.S. Karadžić, *Izabrana dela, op. cit.*, pp. 264-265. It is interesting to note that after the revolt of Miloje Djak (Miloje Popović) of 1825 which was directed against Prince Miloš, it was said in Miloš's court *"that the schools were not necessary because the educated people organize revolts against the government."* The main reasons for such an opinion was because Miloje Popović "knew slightly how to read and write." Some of them, for example, Milosav Lapovac, went so far as to publicly suggest *"that everybody who knows how to read and write should be shot."* (*Ibid.*, p. 264).

49. V. Stojančević, *op. cit.*, pp. 330-301.

50. Prvoš Slankamenac, "Dokumenti o prvim školskim zakonima u Srbiji u vremenu od 1833.do. 1843.godine," *Mešovita gradja*, SAN, Gradja, Knj. XII, Istoriski institut, knj. 9 (Beograd, 1956), p. 91.

51. *Ibid.*

52. AS, KK XXXVIII - 39, pp. 2-3.

53. *Ibid.*, p. 3.

54. *Ibid.*

55. AS, KK XXXVIII - 54.

56. "Nastavlenije direktoru sviju škola u Knjažestvu Srbiji," *ibid.* In Serbia, as in many European countries, secondary school teachers have been called professors.

57. AS, KK XXXVIII - 39, pp. 30-39.

58. P. Slankamenac, *op. cit.*, p. 111.

59. AS, KK XXXVIII - 140.

60. AS, KK XXXVIII - 39, pp. 5-9.

61. AS, KK XXXVIII - 140.

62. "Naznačenije učebni predmeta koji se u školama normalnim za prvo i drugo tečanije školsko predavati imaju"; "Nastavlenije učiteljima praviteljsteveni i obšestveni škola u Knjažestvu Srbiji," Milenko M. Vukićević, "Osnovne škole u Srbiji," *Prosvetni glasnik*, No. 8 (Beograd, 1899), p. 452.

63. M.Dj. Milićević, "Škole u Srbiji," *op cit.*, pp. 8-10.

64. *Ibid.*

65. *Ibid.*, p. 10.

66. *Ibid.*

67. *Glasnik* SUD, knj. VIII, No. 24 (Beograd, 1868), p. 126.

68. S. Ćunković, *op. cit.*, p. 27.

69. B.S. Cunibert, *op. cit.*, pp. 690-700.

70. M. Spasić, *op. cit.*, p. 194.

71. T.R. Djordjević, "Školske prilike u Srbiji," *op. cit.*, p. 274.

72. V. Stojančević, *op. cit.*, p. 300.

73. M. Spasić, *op. cit.*, p. 193; AS, KK XXXVIII -54.

74. M. Spasić, "Štatistični podaci školski zavedenija u Knjažestvu Srbskom," *Glasnik* DSS, No. 9 (Beograd, 1857), p. 166. See Bogoljub Jovanović, "Škole u Srbiji 1836.godine," *Prosvetni glasnik*, No. 21 (Beograd, 1882), p. 806. In this article, Jovanović points out that in that number (72 schools) some grades (classes) were counted as schools. According to him in the school year 1835-36, Serbia had only 62 schools with 72 teachers. It should be noted that the statistical data regarding the teachers' number are not reliable. For instance, according to Petar Radovanić's report of July 8/20, 1836, Serbia did not have 72 but 68 teachers. See As, KK XXXVIII - 140.

75. B. Jovanović, "Stanje javne nastave u Kneževini Srbiji za 1875-76.školsku godinu," *Prosvetni glasnik*, Nos. 12-13 (Beograd, 1881), p. 472.

The statistical data which Vladimir Korać cites in his book *Školovanje u Srbiji i njegovi rezultati* (Beograd, 1886), p. 11, are considerably different. According to him, in 1836 Serbia had 744,686 inhabitants and 62 schools with 2,511 pupils. There was one school for every 12,000 inhabitants, one every 607 square kilometers, and one pupil for every 297 inhabitants. According to the statistical data which were published by the Bureau of Statistics of the Socialist Republic of Serbia in 1834, Serbia had 668,492 inhabitants. See *Stanovništvo Narodne Republike Srbije od 1834-1853*, knj. 1, Serija B. Sveska 1 (Beograd, 1953), p. 11.

76. V. Stojančević, *op. cit.*, p. 301; S. Ćunković, *op. cit.*, p. 27.

77. AS, KK XXXVIII - 39, p. 4.

78. *Ibid.*, pp. 5-6.

79. M. Spasić, "Štatistični podaci školski zavedenija," *op. cit.*, p. 167.

80. *Ibid.*

81. *Ibid.*

82. T.R. Djordjević, "Školske prilike u Srbiji," *op. cit.*, p. 272; B. Jovanović, "Škole u Srbiji 1836.godine," *op. cit.*, p. 847.

83. *Ibid.*, p. 273.

84. *Ibid.*, p. 274.

85. AS, KK XXXVIII - 140.

86. T.R. Djordjević, "Školske prilike u Srbiji," *op. cit.*, p. 275.

87. Otto D. Pirch, *Putovanje po Srbiji u godini 1829.* Translated from German by Dragiša Mijušović (Beograd, 1900), p. 130.

88. *Ibid.*, pp. 275-276.

89. Mihailo S. Petrović, *Beograd pre sto godina* (Beograd, 1930), p. 196.

90. *Ibid.*, p. 198.

91. *Ibid.*

92. Radoslav Medenica, *Počeci nemačke nastave u Srbiji i reforme Jovana St. Popovića* (Beograd, 1936), p. 7.

93. Stojan Novaković, *Srpska bibliografija za noviju književnost, 1741-1867* (Beograd, 1869), p. 210.

94. M.M. Vukićević, *op. cit.*, p. 454.

95. Živojin S. Djordjević, "Naše čitanke u 18. i 19. veku," *Nastava i vaspitanje*, No. 5 (Beograd, 1952), p. 382.

96. *Ibid.*

97. S. Novaković, *op. cit.*, p. 205.

98. M.M. Vukićević, *op. cit.*, p. 454.

99. AS, KK XXXVIII - 66.

100. M. Spasić, "Štatistični podaci školski zavedenija," *op. cit.*, p. 194.

101. *Ibid.*

102. *Stanovništvo Narodne Republike Srbije of 1834 do 1953, op. cit.*, p. 11.

103. Cited by Anastasija Papahristu, "Grčke škole u Beogradu u XIX vek," *Nastava i vaspitanje*, No. 3 (Beograd, 1970), p. 356.

104. T.R. Djordjević, *Srbija pre sto godina, op. cit.*, p. 109.

105. Dušan Sindik, "O jevrejakim školama u Beogradu u XIX veku," *Jevrejski almanah* (Beograd, 1961/62), p. 99.

106. T.R. Djordjević, *Srbija pre sto godina, op. cit.*, pp. 110-112.

107. Stevan Ignijić, *Užička nahija* (Beograd, 1961), p. 120; M. Petrović, *op. cit.*, p. 195.

108. M.M.B., "Prve godine života naše gimnazija," *Prosvetni glasnik*, No. 6 (Beograd, 1898), p. 302.

109. V.S. Karadžić, *Izabrana dela, op. cit.*, p. 263.

110. *Ibid.*

111. S. Ćunković, *op. cit.*, p. 49.

112. AS, KK XXXVIII - 95.

113. M.M.B., "Prve godine života naše gimnazije," *op. cit.*, p. 302.

114. S. Ćunković, *op. cit.*, p. 49.

115. Ž.S. Djordjević, *Škole i prosveta u Srbiji, 1700-1859* (Beograd, 1950), p. 59.

116. B. Jovanović, *op. cit.*, p. 805.

117. *Ibid.*

118. *Ibid.*, p. 804.

119. M. Spasić, "Štatistični podaci školski zavedenija," *op. cit.*, p. 167.

120. Ž.S. Djordjević, *Škole i prosveta u Srbiji, op. cit.*, p. 59.

121. *Ibid.*

122. *Ibid.*, p. 22; Živan Živanović, *Politička istorija Srbije u drugoj polovini XIX veka*, Vol. 1 (Beograd, 1923), p. 7.

123. AS, KK XXXVIII - 66.

124. *Ibid.*

125. AS, KK XXXVIII - 54.

126. V.S. Karadžić, *Izabrana dela, op. cit.*, pp. 263-64.

127. D.K. Petrović, *op. cit.*, p. 10.

128. *Ibid.*, pp. 13-14.

129. *Ibid.*, p. 16.

130. *Ibid.*

131. Cited by Djoko Slijepčević, *Istorija srpske pravoslavne crkve*, Vol. 2 (Minhen, 1966), p. 354.

132. *Ibid.*, p. 377.

133. Radoslav P. Marković, "Stogodišnjica bogoslovije Sv. Save," *Glasnik* JPD, knj. XVII (Beograd, 1936), pp. 6-7.

134. D.K. Petrović, *op. cit.*, p. 30; M. Spasić, "Štatistični podaci školski zavedenija," *op. cit.*, p. 167; T.R. Djordjević, "Školske prilike u Srbiji," *op. cit.*, p. 332. Marković writes that in the first year, the Seminary had forty-six students. See R.P. Marković, "Stogodišnjica bogoslovije Sv. Save," *op. cit.*, p. 9. According to M. Milićević, that number was forty-three; see M.Dj. Milićević, "Škole u Srbiji," *op cit.*, p. 84.

135. R.P. Marković, "Stogodišnjica bogoslovije Sv. Save," *op. cit.*, p. 9.

136. *Ibid.*

137. *Ibid.*, p. 9. By a decree of February 11/23, 1835, Prince Miloš decided to give annually 1,000 talers from the state budget for the help of the poor students. In addition to that, the poor students received the textbooks free. (Milen Nikolić, *Spomenica Kragujevačke gimnazije, 1833-1933* (Kragujevac, 1934), p. 97.

138. *Ibid.*, p. 7.

139. M.Dj. Milićević, "Škole u Srbiji," *op cit.*, p. 380.

140. *Ibid.*, p. 84.

141. Mita Petrović, *Finansije i ustanove obnovljene Srbije do 1842*, Vol. 1 (Beograd, 1897), p. 759.

142. D.K. Petrović, *op. cit.*, (appendix); M.Dj. Milićević, "Škole u Srbiji," *op cit.*, pp. 84-85.

143. Radoslav Marković, *Vojska i naoružanje Srbije kneza Miloša* (Beograd, 1957), p. 274.

144. *Spomenica sedamdesetpetgodišnjice Vojne akademije, 1850-1925* (Beograd, 1925), p. 3. Tihomir R. Djordjević writes that in 1833 Serbia sent thirty young men to Russia "to study military skill." (T.R. Djordjević, *Srbija pre sto godina, op. cit.*, p. 108). It seems that the number of twelve students which is cited in *Spomenica* is more acceptable than the number which Djordjević cited because it was the beginning of the autonomous Serbian state and she, among many difficulties, faced grave financial problems.

145. R. Marković, *Vojska i naoružanje Srbije kneza Miloša , op. cit.*, p. 287. In *Spomenica, op. cit.*, p. 3, was cited the number of thirty-two students, whereas according to Petar Radovanović's letter to Prince Miloš of November 21/December 2, 1837, that number had to be thirty (AS, KK XXXVIII -203). We took Marković's number because we believe that it is more reliable.

146. *Ibid.*

147. *Ibid.*

148. Ž.S. Djordjević, *Škole i prosveta u Srbiji, op. cit.*, p. 23.

149. M.Dj. Milićević, "Škole u Srbiji," *op cit.*, p. 99.

150. *Ibid.*, pp. 294-296.

151. *Ibid.*, p. 296; *Spomenica, op. cit.*, p. 3.

152. AS, KK XXXVIII - 95.

153. *Ibid.*

154. *Sto godina Filozofskog fakulteta* (Beograd, 1963), p. 10.

155. *Novine Srbske*, No. 46 (November 19, 1838).

156. *Ibid.*; AS, KK XXXVIII -828.

157. Kosta Branković, "Razvitak Velike škole," *Glasnik* SUD, knj. 18 (Beograd, 1865), p. 20.

158. Natalija and Platon Dimić, "Nastav u Beogradskom liceju u toku prve dve godine njegovog postojanja," *Savremena škola*, Nos. 1-2 (Beograd, 1959), p. 58.

159. *Ibid.*, p. 59.

160. P. Slankamenac, "Osnivanje i karakter Beogradskog liceja," *Savremena škola*, Nos. 3-4 (Beograd, 1952), p. 19.

161. Ilija A. Pržić, "Osnivanje Pravnog fakulteta u Srbiji," *Arhiv za pravne i društvene nauke*, knj. XLI, Nos. 1-2 (Beograd, 1940), p. 3.

162. Ž.S. Djordjević, *Škole u Srbiji, op. cit.*, p. 63.

163. *Ibid.*

164. Pera Polovina, *Udžbenici francuskog jezika kod Srba do 1914.godine* (Beograd, 1964), p. 28.

165. S. Novaković, *Srpska bibliografija, op. cit.*, p. 216.

166. T.R. Djordjević, "Prvo uputstvo za državne pitomce na strani," *Misao*, Nos. 229-232 (Beograd, 1929), p. 428.

167. Nenad Simić, "Obaveze srpskih državnih pitomaca u inostranstvu sredinom prošlog stoleća," *Zbornik za historiju školstva i prosvete*, No. 6 (Zagreb, 1971), p. 147.

168. N. Simić, *Knez Miloš i srpska umetnost* (Beograd, 1960), p. 13.

169. Jovan Milićević, "Prva grupa srbijanskih studenata, državnih pitomaca školovanih u inostranstvu (1839-1842)," *Istorijski časopis*, knj. IX-X (Beograd, 1960), p. 364.

170. Mihailo Bjelica, "Počeci političke štampe u Srbiji, 1834-1872" (unpublished Ph.D. dissertation, University of Belgrade, 1972), p. 12.

171. Nikola Pijuković, "Sto dvadeset i pet godina od osnivanja državne štamparije u Beogradu," *Godišnjak Muzeja grada Beograda*, knj. IV (Beograd, 1957), p. 383.

172. *Ibid.*, p. 384.

173. *Ibid.*, p. 389.

174. *Ibid.*, pp. 387-389.

175. M. Bjelica, *op. cit.*, p. 13.

176. *Ibid.*

177. *Ibid.*, p. 12.

178. According to Ljubomir Durković-Jakšić, from 1831 to 1835, twenty-nine Serbian books were published in Belgrade and seventeen in Kragujevac, and from 1836 to 1840, another sixty-six were published. (Ljubomir Durković-Jakšić, *Istorija srpskih biblioteka, 1801-1850*, Beograd, 1963, p. 14).

179. V. Stojančević, *op. cit.*, p. 303.

180. *Ibid.*, p. 304; T.R. Djordjević, *Srbija pre sto godina, op. cit.*, p. 40.

181. AS, MPs, VI - 594/1852. In the second quarter of the nineteenth century, V.S. Karadžić began his action for the reformation of the Serbian literary language. He established the fact that the Serbian language contains 30 distinct sounds, for 6 of which the Old Slavonic alphabet had no special letters. He introduced new letters for those special sounds and threw out of the Old Slavonic alphabet 18 letters for which the Serbian language had no use. This reform was opposed by the Church and many conservative authors; under their influence, the Serbian government prohibited printing in this new orthography. The prohibition was removed in 1859.

182. Andrija Radenić, "Prve novine u Srbiji," *Počeci štampe jugoslovenskih naroda* (Beograd, 1969), p. 59.

183. *Ibid.*, p. 63.

184. *Ibid.*; M. Bjelica, *op. cit.*, p. 15.

185. M. Bjelica, *op. cit.*, p. 18.

186. *Ibid.*, p. 17.

187. Gavrilo Kovijanić, "Srpske novine," *Bibliotekar*, No. 1 (Beograd, 1966), p. 154.

188. *Ibid.*

189. Cited by A. Radenić, *op. cit.*, p. 77.

190. N. Pijuković, *op. cit.*, p. 387.

191. M. Bjelica, *op. cit.*, p. 20.

192. M. Petrović, *op. cit.*, p. 201.

193. Lj. Durković-Jakšić, *op. cit.*, p. 98.

194. *Ibid.*

195. G. Kovijanić, "Narodna biblioteka nije osnovana u Vozarovićevoj radnji 1832.godine," *Bibliotekar*, No. 1 (Beograd, 1971), p. 15.

196. M.M. Nikolić, "Prvi prosvetni i kulturni centar obnovljene Srbije," *Šumadija u prošlosti i sadašnjosti* (Subotica, 1932), p. 171.

197. O.D. Pirch, *op. cit.*, p. 152.

198. T.R. Djordjević, *Srbija pre sto godina, op. cit.*, p. 75.

199. M.M. Nikolić, "Prvi prosvetni i kulturni centar obnovljene Srbije," *op. cit.*, p. 174.

200. G. Kovijanić, *Gradja Arhiva Srbije o Narodnom pozorištu u Beogradu, 1835-1914* (Beograd, 1971), p. 16.

CHAPTER II: ELEMENTARY AND SECONDARY SCHOOLS

1. Cited by Miloš V. Radovanović, *Zloupotreba službenog položaja ili ovlašćenja* (Beograd, 1958), p. 57.

2. Slobodan Javanović, *Ustavobranitelji i njihova vlada, 1838-1858* (Beograd, 1933), p. 75.

3. "Ustrojenije javnog učilišnog nastavlenija," *Sbornik zakona i uredaba*, Vol. 2 (Beograd, 1845), p. 315.

4. "Uredaba o prigoru glavnog fonda školskog," *Ibid.*, p. 17.

5. *Ibid.*, pp. 17-29; *Novine Srbske* (1841-1858).

6. AS, MPs, I - 4/1842.

7. *Srbske Novine*, No. 21 (February 19, 1852).

8. Milan Dj. Milićević, *Pogled na narodno školovanje u Srbiji* (Beograd, 1873), p. 13.

9. Živojin S. Djordjević, *Istorija vaspitanja u Srba* (Beograd, 1958), p. 37.

10. Milovan Spasić, "Neki podaci o osnovnim školama u Srbiji od 1845.do 1861.god.," *Glasnik* SUD, knj. 73 (Beograd, 1892), p. 214.

11. According to the law of August 31/September 12, 1855, the official rate of a taler in Serbia was 12 *groše s*, and of a *cvancig* 2 *groše s*. (*Srbski dnevnik*, No. 72, Novi Sad, September 11, 1855).

12. *Sbornik zakona i uredaba*, Vol. 8 (Beograd, 1856), pp. 98-99.

13. *Ibid.*, p. 99.

14. "Ustrojenije glavnog fonda školskog," *Sbornik zakona i uredaba*, Vol. 9 (Beograd, 1857), p. 58.

15. *Ibid.*, p. 59.

16. *Ibid.*, p. 64; *Sbornik zakona i uredaba*, Vol. 5 (Beograd, 1853), p. 93.

17. *Sbornik zakona i uredaba*, Vol. 10 (Beograd, 1857), pp. 61-62.

18. Alimpije Vasiljević, "Moje uspomene," Arhiv Srbije. Pokloni i otkupi, 102/136, pp. 2-3.

19. *Sbornik zakona i uredaba*, Vol. 2 (Beograd, 1845), pp. 317-318.

20. *Ibid.*, Vol. 10 (Beograd, 1857), pp. 62-64.

21. As, MPs, I - 41/1842.

22. *Novine Čitališta Beogradskog*, No. 12 (March 12, 1848), pp. 104-105.

23. *Ibid.*, No. 32 (August 8, 1847).

24. AS, MPs, III - 128/1858. Since the official reports and other sources about the number of elementary schools and their pupils differ, we presented the most acceptable data.

25. M. Dj. Milićević, "Škole u Srbiji," *Glasnik* SUD, knj. VII, No. 24 (Beograd, 1868), p. 12.

26. M. Spasić, *op. cit.*, p. 197.

27. *Ibid.*

28. "Ustrojenije javnag učilišnog nastavlenija," *Sbornik zakona i uredaba*, Vol. 2 (Beograd, 1845), pp. 315-345.

29. *Ibid.*, p. 317.

30. *Ibid.*, pp. 318 and 322.

31. *Ibid.*, pp. 319-322; AS, MPs, V - 74/1844, pp. 3-8.

32. "Nastavlenije za učitelje osnovni učilišta," AS, MPs, V - 74/1844.

33. *Ibid.*, pp. 19-20.

34. Ž. S. Djordjević, *Škole i prosveta u Srbiji, 1700-1850* (Beograd, 1950), p. 70; *Srbske Novine*, No. 30 (April 14, 1845).

35. "Raspoloženje predmeta koji se u osnovnim učilištima predaju po razredima i polugodijama," Srećko Ćunković, *Školstvo i prosveta u Srbiji u XIX veku* (Beograd, 1980), p. 41.

36. AS, MPs, I - 63/1847, p. 6. The Educational Committee was established by Prince Alexander's decree of June 21/July 3, 1845, with the aim of helping the Ministry of Education. We shall say more about it in the next chapter.

37. AS, MPs, I -63/1847, p. 11.

38. *Srbske Novine*, No. 100 (September 2, 1850).

39. *Sbornik zakona i uredaba*, Vol. 9 (Beograd, 1857), p. 58.

40. M. Spasić, *op. cit.*, p. 217.

41. *Ibid.*, p. 222.

42. AS, MPs, V - 74/1844.

43. AS, MPs, VI - 4/1846.

44. *Ibid.*

45. AS, MPs, VI - 41/1844.

46. *Ibid.*

47. "Ustrojenije osnovni škola u knjažestvu Srbiji," *Sbornik zakona i uredaba*, Vol. 10 (Beograd, 1957), pp. 64-65.

48. *Srbski dnevnik*, No. 53 (Novi Sad, July 10, 1858),.

49. *Ibid.*

50. *Novine Čitališta Beogradskog*, No. 4 (January 24, 1847). For example, in 1843, one *oka* (1,280 grams) of bread cost 0,20 *grošes* (1 taler was equal to 10 *grošes*), one *oka* of beef 1,10, one *oka* of lard 4, one *oka* of beans 0,30, and one *oka* of potatoes 0,12 *grošes*. The cost of living rose rapidly so that in 1853 one *oka* of bread cost as much as 1,09 *grošes*, and one *oka* of beef 2,17 *grošes*. (Nikola Vučo, *Raspadanje esnafa u Srbiji*, Vol. 2 (Beograd, 1958), p. 74).

51. Miloš B. Janković, *Pedagoške raprave i članci* (Beograd, 1967), p. 38.

52. *Novine Čitališta Beogradskog*, No. 37 (September 12, 1847).

53. *Sbornik zakona i uredaba*, Vol. 2 (Beograd, 1845), p. 322.
54. *Novine Čitališta Beogradskog*, No. 3 (January 17, 1847).
55. *Srbske Novine*, No. 179 (September 6, 1856).
56. *Ibid.*
57. AS, MPs, I - 45/1844.
58. *Ibid.*
59. M. Spasić, *op. cit.*, p. 196.
60. AS, MPs, IV - 97/1844.
61. AS, MPs, V - 74/1844, p. 24.
62. *Ibid.*
63. AS, MPs, II - 315/1851.
64. AS, MPs, II - 266/1850.
65. Svetozar Marković, "Kako su nas vaspitali," in the Najdan Pašic, ed., *Svetozar Marković - sabrani spisi* (Beograd, 1960), p. 31.
66. *Sbornik zakona i uredaba*, Vol. 10 (Beograd, 1857), p. 71.
67. Ž.S. Djordjević, *op. cit.*, p. 67.
68. *Ibid.*, p. 66.
69. *Ibid.*, p. 67.
70. AS, MPs, I -41/1842.
71. S. Marković, *op. cit.*, p. 33.
72. *Srbske Novine*, No. 133 (November 20, 1852).
73. Vladimir Grujić, *Školsko reformatorski rad J. St. Popovića u Srbiji, 1840-1848* (Beograd, 1956), p. 41.
74. Olga Obradović, "Osnivanje prvih ženskih škola u Beogradu," *Izveštaj V ženske gimnazije u Beogradu za šk. 1939-49.godinu* (Beograd, 1940), p. 41.
75. V. Grujić, *op. cit.*, p. 40.
76. AS, MPs, IV - 68/1844.
77. AS, MPs, I - 26/1845.
78. *Ibid.*
79. *Podunavka*, No. 22 (June 2, 1845).
80. V. Grujić, *op. cit.*, p. 41.
81. "Ustrojenije devojački učilišta," *Srbske Novine*, Nos. 61-62 (August 5 and 8, 1847).
82. O. Obradović, *op. cit.*, p. 43.
83. *Srbske Novine*, No. 137 (December, 1850).
84. M. Spasić, "Državopisni podatci školski zavedenija u Knjaž. Srbskom od 1856/7 do 1860/1 god. školsk.," *Glasnik*, DDS, knj. 14 (Beograd, 1862), pp. 283 and 288.
85. M. Spasić, "Neki podaci o osnovnim školama," *op. cit.*, p. 221.
86. M. Spasić, "Državopisni podatci," *op. cit.*, p. 288.
87. AS, MPs, II - 269/1853.
88. *Srbske Novine*, No. 57 (May 14, 1853).
89. *Ibid.*, No. 83 (July 22, 1858).
90. AS, MPs, V - 47/1858.
91. *Ibid.*
92. "Biografija Nikolić Atanasija, pisana 1874-74," Arhiv SAN, No. 7380/32.
93. AS, MPs, IV -16/1845.
94. *Ibid.*
95. V. Grujić, *op. cit.*, p. 144.
96. AS, MPs, IV -16/1845.
97. V. Grujić, *op. cit.*, p. 143.

98. "Biografija Nikolić Atanasija, pisana 1874-75," *op. cit.*

99. AS, MPs, V - 43/1846.

100. AS, MPs, IV - 57/1846.

101. AS, MPs, V- 43/1846.

102. *Ibid.*

103. *Ibid.*

104. *Ibid.*

105. AS, MPs, VI - 561/1843.

106. AS, MPs, I -45/1844.

107. AS, MPs, VII - 611/1847.

108. Anastasija Papahristu, "Grčke škole u Beogradu u XIX veku," *Nastava i vaspitanje*, No. 3 (Beograd, 1970), p. 358.

109. *Šumadinka*, No. 38 (March 30, 1857).

110. *Ibid.*

111. AS, MPs, VII - 493/1847.

112. AS, MPs, II - 193/1852.

113. *Podunavka*, No. 4 (January, 24, 1847), p. 14.

114. *Spomenica Šabačke realne gimnazije, 1836-1936* (Šabac, 1938), p. 52.

115. AS, MPs, II - 29/1855. *Veliki beogradski kalendar* for the years 1852 and 1853 published different statistical data (see pp. 163 and 224). According to it, in 1852 the Šabac lower gymnasium had 68 students and in 1853, 97 students. We cited data from Simonović's report because it was an official document sent to the Ministry of Education.

116. *Kalendar sa šematizmom Kmjažestva Srbije za 1857* (Beograd, 1857), p. 38.

117. *Kalendar sa šematizmom Kmjažestva Srbije za 1858* (Beograd, 1858), p. 38.

118. AS, MPs, VII - 77/1855.

119. *Spomenica Čačanske realne gimnazije 1837-1937* (Čačak, 1938), pp. 66-73.

120. D.S. Popović, "Povodom stogodišnjice Čačanske gimnazije," *Glasnik*, JPD, knj. XVIII, No. 2 (Beograd, 1937), p. 94.

121. *Ibid.*, p. 95.

122. *Ibid.*

123. AS, MPs, III - 132/1842.

124. *Spomenica Čačanske realne gimnazije*, *op. cit.*, pp. 85-86.

125. Milen M. Nikolić, *Spomenica Kargujevačke gimnazije, 1833-1933* (Kragujevac, 1934), p. 118.

126. *Ibid.*

127. AS, MPs, II - 29/1855. According to *Veliki beogradski kalendar* for the years 1852 and 1853, in 1852 the Kragujevac gymnasium had only 39 students and in 1853, 153 students. (See pp. 163 and 224.)

128. *Kalendar sa šematizmom Knjažestva Srbije za 1855 i 1856.god.* (Beograd, 1855 and 1856), pp. 37 and 37.

129. AS, MPs, VII - 77/1855.

130. M.Dj. Milićević, "Škole u Srbiji," *op. cit.*, pp. 67-68.

131. AS, MPs, II - 29/1855. According to the *Veliki beogradski kalendar* for the years 1852 and 1853, in 1852 Negotin lower gymnasium had 49 students and in 1853, 60 students.

132. *Kalendar sa šematizmom Knjažestva Srbije za 1855.god.* (Beograd, 1855), p. 38.

133. AS, MPs, VII - 77/1855.

134. M. Spasić, "Štatistični podatci školski zavedenija u Knjažestvu Srbskom," *Glasnik*, DSS, knj. 9 (Beograd, 1857), p. 171.

135. *Ibid.*

136. *Kalendar sa šematizmom Knjažestva Srbije za 1855.god* (Beograd, 1855), pp. 37-38.

137. M. Spasić, "Državopisni podatci školskog zavedenija," *op. cit.*, p. 290.

138. AS, MPs, I - 35/1858.

139. AS, MPs, III - 5/1845.

140. AS, MPs, I -120/1856.

141. AS, Sovjet, 721/1857.

142. *Novine Srbske*, No. 40 (September 9, 1839).

143. Petar A. Tipa, *Gimnazija kralja Aleksandra I u XIX veku* (Beograd, 1900), p. 4.

144. M. Spasić, "Štastistični podatci školski zavedenija," *op. cit.*, p. 171.

145. AS, MPs, II - 29/1855.

146. AS, MPs, I - 35/1858.

147. M. Spasić, "Štastistični podatci školski zavedenija," *op. cit.*, p. 171.

148. AS, MPs, VII - 77/1855.

149. M. Spasić, "Državopisni podatci školski zavedenija," *op. cit.*, p. 290.

150. Miodrag Jugović, "Prva Beogradska gimnazija," in *1839-1939 Spomenica o stogodišnjici Prve muške gimnazije u Beogradu* (Beograd, 1939), p. 105.

151. AS, MPs, I - 45/1844.

152. AS, MPs, VII - 77/1845.

153. *Ibid*.

154. Jovan Milićević, "Petrovska skupština 1848.godine," *Istoriski glasnik*, Nos. 1-2 (Beograd, 1959), p. 53.

155. *Srbski dnevnik*, Nos. 63-68 (Novi Sad, 1857).

156. Stojan Bošković, *Za prosvetu i slobodu* (Beograd, 1882), pp. 17 and 19.

157. AS, Sovjet, 596/1857.

158. *Sbornik zakona i uredaba*, Vol. 11 (Beograd, 1858).

159. *Ibid*.

160. *Ibid*., p. 49.

161. *Ibid*., p. 50.

162. AS, MPs, VII - 646/1847.

163. AS, Sovjet, 721/1857.

164. "Sistema predavaeni nauka," Ž. S. Djordjević, *Škole i prosveta u Srbiji, op. cit.*, p. 78.

165. *Sbornik zakona i uredaba*, Vol. 2 (Beograd, 1845), pp. 300-338.

166. *Ibid*., p. 330.

167. *Ibid*., pp. 331-333.

168. "Nastavlenije za profesore gimnazije i polugimnazija," P.A. Tipa, *op. cit.*, pp. 23-34.

169. *Ibid*., p. 28.

170. AS, MPs, IV - 9/1844; M. Jugović, *op. cit.*, p. 81.

171. AS, Sovjet, 77/1841.

172. S. Jovanović, *op. cit.*, p. 86.

173. *Ibid*.

174. P.A. Tipa, *op. cit.*, pp. 24-27.

175. Pera Polovina, *Udžbenici francuskog jezika kod Srba do 1914 godine* (Beograd, 1964), p. 10.

176. *Ibid.*, p. 23.

177. AS, MPs, VI - 445/1842.

178. AS, Sovjet, 180/1842.

179. S. Jovanović, *op. cit.*, p. 85.

180. AS, MPs, II -234/1851.

181. *Ibid.*

182. AS, MPs, VI - 2/1853.

183. "Nastavlenije za glavnog inspektora učilišta," AS, Sovjet, 161/1853.

184. As, Sovjet, 501/1853.

185. As, Sovjet, 516/1854.

186. "Ustrojenije Knjažesko-srbske gimnazije," *Sbornik zakona i uredaba*, Vol. 7 (Beograd, 1854), p. 83.

187. Djordje Maletić, "Istorijiski razvitak gimnazije Beogradske od njenog postanka do danas," *Glasnik* SUD, knj. VII, No. 24 (Beograd, 1868), p. 151.

188. *Sbornik zakona i uredaba*, Vol. 7 (Beograd, 1854), pp. 84-85.

189. Dj. Maletić, *op. cit.*, p. 150.

190. M. Jugović, *op. cit.*, p. 132.

191. AS, MPs, IV - 31/1856.

192. *Srbski dnevnik*, No. 26 (Novi Sad, March 31, 1854).

193. P.A. Tipa, *op. cit.*, p. 75.

194. *Ibid.*, pp. 75-79.

195. M. Jugović, *op. cit.*, p. 67.

196. *Srbske Novine*, No. 25 (February 28, 1850).

197. AS, Sovjet, 308/1849.

198. AS, MPs, IV - 53/1844.

199. Milan Vujačić, "Omladina iz Crne Gore i susjednih oblasti pod Turskom na školovanju u Srbiji 1850-1878.godine i pomoć koju je Srbija pružila tim oblastima," *Arhivski almanah*, Nos. 2-3 (Beograd, 1960), p. 244.

200. M.Dj. Milićević, *Uspomene, 1831-1855* (Beograd, 1952), p. 208.

201. M. Jugović, *op. cit.*, p. 147.

202. *Ibid.;* AS, Sovjet, 355/1846.

203. *Sbornik zakona i uredaba*, Vol. 5 (Beograd, 1853), pp. 1-2.

204. *Ibid.*, Vol. 2 (Beograd, 1845), p. 330.

205. Jovan Dragašević, *Istinski priče-avtobiografija u odlomcima* (Beograd, 1888), pp. 84-85.

206. S. Marković, *op. cit.*, p. 39.

207. *Ibid.*, pp. 34-35.

208. Vladeta M. Tešić, "Moralno vaspitanje u školama Srbije od 1830. do 1878" (Unpublished Ph.D. dissertation, University of Belgrade, 1961), p. 144.

209. AS, MPs, II - 6/1842.

210. AS - Ilija Garašanin, No. 1, 003.

211. *Ibid.*

212. AS, MPs, III - 65/1844.

74. *Sbornik zakona i uredaba*, Vol. 3 (Beograd, 1847), pp. 414-415; AS, MPs, II - 65/1846.

75. *Ibid.*

76. M.Dj. Milićević, "Škole u Srbiji," *op. cit.*, pp. 110-111.

77. "Djeneral Franja A. Zah" (nekrolog), *Šluzbeni vojni list* (Beograd, 1892), pp. 145-146.

78. *Spomenica 75-godišnjice Vojne akademije, 1850-1925* (Beograd, 1925), pp. 5-15.

79. AS, L - 297/1850.

80. AS, MPs, VII - 96/1856; *Zvanične novine Knjažestva Srbije*, No. 54 (August 25, 1856).

81. AS, L - 297/1850.

82. AS, Sovjet, 620/1852.

83. AS, Sovjet, 576/1854.

84. AS, Sovjet, 582/1855.

85. *Ibid.*

86. AS, L - 297/1850.

87. M. Spasić, "Državopisni podatci školski zavedenija u knjaž. srbskom od 1856/7 do 1960/1.god. školsk.," *Glasnik* DSS, knj. 14 (Beograd, 1862), pp. 286-287.

88. *Spomenica 75-godišnjice Vojne akademije, op. cit.*, p. 86.

89. "Djeneral Franja A. Zah," *op. cit.*, pp. 146 and 149.

90. AS, L - 297/1850; AS, MPs, VII - 96/1856; *Kalendar sa šematizmom Knjažestva Srbije za 1852* (Beograd, 1852), p. 155.

91. M. Spasić, "Državopisni podatci školski zavedenija u knjaž.srbskom," *op. cit.*, p. 290.

92. *Srbski dnevnik*, No. 19 (Novi Sad, August 23, 1852).

93. *Srbske Novine*, No. 141 (December 19, 1850).

94. AS, Sovjet, 606/1852.

95. *Ibid.*

96. AS, Sovjet, 9/1853.

97. "Ustrojenije Zemljodelske škole u Topčideru," *Sbornik zakona i uredaba*, Vol. 7 (Beograd, 1854), pp. 3-12.

98. AS, Sovjet, 86/1854.

99. *Sbornik zakona i uredaba*, Vols. 7 and 9 (Beograd, 1854 and 1857), pp. 4-6.

100. Stojan Petrović, *Sto godina poljoprivrednih škola u Srbiji, 1853-1953* (Beograd, 1956), p. 42.

101. *Ibid.*, p. 43.

102. *Srbski dnevnik*, No. 30 (Novi Sad, April 21, 1856).

103. *Ibid.*

104. Andrija Radenić, *Svetoandrejska skupština*, SAN i U, Spomenik CXIII, Odelenje društvenih nauka, Nova serija, No. 15 (Beograd, 1964), pp. 95-96.

105. Vladimir Jovanović (1833-1922) was a liberal and an eminent cultural and political worker in Serbia in the second half of the nineteenth century.

106. "Biografija Nikolića Atanasija, pisana 1874-75," Arhiv SAN, No. 7380/32.

107. A. Radenić, *op. cit.*, p. 8.

108. M.Dj. Milićević, "Škole u Srbiji," *op. cit.*, p. 50.

109. AS, Sovjet, 85/1854.

110. Cited by Svetislav Šumarević, *Pozorište kod Srba* (Beograd, 1939), p. 241.

111. *Srbske Novine*, No. 59 (July 25, 1845).

112. *Ibid.*

113. Ljubomir M. Protić, *Glavni prosvetni savet* (Beograd, 1910), p. 5.

114. *Srbske Novine*, No. 59 (July 25, 1845).

115. *Ibid.*

116. Lj. M. Protić, *op. cit.*, p. 9.

117. *Ibid.*, p. 10.

118. *Ibid.*, p. 11.

119. *Srbske Novine*, No. 16 (February 7, 1850).

120. *Ibid.*

121. Lj. M. Protić, *op. cit.*, p. 15.

122. *Srbske Novine*, No. 63 (May 30, 1850).

123. *Sbornik zakona i uredaba*, Vol. 7 (Beograd, 1854), pp. 90 and 107.

124. Stojan Novaković, *Srpska bibliografija za noviju književnost, 1747-1847* (Beograd, 1869).

125. *Ibid.*, pp. 219-402.

126. *Ibid.*, p. 323.

127. AS, MPs, I - 61/1847.

128. Matija Ban, *Vospitatelj ženskij*, Vol. 1 (Beograd, 1847).

129. S. Novaković, *op. cit.*, pp. 361-362.

130. Miodrag Popović, "Nenadovićeva 'Šumadinka'," *Istoriski glasnik*, No. 4 (Beograd, 1954), pp. 119-120.

CHAPTER IV: HIGHER EDUCATION

1. Archibald A. Paton, *Serbia, the Youngest Member of the European Family* (London, 1845), p. 283.

2. Vladimir Grujić, "Više obrazovanje u Srbiji za prvih sedam decenija XIX veka," *Godišnjak grada Beograda*, knj. XIV (Beograd, 1967), pp. 208-209.

3. *Ibid.*, p. 209.

4. Konstantin Branković, "Razvitak Velike škole," *Glasnik* SUD, knj. 18 (Beograd, 1865), p. 17.

5. Cited by Milen Nikolić, "Licej," *Iz prošlosti Kragujevca* (Subotica, 1926), p. 13.

6. *Novine Srbske*, No. 45 (October 14, 1839).

7. Ilija A. Pržić, "Osnivanje Pravnog fakulteta u Srbiji," *Arhiv za pravne i društvene nauke*, knj. XLI, Nos. 1-2 (Beograd, 1940), p. 4.

8. Svetomir Nikolajević, "Kraljevsko-srpska Velika škola za pedeset njenih godina," *Godišnjica Nikole Čupića*, knj. XII (Beograd, 1891), p. 208.

9. I.A. Pržić, *op. cit.*, pp. 16-17.

10. Princess Ljubica was the wife of Prince Miloš Obrenović.

11. I.A. Pržić, *op. cit.*, p. 4.

12. *Ibid.*

13. V. Grujić, "Prvi profesori 'Pravoslovnog' fakulteta na liceju u Kragujevcu i Beogradu," *Anali Pravnog fakulteta u Beogradu* (October-December, 1955), p. 449.

14. *Novine Srbske*, No. 31 (August 3, 1840).

15. V. Grujić, "Prvi profesori 'Pravoslovnog' fakulteta na liceju u Kragujevcu i Beogradu," *op. cit.*, p. 449.

16. *Ibid.*, p. 450.

17. *Ibid.*, pp. 451-452.

18. V. Grujić, "Pravničko obrazovanje na Liceju u početku njegovog rada," *Anali Pravnog fakulteta u Beogradu*, No. 2 (Beograd, 1954), p. 196.

19. Radovan D. Lukić, "Jovan Sterija Popović - profesor prirodnog prava na Liceju," *Anali Pravnog fakulteta u Beogradu*, No. 1 (Beograd, 1957), pp. 13-14.

20. V. Grujić, "Pravničko obrazovanje na Liceju u početku njegovog rada," *op. cit.*, p. 196.

21. *Ibid.*, p. 197; L - 124/1844.

22. M. Nikolić, *op. cit.*, p. 17.

23. AS, L - 104/1842.

24. AS, Sovjet, 75/1841.

25. *Ibid.*

26. *Sbornik zakona i uredaba*, Vol. 2 (Beograd, 1845), pp. 338-345.

27. *Ibid.*, p. 339.

28. *Ibid.*, pp. 339-340.

29. Prvoš Slankamenac, "Osnivanje i karakter Beogradskog liceja," *Svremena škola*, Nos. 3-4 (Beograd, 1952), p. 20.

30. *Sbornik zakona i uredaba*, Vol. 2 (Beograd, 1845), p. 340.

31. Smilja Mišić, "Iz istorije Beogradskog liceja," *Srpski knjiženi glasnik*, knj. 53, No. 6 (Beograd, 1938), p. 444.

32. AS, MPs, VII - 77/1855; Pera Polovina, *Ubžbenici francuskog jezika kod Srba do 1914.godine* (Beograd, 1964), p. 28.

33. AS, MPs, III - 228/1848; *Srbske Novine*, Nos. 79-80 (August 31 - September 3, 1848).

34. AS, MPs, III - 228/1848.

35. AS, MPs, II - 316/1851; V. Grujić, "Više obrazovanje u Srbiji za prvih sedam decenija XIX veka," *op. cit.*, p. 239; Milan Dj. Milićević, *Pomenik znamenitih ljudi u srpskog naroda novijega doba* (Beograd, 1888), p. 799.

36. AS, MPs, III - 228/1848.

37. AS, MPs, IV - 257/1848.

38. *Ibid.*; V. Grujić, "Više obrazovanje u Srbiji za prvih sedam decenija XIX veka," *op. cit.*, p. 239.

39. "Matićev dnevnik," IBR 595 (University Library "Svetozar Marković," Beograd).

40. *Srbske Novine*, No. 79 (August 31, 1848).

41. "Matićev dnevnik," *op. cit.*

42. *Ibid.*

43. Jovan Skerlić, *Omladina i njena književnost, 1848-1871* (Beograd, 1925), p. 17.

44. M. Dj. Milićević, *Pomenik*, *op. cit.*, pp. 332 and 800.

45. AS, MPs, II - 73/1856.

46. J. Skerlić, *op. cit.*, p. 16.

47. AS, MPs, VII - 77/1855, II - 316/1851.

48. AS, L - 878/1858.

49. AS, MPs, V - 386/1848. During 1848 the professors of the French language at the Belgrade Lyceum were changed very often. After Aleksije Okoljski's death in February, Konstantin Rano, Professor in the Business School, was appointed his successor. On September 16/28, the Ministry of Education replaced him with Djordje Atanasijević. Since Atanasijević did not accept his appointment, for unknown reasons, the Ministry appointed Ljudevit Španić on October 2/14. (AS, L - 237/1848, L - 241/1848).

50. *Ibid.*

51. *Pandects* - a part of the *Corpus Iuris Civilis*, a collection of Roman classical laws gathered during the reign of the Byzantine Emperor Justinian I (527-565).

52. *Sbornik zakona i uredaba*, Vol. 5 (Beograd, 1853), p. 8.

53. *Ibid.*, pp. 9-10.

54. AS, L - 302/1850.

55. AS, MPs, II - 316/1851.

56. AS, L - 303/1850.

57. P. Polovina, *op. cit.*, p. 39.

58. *Ibid.*, p. 40.

59. AS, MPs, II - 405/1851.

60. P. Polovina, *op. cit.*, p. 40.

61. *Srbske Novine*, No. 18 (February 12, 1852).

62. AS, MPs, I - 41/1852.

63. *Sbornik zakona i uredaba*, Vol. 6 (Beograd, 1853), p. 61.

64. AS, MPs, I - 41/1852.

65. AS, L - 388/1851.

66. *Sbornik zakona i uredaba*, Vol. 7 (Beograd, 1854), pp. 98-99.

67. Olga Mučalica, "Osnivanje katedre narodne istorije i književnosti i njen prvi profesor u Liceju," *Arhivski almanah* (Beograd, 1958), p. 178.

68. *Ibid.*, p. 180.

69. *Ibid.*, p. 181.

70. AS, MPs, VII - 77/1855.

71. "Biografija Vukomanović Alekse Društvu srpske slovesnosti," Arhiv SAN, No. 7380/8.

72. *Srbske Novine*, No. 102 (September 6, 1852).

73. Cited by O. Mučalica, *op. cit.*, p. 182.

74. "Ustrojenije Knjažesko-srbskog liceja," *Sbornik zakona i uredaba*, Vol. 7 (Beograd, 1854), pp. 98-112.

75. *Ibid.*, p. 99.

76. *Ibid.*, pp. 99-100.

77. *Ibid.*, pp. 100-101.

78. *Ibid.*, p. 104.

79. Milovan Spasić, "Državopisni podatci školski zavedenija u knjaž. srbskom od 1856/7 do 1860/1 god. školsk.," *Glasnik* DDS, knj. 14 (Beograd, 1862), p. 290.

80. AS, Sovjet, 29/1845.

81. AS, Sovjet, 501/1853.

82. AS, Sovjet, 721/1857.

83. AS, MPs, VII - 77/1855, II - 316/1851; L - 831/1858, L - 878/1858.

84. Aleksandar Matejić, *Pioniri joslovenske nauke* (Beograd, 1966), p. 38.

85. AS, MPs, VII - 77/1855.

86. V. Grujić, "Više obrazovanje u Srbiji za prvih sedam decenija XIX veka," *op. cit.*, p. 240.

87. *Sbornik zakona i uredaba*, Vol. 11 (Beograd, 1858), pp. 47-50.

88. AS, MPs, V - 366/1849.

89. *Ibid.*

90. Stojan Bošković, *Za prosvetu i slobodu* (Beograd, 1882), p. 24.

91. AS, Sovjet, 464/1850.

92. AS, Sovjet, 721/1857.

93. S. Nikolajević, "Kraljevsko-srbska Velika škola za pedeset njenih godina," *op. cit.*, p. 211.

94. AS, MPs, II - 233/1850.

95. *Ibid.*

96. Miodrag Jugović, "Prva beogradska gimnazija," *Spomenica o stogodišnjici prve muške gimnazije u Beogradu, 1839-1939* (Beograd, 1939), p. 114.

97. AS, L - 134/1844.

98. *Spomenica Josifa Pančića* (Beograd, 1939), pp. 3-4.

99. Vladan Djordjević, "Beseda koju je na opelu prof.dr. Josifa Pančića 26 februara 1888. u Sabornoj crkvi govorio dr. Vladan Djordjević," *Otadžbina*, knj. 18 (Beograd, 1888), p. I.

100. AS, MPs, VI - 562/1834, II -70/1848; L -310/1850.

101. AS, L - 715/1857, 83/1858, 836/1858.

102. AS, MPs, VI - 7/1846.

103. *Novine Čitališta Beogradskog*, No. 3 (January 17, 1847).

104. K. Branković, "Razvitak Velike škole," *op. cit.*, p. 20.

105. AS, MPs, II - 29/1855.

106. *Kalendar sa šematizmom Knjažestva Srbije za 1858* (Beograd, 1858), p. 37.

107. *Ibid.*, p. 38.

108. *Stanovništvo Narodne Republike Srbije od 1834-1953*, Vol. 1, Serija B, Sveska 1 (Beograd, 1953), p. 11.

109. AS, Sovjet, 646/1840.

110. AS, MPs, V - 404/1843.

111. AS, MPs, I - 20/1848.

112. AS, MPs, V - 53/1853.

113. AS, MPs, V - 404/1843.

114. AS, Sovjet, 9/1841; L - 526/1854.

115. AS, MPs, V - 388/1847.

116. AS, MPs, VI - 8/1844.

117. "Autobiografija Protić Petra," Arhiv SAN, No. 7380/32.

118. As, L - 611/1855.

119. AS, Sovjet, 616/1839.

120. Dragoljub Novakov, "Prilog istoriji Kragujevačkog liceja 1840.godine," *Zbornik Matice Srpske*, Serija društvenih nauka, No. 8 (Novi Sad, 1954), p. 129.

121. "Učilišni zakon za slušatelje u Liceum Knjažestva Srbskog," AS, L - 341/1851; *Srbske Novine*, No. 105 (September 15, 1851).

122. AS, L - 270/1849.

123. AS, L - 16/1839.

124. AS, L - 54/1841.

125. "Matićev dnevnik," *op. cit.*

126. Dragoslav Stranjaković, ed. *Uspomene i doživljaji Dimitrija Marinkovića, 1846-1869* (Beograd, 1939), pp. 8-9.

127. *Ibid.*, pp. 34-35.

128. Cited by Branislav Dj. Nušić, "'Oda Sultanu' - jedno sećanje iz poluprošlosti," *Srpski književni glasnik*, knj. XXVI, No. 4 (Beograd, 1911), p. 259.

129. *Ibid.*, pp. 262-263.

130. J. Skerlić, "Družina Mladeži Srbske," *Srpski književni glasnik*, No. 15 (Beograd, 1905), p. 428.

131. *Ibid.*, p. 429; Milorad Radević, "Pravila Družine Mladeži Srbske," *Nastava i vaspitanje*, No. 1 (Beograd, 1969), pp. 97, 104-105.

132. *Ibid.*, pp. 104-105.

133. J. Skerlić, "Družina Mladeži Srbske," *op. cit.*, p. 430.

134. *Ibid.*, pp. 430-431.

135. M. Radević, *op. cit.*, p. 98.

136. *Ibid.*, pp. 99 and 103.

137. J. Skerlić, "Družina Mladeži Srbske," *op. cit.*, p. 431.

138. "Hartije Jevrema Grujića," Arhiv IIB, Inv. No. 3/26, Sign. I, I/3.

139. Jevrem Grujić, *Zapisi*, Vol. 1 (Beograd, 1922), p. 3.

140. Cited by Luka Zrnić, *Srpske djačke družine* (Beograd, 1912), pp. 33-34.

141. D. Stranjaković, "Svetozar Miletić i Jevrem Grujić 1848.godine," Matica srpska, *Zbornik* za drustvene nauke, Nos. 13-14 (Novi Sad, 1956), p. 145.

142. Cited by Mihailo Bjelica, "Počeci političke štampe u Srbiji, 1834-1872" (unpublished Ph.D. dissertation, University of Belgrade, 1972), p. 61.

143. *Sto godina Filozofskog fakulteta* (Beograd, 1963), p. 706.

144. M. Radević, "Gradja za istoriju Družine Mladeži Srbske, 1847-1851," *Nastava i vaspitanje*, No. 4 (Beograd, 1969), pp. 469-470.

145. *Ibid.*, pp. 170-171.

146. L. Zrnić, *op. cit.*, p. 57.

147. "Hartije Jevrema Grujića," Arhiv IIB, Inv. No. 3/26, Sign. I, I/3.

148. L. Zrnić, *op. cit.*, p. 52.

149. Information concerning the place of *Neven-Sloga*'s publication differs. For instance, Mihailo Bjelica writes that it was published in Zemun (M. Bjelica, *op. cit.*, p. 62), Luka Zrnić writes that it was published in Karlovci (L. Zrnić, *op. cit.*, p. 52), and its original copy shows that it was published in Belgrade. We accepted Bjelica's information for two reasons: (1) his work is of the latest date, and (2) he is one of the leading experts in the history of the Serbian press in the nineteenth century.

150. *Neven-Sloga* (Beograd, 1849).

151. Jovan Milićević, *Jevrem Grujić, istorijat svetoandrejskog liberalizma* (Beograd, 1964), p. 34.

152. J. Grujić, "Obzor države," *Neven-Sloga* (Beograd, 1849), pp. 175-176.

153. *Ibid.*, pp. 177-178.

154. J. Skerlić, *Omladina i njena književnost*, *op. cit.*, p. 26.

155. M. Radević, "Gradja za istoriju Družine Mladeži Srbske," *op. cit.*, pp. 471-472.

156. "Hartije Jevrema Grujića," Arhiv IIB, Inv. No. 3/18, Sign. I, I/3.

157. D. Stranjaković, "Ukidanje 'Družine Mladeži Srbske'," *Srpski književni glasnik*, knj. XLIX, No. 6 (Beograd, 1936), p. 446; D. Stranjaković, ed., *Uspomene i doživljaji Dimitrija Marinkovića*, *op. cit.*, p. 22.

158. D. Stranjaković, ed., *Uspomene i doživljaji Dimitrija Marinkovića*, *op. cit.*, p. 22.

159. *Ibid.*, p. 23.

160. M. Radević, "Gradja za istoriju Družine Mladeži Srbske," *op. cit.*, p. 466.

161. J. Grujić, *Život Andrije Stamenkovića* (Beograd, 1869), p. 23.

162. M. Radević, "Gradja za istoriju Družine Mladeži Srbske," *op. cit.*, p. 477.

163. D. Stranjaković, ed., *Uspomene i doživljaji Dimitrija Marinkovića*, *op. cit.*, p. 23.

164. *Sbornik zakona i uredaba*, Vol. 7 (Beograd, 1854), p. 112.

165. *Sto godina Filozofskog fakulteta*, *op. cit.*, p. 14.

166. Olga Popović, "Biblioteka srpskog liceja," *Bibliotekar*, Nos. 1-2 (Beograd, 1951), p.4

167. *Ibid.*, p. 6.

168. AS, L - 474/1853.

169. AS, L - 543/1855.

170. AS, L - 799/1857.

171. *Sbornik zakona i uredaba*, Vol. 7 (Beograd, 1854), p. 112.

172. *Sbornik zakona i uredaba*, Vol. 2 (Beograd, 1845), p. 340.

173. AS, L - 164/1845; L - 174/1846.

174. AS, L - 33/1840.

175. Stojan Novaković, *Srpska bibliografija za noviju književnost, 1741-1867* (Beograd, 1869), pp. 219-402.

176. Mihailo Popović, "Konstantin Branković, profesor filosofije i pasac prvog udžbenika logike na Beogradskoj Velikoj školi," *Zbornik Filozofskog fakulteta*, knj. 3 (Beograd, 1955), p. 594.

177. Andrija Stojković, *Razvitak filozofije u Srba, 1804-1944* (Beograd, 1972), p. 110.

178. *Ibid.*

179. *Ibid.*, p. 111.

180. *Ibid.*, p. 110.

181. Ilija Ivačković, *Jedan srpski filozof* (Sremski Karlovci, 1908), p. 54.

182. *Ibid.*, p. 56.

183. Dimitrije Matić, *Načela umnog dražvnog prava* (Beograd, 1851), p. 125.

184. *Ibid.*, p. 43.

185. Kosta P.L. Cukić, *Državna ekonomija*, Vol. 3 (Beograd, 1853), p. 109.

186. *Dodatak k Srbskim Novinama*, No. 33 (August 16, 1841).

187. Cited by Stojan Bošković, "U spomen Dimitriju Matiću," *Glasnik* SUD, No. LXIX (Beograd, 1899), p. 196.

188. K. Branković, "Razvitak Velike škole," *op. cit.*, pp. 20-21.

CHAPTER V: THE EDUCATION OF SERBIA'S YOUTH ABROAD

1. AS, MPs, No. 400/1839.

2. *Ibid.*

3. *Ibid.*

4. *Ibid.*

5. *Ibid.*

6. *Ibid.*

7. Milan Dj. Milićević, "Škole u Srbiji," *Glasnik* SUD, knj. VII, No. 24 (Beograd, 1868), p. 21.

8. AS, MPs, No. 126/1840.

9. "Nastavlenije mladićima, koji se u strane države izučenija radi različni polezni znanija pošilju," AS, MPs - 400/1839.

10. Vladeta Tešić, "Moralno vaspitanje u školama Srbije od 1830. do 1878" (unpublished Ph.D. dissertation, University of Belgrade, 1961), p. 67.

11. As, MPs, No. 126/1840.

12. *Ibid.*

13. Golub Dobrašinović, ed., *Arhivska gradja o Vuku Karadžiću, 1813-1864* (Beograd, 1970), p. 271.

14. Sreten L. Popović, *Putovanje po novoj Srbiji* (Beograd, 1950), p. 208.

15. On their way to Vienna, the Serbian students visited Pozsony where they were welcomed by a group of Slovakian students who prepared a party for them.

16. S.L. Popović, *op. cit.*, p. 209.

17. Cited by Tihomir R. Djordjević, *Srbija pre sto godina* (Beograd, 1946), p. 72.

18. G. Dobrašinović, *op. cit.*, p. 274. Since we could not always establish which calendar (Julian or Gregorian) the Serbian students abroad used in their correspondence with the government, we shall cite all dates regarding their correspondence from abroad as they appeared on the original letters.

19. AS, MPs, II - 117/1849.

20. AS, Sovjet, 263/1850.

21. Slobodan Jovanović, *Ustavobranitelji i njihova vlada, 1838-1858* (Beograd, 1933), p. 94.

22. AS, MPs, V - 5/1857.

23. *Ibid.*

24. AS, Sovjet, 510/1843.

25. Svetozar Vuković, "Srpski pitomci na Halci u XIX i XX veku," *Glasnik* službeni list Srpske pravoslavne patrijaršije (Beograd, 1954), pp. 200-202.

26. Michael B. Petrovich, *The Emergence of Russian Panslavism, 1856-1870* (New York, 1956), pp. 96-102.

27. AS, Sovjet, 652/1844.

28. AS, MPs, VI - 414/1842.

29. *Srbski dnevnik*, No. 58 (Novi Sad, July 27, 1858).

30. "Matićev dnevnik," IBR 595 (University Library "Svetozar Marković," Beograd).

31. AS, MPs, I - 42/1847.

32. "Memoari Koste Magazinovića," Arhiv SAN, No. 9288.

33. "Biografija Petra Protića," Arhiv SAN, No. 7380/42.

34. Nenad Simić, "Obaveze srpskih državnih pitomaca u inostranstvu sredinom prošlog stoleća," *Zbornik za historiju školstva i prosvete*, No. 6 (Zagreb, 1971), p. 149.

35. AS, Sovjet, 540/1858.

36. AS, MPs, No. 400/1839.

37. AS, Sovjet, 289/1858.

38. "Matićev dnevnik," *op. cit.*

39. *Ibid.*

40. Jevrem Grujić, *Zapisi*, Vol. 1 (Beograd, 1922), p. 21.

41. "Matićev dnevnik," *op. cit.*

42. Cited by Uroš Džonić, "Školovanje Jovana Ilića u inostranstvu," *Prilozi za književnost, jezik, istoriju i folklor*, knj. XIX, Sv. 1-2 (Beograd, 1939), p. 123.

43. "Matićev dnevnik," *op. cit.*

44. Branko Petrović, *Jovan Ristić, biografske i memoarske beleške* (Beograd, 1912), p. 1.

45. Momčilo Ivanić, "Stojan Bošković," *Godišnjica Nikole Čupića*, No. XXVIII (Beograd, 1909), p. 67.

46. J. Grujić, *op. cit.*, Vol. 1, p. 22.

47. Ïankovitch and Grouïtch, *Slaves du Sud* (Paris, 1853), p. 115.

48. J. Grujić, *op. cit.*, p. 22.

49. Ïankovitch and Grouïtch, *op. cit.*, p. 131.

50. AS, MPs, II - 329/1853.

51. *Ibid.*

52. AS, MPs, II - 132/1849.

53. AS, MPs, V - 58/1856.

54. AS, MPs, II - 136/1847.

55. AS, MPs, I - 24/1855.

56. Vasilj Popović, "Djački putopis mitropolita Mihaila," *Prilozi za književnost, jezik, istoriju i folklor*, knj. SVIII (Beograd, 1938), p. 447.

57. AS, MPs, No. 126/1840.

58. AS, Sovjet, No. 640/1840.

59. AS, MPs, II - 86/1843.

60. AS, MPs, II - 133/1849.

61. AS, MPs, VI - 434/1847.

62. *Srbske Novine*, No. 31 (April 18, 1845).

63. AS, MPs, II - 197/1852.

64. AS, Sovjet, 32/1852.

65. AS, MPs, V - 366/1849.

66. S. Jovanović, *op. cit.*, p. 93.

67. AS, MPs, No. 400/1839.

68. "Memoari Koste Magazinovića," *op. cit.*; AS, MPs, III - 23/1844.

69. AS, Sovjet, 126/1856.

70. AS, Sovjet, 244/1849; AS, MPs, IV - 343/1849.

71. AS, MPs, II - 329/1853.

72. "Matićev dnevnik," *op. cit.*

73. Jovan M. Milićević, "Prva grupa srbijanskih studenata, državnih pitomaca školovanih u inostranstvu (1839-1842)," *Istorijski časopis*, knj. IX-X (Beograd, 1960), p. 373.

74. Dragoslav Stranjaković, ed., *Uspomene i doživljaji Dimitrija Marinkovića, 1846-1869* (Beograd, 1939), p. 17.

75. Cited by S. Jovanović, *op. cit.*, p. 97.

76. Stojan Bošković, *Za prosvetu i slobodu* (Beograd, 1882), pp. 24-25.

77. Svetozar Marković, "Kako su nas vaspitali," in Najdan Pašić, ed., *Svetozar Marković-sabrani spisi* (Beograd, 1960), p. 57.

78. Vladimir Jovanović, *Srbenda i gotovan* (Novi Sad, 1864), pp. 5-6. This pamphlet is Vladimir Jovanović's speech which he intended to deliver at the annual meeting of the Serbian Learned Society held in Belgrade on January 26/February 7, 1864. However, its president, Konstantin Cukić, did not allow him to speak.

79. S. Jovanović, *op. cit.*, p. 96.

CHAPTER VI: CULTURAL INSTITUTIONS AND SOCIETIES

1. Ljubomir Durković-Jakšic, *Istorija srpskih biblioteka, 1801-1850* (Beograd, 1963), pp. 106-107.

2. *Srbske Novine*, No. 91 (November 13,1843).

3. *Ibid.*

4. Lj. Durković-Jakšić, "O Stevanu Hrkaloviću," *Istorijski časopis*, knj. XVI-XVII, 1966-67 (Beograd, 1970), p. 123.

5. A secret democratic Panslavic club was established in Belgrade at the end of 1844. Its members were cultural and political figures of Serbia. Some of them were Serbs from Serbia, and some Slavs from different Slavic territories who lived in Serbia. In addition to Hrkalović, František Zách, Janko Šafarik, Paja Čavlović, and Miloš Popović can be mentioned. They advocated a Slavic, especially South Slavic, policy based on mutual respect and solidarity. Their activities were supported by Prince Alexander Karadjordjević and several leading Serbian statesmen. (Lj. Durković-Jakšić, "O Stevanu Hrkaloviću," *op. cit.*, p. 118).

6. Lj. Durković-Jakšić, "O Stevanu Hrkaloviću," *op. cit.*, pp. 123-124.

7. Branislav Dj. Nušić, "Iz prošlosti," *Sabrana dela*, Vol. 2 (Beograd, 1935), p. 209.

8. *Srbske Novine* (October 29, 1846).

9. Milan Dj. Milićević, "Crtice za raniju sliku srpske prestonice," *Godišnjica Nikole Čupića*, knj. 22 (Beograd, 1903), p. 53.

10. *Postanak i razvitak Beogradske čitaonice* (Beograd, 1872), p. 12. The sources regarding the operation of *Kasina* are very poor. They indicate that it was not accessible to everyone without giving particular reasons for this. On the basis of the available sources, it may be concluded that it was not accessible for everyone for two reasons: first, it was more or less a place for political meetings; second, its membership fee, amounting to 3 florins per month, was too high. Lj. Durković-Jakšić, "O Stevanu Hrkaloviću," *op. cit.*, p. 124.

11. *Srbske Novine* (January 8, August 16, and October 29, 1846),

12. *Postanak i razvitak Beogradske čitaonice, op. cit.*, p. 5.

13. *Ibid.*

14. *Ibid.*

15. Bosiljka Janković, "Čitalište Beogradsko," *Bibliotekar*, Nos. 1-3 (Beograd, 1954), p. 11.

16. *Ibid.*, pp. 11-13; M.Dj. Milićević, *op. cit.*, p. 34.

17. Cited by Svetislav Šumarević, *Čitalište* (Beograd, 1938), p. 25.

18. M.Dj. Milićević, *op. cit.*, p. 34.

19. Jakov Ignjatović, *Memoari-Rapsodija iz prošlosti srpskog života* (Beograd, 1966), p. 304.

20. *Srbske Novine*, No. 43 (May 31, 1846).

21. M.Dj. Milićević, *Uspomene, 1831-1855* (Beograd, 1952), p. 204.

22. M.Dj. Milićević, "Crtice za raniju sliku srpske prestonice," *op. cit.*, p. 54.

23. *Srbske Novine*, No. 43 (May 31, 1846).

24. *Ibid.*

25. *Ibid.*

26. Lj. Durković-Jakšić, *Istorija srpskih biblioteka, op. cit.*, p. 116.

27. *Srbske Novine*, No. 16 (February 10, 1851).

28. *Stanovništvo Narodne Republike Srbije od 1834-1953*, Vol. 1, Serija B, Sveska 1 (Beograd, 1953), p. 11.

29. *Srbske Novine*, No. 16 (February 10, 1851).

30. *Ibid.*

31. *Ibid.*

32. *Postanak i razvitak Beogradske čitaonice, op. cit.*, p. 18.

33. *Stanovništvo Narodne Republike Srbije, op. cit.*, p. 11.

34. *Srbske Novine*, Nos. 42, 43, and 44 (April 13, 16, and 18, 1857).

35. *Srbske Novine*, No. 44 (April 18, 1857).

36. *Srbske Novine*, No. 34 (March 19, 1853).

37. AS, MPs, III - 42/1846.

38. B. Janković, *op. cit.*, p. 14.

39. *Srbske Novine*, No. 37 (March 26, 1853).

40. *Novine Čitališta Beogradskog*, No. 5 (January 31, 1847).

41. *Ibid.*

42. B. Janković, *op. cit.*, p. 145.

43. AS, MPs, II - III/1847.

44. *Postanak i razvitak Beogradske čitaonice, op. cit.*, p. 18.

45. *Ibid.*

46. *Ibid.*

47. AS, MPs, IV - 38/1846.

48. B. Janković, *op. cit.*, p. 148.

49. S. Šumarević, *op. cit.*, p. 35.

50. M.Dj. Milićević, *Uspomene, 1831-1855, op. cit.*, p. 206.

51. Cited by Adrija Radenić, "Prve novine u Srbiji," *Počeci štampe jugoslovenskih naroda* (Beograd, 1969), p. 103.

52. *Ibid.*

53. *Ibid.*, p. 104.

54. Mihailo Bjelica, "Počeci politčke štampe u Srbiji, 1834-1872" (unpublished Ph.D. dissertation, University of Belgrade, 1972), p. 56.

55. *Ibid.*, pp. 329-330.

56. *Ibid.*, p. 57.

57. Gavrilo Kovijanić, *Gradja Arhiva Srbije o Narodnom pozorištu u Beogradu, 1835-1914* (Beograd, 1971), p. 46.

58. *Ibid.*

59. *Ibid.*

60. Borivoje S. Stojković, "Pozorište-od prvih početaka do 1914," *Enciklopedija Jugoslavije*, Vol. 7 (Zagreb, 1968), p. 566.

61. *Ibid.*; S. Šumarević, *Pozorište kod Srba* (Beograd, 1939), pp. 238-239.

62. Jovan Ristić, *Spoljašnji odnošaji Srbije novijega vremena*, Vol. 1 (Beograd, 1887), pp. 9-10.

63. *Postanak i razvitak Beogradske čitaonice, op. cit.*, p. 15.

64. B.Dj. Nušić, "Iz prošlosti," *op. cit.*, pp. 123-124.

65. *Srbske Novine*, No. 32 (March 15, 1858).

66. *Srbske Novine*, No. 43 (May 31, 1846).

67. *Srbske Novine*, No. 90 (August 9, 1858).

68. AS, MPs, III - 65/1846.

69. AS, MPs, II - 102/1848.

70. Miraš Kićović, "Prvi rukovodioci Narodne biblioteke u Beogradu," *Godišnjak Muzeja grada Beograda*, knj. IV (Beograd, 1957), p. 261.

71. *Ibid.*, p. 268.

72. "Biografija Nikolić Atanasija pisana 1874-75." Arhiv SAN, No. 7380/32.

73. Lj. Durković-Jakšić, *Istorija srpskih biblioteka, op. cit.*, pp. 149-150.

74. M. Kićović, *op. cit.*, pp. 262-265.

75. *Ibid.*, p. 271.

76. *Ibid.*, p. 281.

77. *Ibid.*; *Stanovništvo Narodne Republike Srbije, op. cit.*, p. 11.

78. *Srbske Novine*, No. 26 (March 2, 1850).

79. G. Kovijanić, *op. cit.*, pp. 16-17.

80. S. Šumarević, *op. cit.*, p. 184.

81. G. Kovijanić, *op. cit.*, pp. 52-53.

82. *Srbske Novine*, No. 79 (July 14, 1851).

83. G. Kovijanić, *op. cit.*, p. 53.

84. B.S. Stojković, *op. cit.*, p. 567.

85. G. Kovijanić, *op. cit.*, p. 84.

86. Cited by S. Šumarević, *Pozorište kod Srba, op. cit.*, p. 194.

87. Vladimir Korać, *Srbija-opis zemlje, naroda i države* (Beograd, 1887), p. 306.

88. B.Dj. Nušić, "Iz prošlosti," *op. cit.*, p. 227.

89. *Ibid.*, p. 291.

90. Cited by Tihomir R. Djordjević, *Srbija pre sto godina* (Beograd, 1946), p. 42.

91. Cited by Branislav Miljković, "Društvo Srpske Slovesnosti of 1841-1864," *Članci i prilozi o srpskoj književnosti prve polovine XIX veka*, knjiga Matice sprske, No. 46 (Novi Sad, 1914), p. 26.

92. *Ibid.*, p. 30.

93. *Ibid.*, p. 31.

94. *Ibid.*, pp. 34-35.

95. *Dodatak k Srbskim Novinama*, No. 27 (July 4, 1842).

96. *Novine Srbske*, No. 24 (July 13, 1842).

97. *Ibid.*

98. Lj. Durković-Jakšić, *Srbijansko-crnogorska suradnja, 1830-1851* (Beograd, 1957), p. 143.

99. B. Miljković, *op. cit.*, p. 33.

100. *Ibid.*, p. 42.

101. *Sbornik zakona i uredaba*, Vol. 4 (Beograd, 1849), p. 26.

102. *Podunavka*, No. 6 (February 10, 1845).

103. Jovan S. Popović, "Razlozi o nazivoslovnim rečima," *Glasnik* DSS, No. 1 (Beograd, 1847), p. 11.

104. *Ibid.*, p. 15.

105. B. Miljković, *op. cit.*, p. 43.

106. *Glasnik* DSS, No. 1 (Beograd, 1847).

107. AS, Sovjet, 263/1847.

108. AS, MPs, III - 5/1845, V - 366/1849.

109. AS, Sovjet, 440/1856, 721/1857.

110. AS, MPs, I - 98/1846, VII - 646/1847; Sovjet, 457/1847, 382/1848, 308/1849, 464/1850, 620/1852, 501/1853, 516/1854; MPs, I - 120/1856.

BIBLIOGRAPHY

I. PRIMARY SOURCES

ARCHIVES

Arhiv grada Beograda

Arhiv Istorijskog instituta u Beogradu

Arvhiv Srbije

Arhiv Srpske akademije nauka i umetnosti

MEMOIRS AND BIOGRAPHIES IN MANUSCRIPT

"Autobiografija Atanasija Nikolića." Arhiv SAN, No. 7380/32.

"Autobiografija Petra Protića." Arhiv SAN, No. 7380/42.

"Biografija Filipa Hristića." Arhiv SAN, No. 7380/52.

"Biografija Vukomanović Alekse." Arhiv SAN, No. 8107/1-40.

"Matićev dnevnik." Univerzitetska bibiloteka "Svetozar Marković" -
Beograd, IBR 595.

"Memoari Djordja Protića." Arhiv SAN, No. 751.

"Memoari Koste Magazinovića." Arhiv SAN, No. 9288.

Vasiljević, Alimipje. "Moje uspomene." Arhiv Srbije, Fond-Pokloni i
otkupi, 102/136.

"Zaostavština Alekse Vukomanovića." Arhiv SAN, No. 9261.

PUBLISHED DOCUMENTS AND MEMOIRS

Alimpić, Mileva. *Život i rad generala Ranka Alimpića*. Beograd, 1892.

Dobrašinović, Golub, ed. *Arhivska gradja o Vuku Karadžiću, 1813-1864.* Beograd, 1970.

Dragašević, Jovan. *Istinske priče.* Beograd, 1888.

Državopis Srbije. Vol. 1, Beograd, 1863.

Djordjević, Vladan. *Uspomene-kulturne skice iz druge polovine XIX veka.* Vol. 1, Novi Sad, 1927.

Djurdjev, Branislav-Vasić, Milan, ed. *Jugoslavenske zemlje pod turskom vlašću (do kraja XVIII stoljeća).* Zagreb, 1962.

Gradja za istoriju srpskog pokreta u Vojvodini 1848-1849. Vol. 1, Beograd, 1952.

Grujić, Jevrem. *Zapisi.* Vol. 1, Beograd, 1922.

Hristić, Kosta N. *Zapisi starog Beogradjanina.* 2 Vols., Beograd, 1923, 1925.

Ignjatović, Jakov. *Memoari-rapsodija iz prošlog srpskog života.* Beograd, 1966.

Ivić, Aleksa. *Arhivska gradja o jugoslovenskim književnim i kulturnim radnicima.* Vols. 4-5, Beograd, 1935, 1936.

Kaljević, Ljubomir. *Moje uspomene.* Beograd, 1908.

Kovijanić, Gavrilo. *Gradja Arhiva Srbije o Narodnom pozorištu u Beogradu, 1835-1914.* Beograd, 1971.

Maletić, Djordje. *Gradja za istoriju Srpskog narodnog pozorišta u Beogradu.* Beograd, 1884.

Milićević, Milan Dj. *Iz svojih uspomena-beleške za prosvetnu istoriju Beograda.* Beograd, 1895.

__________. *Iz svojih uspomena-dve godine u službi učiteljskoj.*

Milićević, Milan Dj. *Iz svojih uspomena-prve grupe-mesto mojega rodjenja, detinjstvo, sa stanom, u školi u Ripnju, u gimanziji, u Beogradu.* Beograd, 1894.

__________. *Uspomene, 1831-1855.* Beograd, 1952.

Nenadović, Mateja. *Memoari.* Beograd, 1966.

Pecić, Josip. *Prosvetni zbornik zakona i uredaba.* Beograd, 1887.

Popović, Aleksandar. "Prilog gradji za istoriju biblioteka u Srbiji XIX i XX veka." *Bibliotekar*, Nos. 1-2, Beograd, 1953, pp. 10-20.

Popović, Kosta. *Uspomene.* Novi Sad, 1927.

Protić, Djordje. *Istoričesko opisanije.* Zemun, 1854.

Prva knjiga prečišćenog izdanja Zbornika zakona i uredaba od 1835-1896 godine. Beograd, 1897.

Radenić, Andrija. *Svetoandrejska skupština.* Beograd, 1964.

Radević, Milorad. "Gradja za istoriju Družine Mladeži Srbske 1847-1851." *Nastava i vaspitanje*, No. 4, Beograd, 1969, pp. 458-477.

__________. "Pravila Družine Mladeži Srbske." *Nastava i vaspitnaje*, No. 1, Beograd, 1969, pp. 97-105.

Ristić, Jovan. *Istoriski spisi.* Beograd, 1940.

Sbornik zakona i uredaba. Vols. 1-11, Beograd, 1840, 1845, 1847, 1849, 1853, 1854, 1856, 1857, 1858.

Slankamenac, Prvoš. "Dokumenti o prvim školskim zakonima u Srbiji u vremenu of 1833-1843 godine." SAN, Gradja knj. XII, Istorijski institut, knj. IX, *Mešovita gradja*, Beograd, 1956, pp. 91-120.

Stanovništvo Narodne Republike Srbije od 1834-1953. Serija B, No. 1, Beograd, 1953.

Stojanović, Ljubomir, ed. *Vukova prepiska.* 7 Vols., Beograd, 1907, 1908, 1909, 1910, 1912, 1913.

Stranjaković, Dragoslav, ed. *Uspomene i doživljaji Dimitrija Marinkovića, 1846-1869*. Beograd, 1939.

Školski zbornik zakona, pravila i naredaba. Beograd, 1875.

Šurmin, Djuro. "Dokumenti o Srbiji od 1842 do 1848." *Spomenik Srpske Kraljevske Akademije*, No. 69, Beograd, 1929.

Živanović, Živan, ed. *Memoari Stefan-Stevice Mihailovića*. Beograd, 1928.

NEWSPAPERS AND PERIODICALS

Čiča Srećkov List.

Dodatak k Srbskim Novinama.

Golubica s cvetom Knjažestva srbskog. Beograd, 1839, 1840, 1841, 1842, 1843, 1844.

Kalendar sa šematizmom Knjažestva Srbije. Beograd, 1852, 1853, 1855, 1856, 1857, 1858.

Neven-sloga. Beograd, 1849.

Novine Čitališta Beogradskog.

Novine Srbske (after 1843, *Srbske Novine*).

Podunavka.

Prosvetne novine sa državonarodnim pratiocem.

Srbski Dnevnik.

Šumadinka.

Veliki Beogradski Kalendar.

Vila. No. 2, Beograd, 1865.

Zvanične novine Knjažestva Srbije.

II. SECONDARY SOURCES

BOOKS, PAMPHLETS, AND DISSERTATIONS

Alimpić, D. Dj. *Istoriski razvitak policijskih vlasti u Srbiji (1739-1869)*. Beograd, 1905.

Anderson, M.S. *The Eastern Question, 1774-1923*. New York, 1966.

Arnautović, Aleksandar. *Štamparije u Srbiji u XIX veku*. Beograd, 1912.

Arsenijević-Batalaka, Lazar. *Istorija srpskog ustanka*. 2 Vols., Beograd, 1898, 1899.

Ban, Matija. *Vospitatelj ženskij*. Vol. 1, Beograd, 1847.

Belić, Vladimir J. *Ratovi srpskog naroda u XIX i XX veku*. Beograd, 1938.

Beseda, koju je na opelu g. Koste Cukića govorio Čedomilj Mijatović. Beograd, 1879.

Bjelica, Mihailo. "Počeci političke štampe u Srbiji (1834-1872)." Unpublished Ph.D. dissertation, University of Belgrade, 1972.

Bogdanović, Kosta. *Istorija srbskog ustava*. Novi Sad, 1861.

Bošković, Stojan. *Za prosvetu i slobodu*. Beograd, 1882.

Božić, Ivan, Sima Ćirković, Milorad Ekmečić, and Vladimir Dedijer. *Istorija Jugoslavije*. Beograd, 1972.

Cukić, Kosta. *Državna ekonomija*. 3 Vols., Beograd, 1851, 1852, 1853.

Cunibert, Barthélemy S. *Srpski ustanak i prva valdavina Miloša Obrenovića, 1804-1850*. Translated from the French by M.R. Vesnić. Beograd, 1901.

Cvetičanin, Milan. *Zaječarska gimnazija, 1836-1936 godine*. Zaječar, 1937.

Cvijetić, Leposava. *Završni računi Kneževine Srbije od 1835 do 1859*. Beograd, 1955.

Čubrilović, Vaso. *Istorija političke misli u Srbiji XIX veka.* Beograd, 1958.

Čubrilović, Vaso and Vladimir Ćorović. *Srbija od 1858 do 1903.* Beograd.

Ćorović, Vladimir. *Istorija Jugoslavije.* Beograd, 1933.

————. *Velika Srbija.* Beograd, 1925.

Ćunković, Srećko. *Školstvo i prosveta u Srbiji u XIX veku.* Beograd, 1970.

Deli-Gruić. *Preobražaj Beogradske bogoslovije.* Beograd, 1893.

Despotović, Petar. *Istorika pedagogika.* Beograd, 1902.

Durković-Jakšić, Ljubomir. *"Branislav," prvi jugoslovenski ilegalni list 1844-1845.* Beograd, 1968.

————. *Istorija srpskih bilbioteka 1800-1850.* Beograd, 1963.

————. *Prvi srpski pitomci bogoslovi u Rusiji.* Beograd, 1945.

————. *Razvitak osnovnog crkvenog zakona u Šumadiji u prvoj polovini XIX veka (1804-1847).* Beograd, 1947.

————. *Srbijansko-crnogorska saradnja (1830-1851).* Beograd, 1957.

Džambazovski, Kliment. *Kulturno-opštestvenite vrski na Makedoncite so Srbija vo tekot na XIX vek.* Skopje, 1960.

Djordjević, Dimitrije. *Révolutions nationales des peuples Balkaniques, 1804-1914.* Beograd, 1965.

Djordjević, Dragoslav P., ed. *Šumadija u prošlost i sadašnjosti.* Subotica, 1932.

Djordjević, Tihomir R. *Medicinske prilike u Srbiji za vreme prve vlade kneza Miloša Obrenovića (1815-1839).* Beograd, 1921.

————. *Srbija pre sto godina.* Beograd, 1946.

Djordjević, Vladan. *Grčka i srpska prosveta.* Beograd, 1896.

Djordjević, Živojin S. *Istorija vaspitanja u Srba*. Beograd, 1958.

__________. *Škole i prosveta u Srbiji 1700-1850*. Beograd, 1950.

Gavrilović, Andra. *Beogradska Velika škola, 1808-1813*. Beograd, 1902.

__________. *Narodne škole u Srbiji, 1803-1815*. Beograd, 1903.

Gavrilović, Mihailo. *Miloš Obrenović*. 3 Vols., Beograd, 1908, 1909, 1912.

__________. *Počeci diplomatskih odnosa Velike Britanije i Srbije*. Beograd, 1926.

Grujić, Djordje. *Društveno posvećivanje*. Novi Sad, 1912.

Grujić, Jevrem. *Život Andrije Stamenkovića*. Beograd, 1969.

Grujić, Vladimir. *Školsko-reformatorski rad Jovana St. Popovića u Srbiji 1840-1848*. Beograd, 1956.

Guzina, Ružica. *Knežina i postanak srpske buržoaske države*. Beograd, 1955.

Herceg, Jakša. *Ilirizam*. Beograd, 1935.

Ïankovitch-Grouïtch. *Slaves du sud ou le peuple Serbe avec les Croates et les Bulgares*. Paris, 1853.

Ignjatović, Djordje. "Srbija i bugarski preporod-književne i kulturno-prosvetne veze Srba i Bugara u XVIII i XIX veku (1762-1878)." Unpublished Ph.D. dissertation, University of Belgrade, 1964.

Ignjić, Stevan. *Užička nahija*. Beograd, 1961.

Ilić, Aleksa. *Petar Jovanović, mitropolit Beogradski-njegove život i rad 1833-1859 god*. Beograd, 1911.

Ivačković, Ilija. *Jedan srpski filozof*. Sremski Karlovci, 1908.

Ivić, Aleksa. *Iz doba Karadjordjeva i sina mu Aleksandra*. Beograd, 1926.

Jakšić, Grgur. *Iz novije srpske istorije*. Beograd, 1953.

Jakšić, Grgur. *Prepiska Ilije Garašanina*. Beograd, 1950.

Jakšić, G. and V.J. Vučković. *Spoljna politika Srbije za vlade kneza Mihaila (Prvi Balkanski savez)*. Beograd, 1963.

Jakšić, Vladimir. *Postanak i razviće štampe u Srbiji*. Beograd, 1873.

Janča, Ivanka. *Izložba Licej, Velika škola i Beogradski univerzitet kroz arhivsku gradju rektorata (1838-1841)*. Beograd, 1959.

Janković, Dragoslav. *Istorija države i prava Srbije u XIX veku*. Beograd, 1952.

__________. *O političkim strankama u Srbiji XIX veka*. Beograd, 1951.

Janković, Miloš B. *Djački socijalistički pokret u Srbiji*. Beograd, 1954.

__________. *Pedagoške rasprave i članci*. Beograd, 1967.

__________. *Pedagoški pogledi prvih srpskih socijalista Živojina Žujovića, Svetozara Markovića i Vase Pelagića*. Beograd, 1952.

Jelavich, Barbara. *A Century of Russian Foreign Policy, 1814-1914*. Philadelphia-New York, 1964.

Jelavich, Charles. *Tsarist Russia and Balkan Nationalism: Russian Influence in the Internal Affairs of Bulgaria and Serbia, 1879-1886*. Berkley, CA: University of California Press, 1958.

Jelavich, Charles and Barbara, eds. *The Balkans in Transition*. Berkley, CA: University of California Press, 1963.

Jelenić, Djurdje. *Nova Srbija i Jugoslavia*. Beograd, 1923.

Jireček, Konstantin. *Istoria Srba*. 2 Vols. Translated by Jovan Radonić. Beograd, 1923, 1925.

Jovanović, Jovan M. *Južna Srbija od kraja XVIII veka do oslobodjenja*. Beograd, 1938.

Jovanović, Kosta. *Da li da se ukinu okružna načelstva*. Beograd, 1887.

Jovanović, Slobodan. *Druga vlada Miloša i Mihaila*. Beograd, 1923.

__________. *Političke i pravne rasprave*. 2 Vols. Beograd, 1908, 1910.

__________. *Ustavobranitelji and njihova vlada (1838-1858)*. Beograd, 1912.

Jovanović, Vladimir. *Srbenda i gotovan*. Novi Sad, 1864.

Jugoslovenska štampa. Beograd, 1911.

Jugović, Miodrag. *Prva Beogradska gimnazija, 1839-1939*. Beograd, 1939.

Kaper, Sigfrid. *Po našem podunavlju*. Translated from the German by
    Djordje Stratimiriović. Beograd, 1935.

Karadžić, Vuk. S. *Izabrana dela*. Beograd, 1964.

__________. *Pismo knezu Milošu*. Beograd, 1947.

__________. *Srpski rječnik istumačen njemačkijem i latinskijem riječima*.
    Beograd, 1898.

Karić, Vladimir. *Kraljevina Srbija*. Beograd, 1887.

__________. *Srbija i Balkanski savez*. Beograd, 1893.

__________. *Srbija-opis zemlje, naroda i države*. Beograd, 1887.

__________. *Školovanje u Srbiji i njegovi rezultati*. Beograd, 1886.

Kićović, Miraš. *Istorija Narodne biblioteke u Beogradu*. Beograd, 1960.

__________. *Jovan Hadžić (Miloš Svetić)*. Novi Sad, 1930.

Kohn, H. *The Idea of Nationalism*. New York, 1944.

__________. *Panslavism*. New York, 1960.

Kukiel, Mavian. *Czartoryski and European Unity, 1770-1861*. Princeton,
    NJ: Princeton University Press, 1955.

Lapčević, Dragiša. *Istorija socijalizma u Srbiji*. Beograd, 1922.

Lovčević, St., ed. *Pisma Ilije Garašanina Jovanu Marinoviću*. 2 Vols., Beograd, 1931.

MacKenzie, David. *The Serbs and Russian Pan-Slavism 1875-1878*. Ithaca, NY: Cornell University Press, 1967.

Maksimović, St. *Sudjenje u Kneževini Srbiji pre pisanih zakona*. Požarevac, 1898.

Malenić, Milivoj J. *Posle četrdeset godina* (U spomen proslave četrdeset - godišnijce Sv. Andrejske velike narodne skupštine). Beograd, 1901.

Marković, Radoslav. *Vojska i naoružanje Srbije kneza Miloša*. Beograd, 1957.

Markićević, S. *Predreforma u našim bogoslovijama*. Beograd, 1939.

Marković, Svetozar. *Izabrana dela*. Beograd, 1968.

__________. *Srbija na Istoku*. Zagreb, 1946.

Marriot, J.A.R. *The Eastern Question: An Historical Study in European Diplomacy*. Oxford, 1940.

Matić, Aleksander. *Pioniri jugoslovenske nauke*. Beograd, 1966.

Matić, Dimitrije. *Javno pravo Knjaževstva Srbije*. Beograd, 1851.

__________. *Načela umnog državnog prava*. Beograd, 1851.

__________. *Objašnenije Gradjanskog zakonika*. Beograd, 1850.

Medenica, Radosav. *Počeci nemačke nastave u Srbiji i reforme Jovana St. Popovića*. Beograd, 1936.

Micić, Zagorka. *Naša kulturna politika*. Vol. 1, Beograd.

Milenković-Alavantić. *Katanska buna u Šapcu 1844*. Beograd, 1889.

Milić, Danica. *Strani kapital u rudarstvu Srbije do 1918*. Beograd, 1970.

Milić-Miljković, Danica. *Trgovina Srbije (1815-1839)*. Beograd, 1959.

Milićević, Jovan. *Gospodin Garašanin i državna administracija*. Beograd, 1885.

Milićević, Jovan. *Jevrem Grujić: Istorijat Svetoandrejskog liberalizma*. Beograd, 1964.

Milićević, Milan Dj. *Istorija pedagogije*. Beograd, 1871.

__________. *Kneževina Srbija*. Beograd, 1876.

__________. *Opštine u Srbiji*. Beograd, 1878.

__________. *Pogled na narodno školovanje u Srbiji*. Beograd, 1873.

__________. *Pomenik znamenitih ljudi u srpskog naroda novijega doba*. Beograd, 1888, 1959.

Miller, William. *The Balkans: Roumania, Bulgaria, Servia and Montenegro*. London, 1908.

__________. *The Ottoman Empire and Its Successors, 1801-1927*. Cambridge, 1927.

Mitranović, Danka. *Pančićev život*. Beograd, 1964.

Mitrović, Andrej, et al. *Studenti Beogradskog universiteta 1838-1941, hronologija političkog života*. Beograd, 1971.

Mousset, Jean. *La Serbie et son église (1830-1904)*. Paris, 1938.

Nedeljković, Milorad. *Istorija srpskih državnih dugova*. Beograd, 1909.

Nenadović, Ljubomir. *Odabrana dela*. Novi Sad, 1959.

Nikić, Fedor. *Lokalna uprava Srbije u XIX i XX veku*. Beograd, 1927.

Nikolić, Milen. *Spomenica Kragujevačke gimnazije (1833-1933)*. Kragujevac, 1934.

Novaković, Stojan. *Jovan Sterijin Popović (1806-1856)*. Beograd, 1907.

Novaković, Stojan. *Srpska bibliografija za noviju književnost 1741-1867*. Beograd, 1869.

Paton, Andrew Archibald. *Servia, the Youngest Member of the European Family*. London, 1845.

Petković-Popović, Radmila-Šalipurović, Vukoman. *Srpske škole i prosveta u zapadnim krajevima stare Srbije u XIX veku*. Priboj, 1970.

Petrovich, Michael B. *The Emergence of Russian Panslavism, 1856-1870*. New York, 1956.

__________. "A History of Modern Serbia, 1804-1918." (Manuscript)

Petrovich, Woislav. *Serbia, Her People, History, and Aspirations*. London, 1915.

Petrović, Branko. *Jovan Ristić*. Beograd, 1912.

Petrović, Dušan K. "Spomenica Beogradske bogoslovije, 1836-1936." Manuscript, Bogoslovija "Sv. Savo," Beograd.

Petrović, Mihailo S. *Beograd pre sto godina*. Beograd, 1930.

Petrović, Mita. *Finansije i ustanove obnovljene Srbije do 1842*. 3 Vols, Beograd, 1897, 1898, 1899.

Petrović, Stojan. *Sto godina poljoprivrednih škola u Srbiji*. Beograd, 1956.

Pirch, Otto Dubislav. *Putovanje po Srbiji u godini 1829*. Translated from the German by Dragiša Mijušković. Beograd, 1900.

Polovina, Pera. *Udžbenici francuskog jezika kod Srba do 1914*. Beograd, 1964.

Popov, Nil. *Rossiia i Serbiia*. 2 Vols., Moscow, 1869.

__________. *Srbija i Rusija od Kočine krajine do Sv. Andrejevske skupštine*. 4 Vols., Beograd, 1870.

__________. *Srbija posle Pariskog mira*. Beograd.

Popović, Dušan J. *Srbija i Beograd*. Beograd, 1950.

Popović, Gavrilo. *Politički programi u prošlosti i sadašnjosti*. Beograd, 1889.

Popović, Miodrag. *Djura Daničić*. Beograd, 1959.

__________. *Vuk Stef. Karadžić*. Beograd, 1972.

Popović, Pavle. *Univerzitet i njegov materijalni razvitak*. Beograd, 1925.

Popović, Streten L. *Putovanje po novoj Srbiji*. Beograd, 1950.

Popović, Vasilj. *Evropa i srpsko pitanje u periodu oslobodjenja (1804-1918)*. Beograd, 1937.

__________. *Istočno pitanje*. Beograd, 1928.

Posniković, Dragutin. *Život i dela vrsnih Srba*. Beograd, 1880.

Potkozarac, Jovan. *Srbi u prošlosti*. 2 Vols, Beograd, 1969.

Predlog Prvozovno-andrejskoj narodnoj skupštini 1858 god. podnesen Vladimirom Jakšićem. Beograd, 1858.

Prodanović, Jaša. *Istorija političkih stranaka i struja u Srbiji*. Beograd, 1947.

__________. *Ustavni razvitak i ustavne borbe u Srbiji*. Beograd, 1936.

Protić, Ljubomir M. *Gimnazija Miloša Velikog*. Beograd, 1900.

__________. *Glavni prosvetni savet*. Beograd, 1910.

Pržić, Ilija. *Spoljašnja politika Srbije, 1804-1914*. Beograd, 1939.

Radovanović, Miloš V. *Zloupotreba službenog položaja ili ovlašćenja*. Beograd, 1858.

Ranke, Leopold. *Srbija i Turska u devetnaestom veku*. Translated from German by Stojan Novaković. Beograd, 1892.

Ruvarac, Ilarion. *Šta se i kako se i s koje strane pokušavalo da se kod nas osnuje seminarija za kandidate svešteničkog reda*. Sremski Karlovci, 1887.

Schevill, Ferdinand. *History of the Balkan Peninsula*. New York, 1966.

Simić, Nenad. *Knez Miloš i srpska umetnost*. Beograd, 1960.

Simić, Vasilije. *Iz skorašnje prošlosti rudarstva u Srbiji*. Beograd, 1960.

Skerlić, Jovan. *Omladina i njena književnost*. Beograd, 1925.

Slijepčević, Djoko. *Istorija srpske pravoslavne crkve*. 2 Vols, Munich, 1966.

Spasić, Milovan. *Pedagogično-metodično nastavlenije za učitelje osnovni škola*. Beograd, 1857.

Spomenica Čačanske realne gimnazije (1837-1937). Čačak, 1938.

Spomenica Josifa Pančića. SKA, Posebna izdanja, knj. CXXVIII, Beograd, 1939.

Spomenica sedamdesetpetogodišnjice Vojne akademije, 1850-1925. Beograd, 1925.

Spomenica - Srpske novine 1834-1934. Beograd, 1934.

Spomenica Stojana Novakovića. Beograd, 1921.

Spomenica Šabačke gimnazije, 1836-1936. Šabac, 1938.

Stavrianos, L.S. *Balkan Federation: A History of the Movement toward Balkan Unity in Modern Times*. Smith College Studies in History, Vol. XXVII, Northampton, MA, 1944.

__________. *The Balkans, 1815-1914*. New York, 1963.

__________. *The Balkans Since 1453*. New York, 1965.

Stojadinović, Rajko-Živković, Milovan, ed. *125.godišnjica Knjažesko-srbskog teatra u Kragujevcu*. Kragujevac, 1960.

Stojančević, Vladimir. *Miloš Obrenović i njegovo doba*. Beograd, 1966.

Stojanović, Ljuba. *Život i rad Vuka Stefanovića Karadžića*. Beograd, 1924.

Stojković, Andrija. *Razvitak filozofije u Srba, 1804-1944*. Beograd, 1972.

Stranjaković, Dragoslav. *Jugoslovenski nacionalni državni program kneževine Srbije 1844*. Novi Sad, 1931.

__________. *Srbija Pijemont južnih Slovena, 1842-1853*. Beograd, 1932.

__________. *Vlada ustavobranitelja, 1842-1858*. Beograd, 1932.

__________. *Vučićeva buna 1842.god*. Beograd, 1936.

Sumner, B.H. *Russia and the Balkans, 1870-1880*. Oxford, 1937.

Šlang, Ignjat. *Jevreji u Beogradu*. Beograd, 1926.

Štedimlija, S.M. *Kulturnopolitičla razmatranja*. Zagred, 1939.

Šumarević, Svetislav. *Čitalište*. Beograd, 1938.

__________. *Dimitrije Davidović, biografski momenti*. Beograd, 1934.

__________. *Podunavka-dokumentarni prilog istoriji srpske štampe*. Beograd, 1938.

__________. *Pozorište kod Srba*. Beograd, 1939.

Tartalja, Ivo. *Počeci rada na istoriji opšte književnosti kod Srba*. Beograd, 1964.

Temperley, Harold W.V. *History of Serbia*. London, 1917.

Tešić, Vladeta M. "Moralno vaspitanje u školama Srbije of 1830.do 1878." Unpublished Ph.D. dissertation, University of Belgrade, 1961.

__________. *Škole u Beogradu pre sto godina*. Beograd, 1967.

Tipa, Petar A. *Gimnazija kralja Aleksandra I u XIX veku*. Beograd, 1900.

Tokin, Milan. *Jovan Sterija Popović*. Beograd, 1956.

Tomašević, Jozo. *Peasants, Politics and Economic Change in Yugoslavia.* Stanford, CA, 1954.

Vasiljević, Alimpije. *Beseda koju je govorio G.A.Vasiljević, državni savetnik, pri opelu Dimitrija Matića, državnog savetnika.* Beograd, 1884.

__________. *Istorija narodnog obrazovanja kod Srba.* Vol. 1, Beograd, 1867.

__________. *Narodno obrazovanje kod Srba.* Vol. 1, Beograd, 1867.

__________. *Sveto-andrejska skupština.* Beograd, 1899.

Vivian, Herbert. *Servia, the Poor Man's Paradise.* London, 1897.

Vrhovac, R. *Karakter i rad Djure Daničića.* Novi Sad, 1923.

Vučković, Vojislav. *Srpska kriza u istočnom pitanju (1842-1843).* Beograd, 1957.

Vučo, Nikola. *Privredna istorija Srbije do I svetskog rata.* Beograd, 1955.

__________. *Raspadanje esnafa u Srbiji.* 2 Vols, Beograd, 1954, 1958.

Vukićević, Milenko. *Spomenica o otvaranju Universiteta.* Beograd, 1906.

__________. *Škole i školovanje za vreme Prvog ustanka, 1804-1813.*

Zhigarev, Sergei. *Russkaia politka v Vostochnom voprose.* 2 Vols., Moscow, 1896.

Zrnić, Luka. *Srpske djačke družine.* Beograd, 1912.

Živadinović, Milan Z. *Srpski advokati u XIX veku.* Beograd, 1969.

Živanović, Jakov. *Nadgrobno slovo Dimitriju Isailoviću.* Beograd, 1853.

Živanović, Živan. *Politička istorija Srbije u drugoj polovini XIX veka.* Beograd, 1923.

Živković, Dragiša. *Počeci srpske književne kritike (1817-1860)*. Beograd, 1957.

ARTICLES

Auty, Phyllis. "Neobjavljeni dokumenti engleskog ministarstva spoljnih poslova o Srbiji, 1837-1911." *Istorijski časopis*, knj. XII-XIII, Beograd, 1963, pp. 413-443.

Bajić, Slobodan. "Škola u Velikom selu - jedna od najstarijih u okolini Beograda." *Nastava i vaspitanje*, Nos. 9-10, Beograd, 1962, pp. 473-476.

Ban, Matija. "Život majora Miše Anastasijevića." *Glasnik* SUD, No. 71, Beograd, 1890, pp. 259-291.

Bodganović, Katarina. "Dimitrije Davidović." *Srpski književni glasnik*, knj. XXV, Nos. 230-231, Beograd, 1910, pp. 278-292; 359-372.

Borisavljević, Miloje K. "Zabrana 'Šumadinke' (1850.godine) - književno-istoriska slika." *Godišnjica Nikole Čupića*, knj. XXX, Beograd, 1911, pp. 181-201.

Bošković, Stojan. "U spomen Dimitriju Matiću." *Glasnik* SUD, No. LXIX, Beograd, 1889, pp. 163-242.

Bourchier, J.D. "A Balkan Confederation." *Fortnightly Review*, No. LVI (September, 1891), pp. 365-377.

Boyle, E. "Towards Balkan Unity." *Contemporary Review*, No. 151 (April, 1937), pp. 404-409.

Branković, Kosta. "Razvitak Velike škole." *Glasnik* SUC, No. XVIII, Beograd, 1865, pp. 1-24.

Cvijetić, Leposava. "Pokušaji osnivanja prvih banaka u Srbiji." *Finansije*, No. 1, Beograd, 1965, pp. 117-123.

__________. "Poreska reforma u Srbiji i stav Vuka Karadžića." *Finansije*, No. 1, Beograd, 1965, pp. 103-119.

Čubrilović, Vaso. "Garašanin Ilija." *Enciklopedija Jugoslavije*, Vol. 3, Zagreb, 1958, pp. 428-429.

__________. "Garašaninovo Načertanije." *Enciklopedija Jugoslavije*, Vol. 3, Zagreb, 1958, p. 429.

Ćorović, Vladimir. "Jedan memorandum Ljudevita Gaja o prilikama u Srbiji 1846.godine." *Spomenik*, No. 62, Beograd, 1925, pp. 71-77.

Dimić, Natilija and Platon. "Nastava u Beogradskom liceju u toku prve dve godine njegovog postojanja." *Savremena škola*, Nos. 1-2, Beograd, 1959, pp. 57-68.

Drobnjaković, B.M. "Prvi naš muzejski inventar." *Muzeji*, Nos. 3-4, Beograd, 1949, pp. 35-46.

Durković-Jakšić, Ljubomir. "Austrija i pitanje jurisdikcije nad rimokatolicima u kneževini Srbiji, 1851-1860." *Istorijski glasnik*, No. 2, Beograd, 1956, pp. 44-56.

__________. "Gajev pokušaj da izdaje 'Narodne novine' ćirilicom." *Istorijski časopis*, knj. IV, Beograd, 1954, pp. 95-129.

__________. "Ljubomir Nenadović i Poljaci (1845-1849)." *Istorijski glasnik*, Beograd, 1949, pp. 75-80.

__________. "O počecima Svetosavske proslave u školi." *Glasnik*, službeni list Srpske pravoslavne patrijaršije, Beograd, 1953, pp. 41-44.

__________. "O prvim srpskim štampanim knjigama u Trstu." *Bibliotekar*, Nos. 3-4, Beograd, 1955, pp. 147-153.

__________. "O Stevanu Hrkaloviću." *Istorijski časopis*, Nos. XVI-XVII, Beograd, 1970, pp. 109-132.

__________. "Objavljivanje prvog srpskog kalendara u Trstu." *Bibliotekar*, No. 4, Beograd, 1954, pp. 224-229.

__________. "Objavljivanje srpskih bukvara u Trstu 1849." *Bibliotekar*, Nos. 1-2, Beograd, 1953, pp. 21-26.

Durković-Jakšić, Ljubomir. "Osnivanje Univerzitetske biblioteke u Beogradu." *Godišnjak grada Beograda*, knj. XIII, Beograd, 1966, pp. 229-252.

________. "Proglašenje i proslava školskog patrona u Srbiji 1840.god." *Glasnik*, službeni list Sprske pravoslavne patrijaršije, Beograd, 1947, pp. 34-36.

________. "Prvi štampani plakat za priredbe i prikazivanja u knjaževini Srbiji." *Bibliotekar*, Nos. 1-3, Beograd, 1961, pp. 74-76.

________. "Učestvovanje poljskih revolucionara u životu Beograda početkom druge polovine XIX veka." *Godišnjak grada Beograda*, knj. XIV, Beograd, 1967, pp. 45-60.

Džambazovski, Kliment. "Nekoliko priloga o prvim koracima na kulturno-političkoj saradnji srpskog i bugarskog naroda u prvoj polovini XIX veka." *Istorijski časopis*, Nos. XVI-XVII, Beograd, 1970, pp. 91-109.

________. "Školovanje bugarskog svešteničkog kadra u kneževini Srbiji." *Balkanika*, Vol. 2, Beograd, 1971, pp. 175-193.

Džonić, Uroš. "Družina 'Omladina licejska'." SAN *Zbornik radova*, knj. XVII, Beograd, 1952, pp. 351-369.

________. "Jovan Ilić kao licejac." *Prilozi za književnost, jezik i folklor*, knj. XVIII, Nos. 1-2, Beograd, 1938, pp. 190-196.

________. "Školovanje Jovana Ilića u inostranstvu." *Prilozi za književnost, jezik i folklor*, knj. XIX, Nos. 1-2, Beograd, 1939, pp. 121-141.

Džuverović, Miodrag. "Školstvo u Beogradu." *Godišnjak Muzeja grada Beograda*, Vol. 1, Beograd, 1954, pp. 372-381.

"Djeneral Franja A. Zah (nekrolog)." *Službeni vojni list*, Beograd, 1892, pp. 142-151.

Djordjević, Božidar. "Univerzitet u Beogradu, 1863-1963." *Godišnjak grada Beograda*, knj. IX-X, Beograd, 1963, pp. 5-79.

Djordjević, Jovan. "O Matiji Banu, povodom proslave 50-godišnjice njegovog književnog rada." *Glasnik SUD*, No. 65, Beograd, 1886, pp. 12-35.

Djordjević, Tihomir R. "Jevreji u Srbiji za vreme prve vlade kneza Miloša (1815-1839)." *Godišnjica Nikole Čupića*, knj. XXXV, Beograd, 1923, pp. 202-211.

__________. "Književne prilike u Srbiji pre sto godina." *Srpski književni glasnik*, Nos. 3, 4, 5, Beograd, 1932, pp. 174-181; 262-271; 338-350.

__________. "Profesori i učitelji u Srbiji 1836.godine." *Učetilj*, No. 8, Beograd, 1923, pp. 553-570.

__________. "Prvo uputstvo za državne pitomce na strani." *Misao*, Nos. 228-232, Beograd, 1929, pp. 228-231.

__________. "Školske prilike u Srbiji za vreme prve vlade kneza Miloša Obrenovića (1815-1839)." *Prosvetni glasnik*, Nos. 5-6, Beograd, 1920, pp. 265-276; 329-337.

Djordjević, Vladan. "Beseda koju je na opelu prof.dr. Josifa Pančića 26.februara 1888. u Sabornoj crkvi govorio dr. Vladan Djordjević." *Otadžbina*, knj. 18, Beograd, 1888, pp. I-VII.

__________. "Jedan memorandum Ljudevita Gaja o prilikama u Srbiji iz 1846.godine." *Spomenik Srpske Kraljevske Akademije*, No. 62, Beograd, 1925, pp. 71-77.

Djordjević, Živojin S. "Istorijski pregled nastavnih planova i programa za osnovne škole u Srbiji." *Nastava i vaspitanje*, No. 1, Beograd, 1952, pp. 79-86.

__________. "Naše čitanke u 18. i 19. veku." *Nastava i vaspitanje*, No. 5, Beograd, 1952, pp. 381-385.

__________. "Naši stari udžbenici za osnovne i srednje škole." *Nastava i vaspitanje*, Nos. 1-2, Beograd, 1953, pp. 108-110.

__________. "Škole u Karadjordjevoj Srbiji, 1804-1813." *Učitelj*, No. 6, Beograd, 1935, pp. 426-438.

Djordjević, Živojin S. "Škole u Šumadiji u prošlosti." *Šumadija u prošlosti i sadašnjosti*, Subotica, 1932, pp. 175-201.

__________. "Velika škola i Bogoslovija u Karadjordjevo doba." *Učitelj*, No. 7, Beograd, 1935, pp. 503-507.

Djurić, Hajrudin. "Obrenovići i Šafarik." *Glasnik Jugoslovenskog profesorskog društva*, knj. XX, No. 1, Beograd, 1939, pp. 20-21.

Djurković, Olga. "Djordje Mušicki - profesor fizike na Liceumu (1841-1843)." *Hemijski pregled*, knj. VII, Nos. 4-5, Beograd, 1956, pp. 71-76.

__________. "Mihail Rašković prvi profesor hemije i tehnologije na Liceumu i Velikoj školi u Beogradu." *Glasnik hemijskog društva*, knj. 19, No. 8, Beograd, 1954, pp. 461-489.

__________. "Prilog istoriji nastave iz fizike i hemije na Liceumu, 1839-1863." *Glasnik hemijskog društva*, knj. 20, No. 9, Beograd, 1955, pp. 585-607.

__________. "Uvodjenje nastave iz 'Jestestvoslovnotehničkih nauka' na Liceumu drugom polovinom XIX stoleća." *Hemijski pregled*, knj. VI, No. 6, Beograd, 1955, pp. 121-125.

__________. "Vuk Marinković, profesor fizike na Liceumu (1849-1859)." *Hemijski pregled*, knj. VII, No. 6, Beograd, 1956, pp. 119-124.

"Djuro Daničić (nekrolog)." *Prosvetni glasnik*, No. 22, Beograd, 1882, pp. 817-819.

Ekmečić, Milorad. "Nacionalna politika Srbije prema Bosni i Hercegovini i agrarno pitanje (1844-1875)." *Godišnjak istorijskog društva Bosne i Hercegovine*, No. X, Sarajevo, 1959, pp. 197-219.

Feher, Ipolj. "Srednje škole u Srbiji." Translated from Hungarian. *Letopis Matice srpske*, knj. 158, No. 2, Novi Sad, 1889, pp. 115-137.

Gavrilović, Andra. "Iz života Dimitrija Davidovića po arhivskim podacima." *Godišnjica Nikole Čupića*, knj. XXXI, Beograd, 1912, pp. 107-124.

Gavrilović, Andra. "Iz života Dr. J. Pančića." *Godišnjica Nikole Čupića*, knj. XXXIII, Beograd, 1913, pp. 74-81.

__________. "'Šumadinka,' kulturno istoriska slika." *Godnišjica Nikole Čupića*, knj. 19, Beograd, 1899, pp. 25-33.

Gavrilović, Bogdan. "Evolucija više nastave u Srbiji." *Spomenica o otvaranju univerziteta*, Beograd, 1906, pp. 1-14.

Gavrilović, Jovan. "Glavni izvod popisa u Srbii godine 1854/5." *Glasnik*, DSS, Beograd, 1857, pp. 224-226.

__________. "Prilog za geografiju i statsiku Srbije." *Glasnik*, DSS, knj. 3, Beograd, 1851, pp. 186-190.

Gavrilović, Mihailo. "The Diplomatic Relations of Great Britain and Serbia." *Slavonica Review*, No. 1 (June, 1922), pp. 86-109.

Grujić, Vladimir. "Josif Pančic kao profesor Liceja i Velike škole u Beogradu." *Godišnjak grada Beograda*, Beograd, 1963, pp. 99-123.

__________. "Jovan St. Popović kao pisac udžbenika." *Zbornik Filozofskog fakulteta*, knj. IV-I, Beograd, 1956, pp. 337-352.

__________. "Jovan St. Popović profesor prava na liceju u Kragujevcu i Beogradu." *Književnost*, knj. XXIII, Nos. 7-8, Beograd, 1956, pp. 141-151.

__________. "Kulturne veze Beograda sa Bosnom i Hercegovinom sredinom XIX veka." *Godišnjak grada Beograda*, knj. XIII, Beograd, 1966, pp. 73-103.

__________. "Nekolike kulturne veze Srbije i Crne Gore sredinom prošlog veka." *Nastava i vaspitanje*, Nos. 1-2, Beograd, 1954, pp. 125-128.

__________. "Nastava egzaktnih nauka na početku delovanja Liceja." *Nauka i priroda*, No. 8, Beograd, 1954, pp. 353-360.

__________. "Nastava Filozofskog fakulteta Liceja od osnivanja do polovine prošlog veka." *Godišnjak Muzeja grada Beograda*, knj. IV, Beograd, 1957, pp. 295-312.

Grujić, Vladimir. "'Nastavlenije' i prva knjiga u obliku udžbenika za pedagogiju štampana u Beogradu." *Godišnjak Muzeja grada Beograda*, knj. V, Beograd, 1958, pp. 95-112.

__________. "O prvom školskom zakonu Srbije, Ustrojeniju javnog učilišnog nastavlenija." *Nastava i vaspitanje*, No. 1, Beograd, 1955, pp. 44-49.

__________. "Početak rada na predškolskom vaspitanju u Beogradu." *Godišnjak Muzeja grada Beograda*, knj. VII, Beograd, 1960, pp. 107-113.

__________. "Pravničko obrazovanje na Liceju posle 1844." *Anali Pravnog fakulteta u Beogradu*, Beograd, 1955, pp. 77-85.

__________. "Pravničko obrazovanje na Liceju u početku njegovog rada." *Anali Pravnog fakulteta u Beogradu*, No. 2, Beograd, 1954, pp. 194-205.

__________. "Pravoslovne nauke na Liceju u njihovom zasnivanju." *Arhiv za pravne i društvene nauke*, No. 4, Beograd, 1951, pp. 672-676.

__________. "Prve naučne 'Ekspedicije Jestestvoslova' sa Liceja u 1857-1863.godini." *Nauka i priroda*, No. 10, Beograd, 1953, pp. 457-466.

__________. "Prvi profesori egzaktno-prirodnih nauka na Liceju." *Nauka i priroda*, No. 9, Beograd, 1954, pp. 409-414.

__________. "Prvi profesori 'Pravoslovnog' fakulteta na Liceju u Kragujevcu i Beogradu." *Anali pravnog fakulteta u Beogradu*, Beograd, 1955, pp. 448-455.

__________. "Rad Jovana St. Popovića na osnivanju akademije nauka, naučnih zbirki i nekih socijalnih ustanova." *Istorijski glasnik*, No. 4, Beograd, 1965, pp. 93-98.

__________. "Rad Jovana St. Popovića u Društvu srpske slovesnosti." *Književnost*, knj. XXII, No. 2, Beograd, 1956, pp. 186-192.

__________. "Školsko pitanje na Petrovskoj skupštini 1848.godine u Kragujevcu i neke posledice." *Pedagoška stvarnost*, No. 9, Novi Sad, 1956, pp. 593-598.

Grujić, Vladimir. "Više obrazovanje u Srbiji za prvih sedam decenija XIX veka." *Godišnjak grada Beograda*, knj. XIV, Beograd, 1967, pp. 203-254.

__________. "Zamisao 'Seminarijuma učiteljskog' u 1846.god." *Nastava i vaspitanje*, No. 4, Beograd, 1952, pp. 296-297.

Guzina, Ružica. "Istorijski osvrt na karakter i značaj srpskog gradjanskog zakonika od 1844.godine." *Istorijski glasnik*, No. 2, Beograd, 1949, pp. 22-37.

Ignjić, Stevan. "Iz istorije užičkih škola-prva polovina XIX veka." *Nastava i vaspitanje*, No. 4, Beograd, 1959, pp. 224-229.

Ivanić, Momčilo. "Stojan Bošković." *Godišnjica Nikole Čupića*, No. XXVIII, Beograd, 1909, pp. 305-322.

__________. "Život i književni rad Vuk Stefanovića Karadžića." *Otadžbina*, knj. 20, Beograd, 1888, pp. 321-334.

Jaćimović, Olga. "Kancelarijsko poslovanje u Srbiji prve polovine XIX veka." *Arhivist*, Nos. 3-4, Beograd, 1957, pp. 49-59.

Jakšić, Grgur. "Izveštaj Ljudevita Gaja o Srbiji 1847." *Srpski književni glasnik*, No. 11, Beograd, 1924, pp. 368-377.

Janković, Bosiljka. "Čitalište beogradsko." *Bibliotekar*, Nos. 1-3, Beograd, 1954, pp. 10-16; 78-85; 145-153.

Janković, Miloš B. "Izdržavanje narodnih škola." *Učiteljska borba*, No. 1, Beograd, 1911, pp.199-204.

__________. "Petar Karić (1838-1871)." *Savremena škola*, No. 8, Beograd, 1953, pp. 459-464.

__________. "Škola za vreme prvog ustanka." *Savremena škola*, No. 8, Beograd, 1953, pp. 614-623.

__________. "Učitelji u Srbiji (1815-1870)." *Savremena škola*, No. 9, Beograd, 1954, pp. 347-361.

Janković, Miloš B. "Veliki prilog Vuka Karadžića istoriji školstva." *Prosvetni pregled*, No. 4, Beograd, 1964.

__________. "Vuk Karadžić o učiteljima u doba kneza Miloša." *Prosvetni pregled*, Nos. 7-8, Beograd, 1964.

Jeftić, Pavle M. "Sterijina delatnost na podizanju prosvete i kulture." *Pedagoška stvarnost*, No. 4, Novi Sad, 1956, pp. 248-256.

Jovanović, Aleksa. "Srpske škole pod Turcima." *Spomenica dvadesetpetogodišnjice oslobodjenja Južne Srbije 1912-1937*, Skoplje, 1937, pp. 241-270.

Jovanović, Bogoljub. "Privatne škole u Kraljevini Srbiji." *Prosvetni glasnik*, No. XV, Beograd, 1885, pp. 450-459; 505-509.

__________. "Stanje javne nastave u Kneževini Srbiji za 1875-76.školsku godinu." *Prosvetni glasnik*, Nos. 8, 9, 11, 12, 13, Beograd, 1881, pp. 299-303; 341-351; 415-423; 446-449; 470-476.

Jovanović, Ljubomir. "Pregled nacionalno-političkog života srpskog u XX veku." *Srpski književni glasnik*, Nos. 1-3, Beograd, 1901, pp. 346-353.

Jovanović, Slobodan. "Serbia in the Early Seventies." *Slavonic Review*, No. IV (December, 1925), pp. 385-395.

__________. "Spoljašna politika Ilije Garašanina." *Srpski književni glasnik*, No. 34, Beograd, 1931, pp. 422-431.

Jovanović, Vladimir. "Alimpije Vasiljević." *Srpski književni glasnik*, knj. XXVI, Nos. 8-9, Beograd,1911, pp. 596-608; 698-711.

__________. "Stojan Bošković." *Srpski književni glasnik*, No. 172 (XX,6), Beograd, 1908, pp. 422-435.

Kićović, Miraš. "Prvi rukovodioci Narodne biblioteke u Beogradu." *Godišnjak Muzeja grada Beograda*, knj. IV, Beograd, 1957, pp. 261-294.

Kirilović, Dimitrije. "Naše stare škole po opisu njihovih učenika." *Pedagoška stvarnost*, No. 5, Novi Sad, 1956, pp. 307-312.

Knežević, Milivoje. "Iz autobiografije Milovana Spasića." *Nastava i vaspitanje*, No. 9, Beograd, 1956, pp. 548-552.

Kolarić, Miodrag. "Strani umetnici u Beogradu u XVIII i XIX veku." *Godišnjak grada Beograda*, knj. VII, Beograd, 1960, pp. 197-307.

Kostić, Milan P. "Dr. Atanasije Teodorović prvi profesor Liceja." *Naučni zbornik Matice srpske*, No. 1, Novi Sad, 1950, pp. 81-92.

Kovačević, Božidar. "O Jeverjima u Srbiji." *Jevrejski almanah*, Beograd, 1959/60, pp. 105-113.

Kovijanić, Gavrilo. "Narodna biblioteka nije osnovana u Vozarovićevoj radnji 1832.godine." *Bibliotekar*, No. 1, Beograd, 1971, pp. 5-16.

__________. "Srspke novine." *Bibliotekar*, Nos. 1-3, Beograd, 1966, pp. 153-163.

L.St. "Stojan Bošković." *Delo*, No. XLVI, Beograd, 1908, pp. 386-390.

Lukić, Radomir D. "Jovan Sterija Popović - profesor prirodnog prava na Liceju." *Anali Pravnog fakulteta u Beogradu*, No. 5, Beograd, 1957, pp. 1-14.

M.M.B. "Prve godine života naših gimnazija." *Prosvetni glasnik*, No. 6, Beograd, 1989, pp. 302-308.

Maksimović, Branko. "Arhitektonska teorija Emilijana Josimovića." *Godišnjak Muzeja grada Beograda*, knj. III, Beograd, 1956. pp. 295-301.

Maletić, Djordje. "Istorijski razvitak gimnazije beogradske." *Glasnik* SUD, knj. VII, No. 24, Beograd,1868, pp. 136-163.

Marić, Dragomir. "Osnivanje bogoslovije u Srbiji za vreme kneza Miloša." *Hrišćanska misao*, Beograd, 1936, pp. 126-128.

Marinović, Jovan. "Stanje javnog nastavlenija u Knjažestvu Serbii." *Glasnik*, DSS, No. 1, Beograd, 1847, pp. 201-205.

Marković, Ljubomir M. "Milendžanska škola." *Nastava i vaspitanje*, Nos. 5-6, Beograd, 1959, pp. 331-343.

Marković, Radosav P. "Iz uspomena Nićifora Ninkovića." *Naučni zbornik Matice srpske*, No. 7, Novi Sad, 1954, pp. 146-156.

__________. "Sto godina gimnazije gospodara Jevrema u Šapcu." *Glasnik Jugoslovenskog profesorskog društva*, knj. XVIII, Beograd, 1937, pp. 33-44.

__________. "Stogodišnjica bogoslovije Sv.Save." *Glasnik Jugoslovenskog profesorskog društva*, knj. XVIII, Beograd, 1936, pp. 1-11.

__________. "Školski patronat Sv.Save - prvo zvanično proglašenje u Kneževini Srbiji." *Glasnik Jugoslovenskog profesorskog društva*, knj. XVII, Beograd, 1936, pp. 296-314.

Marković, Svetozar. "Kako su nas vaspitali." In Najdan Pašić, ed. *Svetozar Marković - sabrani spisi*. Beograd, 1960, pp. 30-57.

McDonald, H.M. "Karl Marx, Friedrich Engles, and the South Slavic Problem in 1848-1849." *University of Toronto Quarterly*, No. VIII (July, 1939), pp. 452-460.

Medaković, Dejan. "Iz prošlosti srpskih muzeja." *Delo*, No. 4, Beograd, 1955, pp. 429-436.

__________. "Ka liku Anastasa Jovanovića." *Istorijski glasnik*, No. 1, Beograd, 1949, pp. 87-90.

Mijatovics, E.L. "Panslavism: Its Rise and Decline." *Fortnightly Review*, No. IX (July, 1873), pp. 94-112.

Milićević, Jovan. "Istorija Katanske bune." *Zbornik Filozofskog fakulteta*, knj. V/1, Beograd, 1960, pp.269-311.

__________. "Narodne skupštine u Srbiji, 1839-1843." *Zbornik Filozofskog fakulteta*, knj. IV/1, Beograd, 1956, pp. 157-194.

__________. "Petrovska skupština." *Istorijski glasnik*, Nos. 1-2, Beograd, 1959, pp. 41-59.

__________. "Prilog pozanavanju ustavne krize u Srbiji uoči revolucije 1848." *Zbornik Filozofskog fakulteta*, knj. 8, No. 2, Beograd, 1964, pp. 665-670.

Milićević, Jovan. "Prve grupe srbijanskih studenata, državnih stipendista školovanih u inostranstvu (1839-1842)." *Istorijski časopis*, Nos. IX-X, Beograd, 1960, pp. 363-373.

__________. "Toma Vučić-Perišić." *Istorijski glasnik*, Nos. 1-2, Beograd, 1957, pp. 108-113.

Milićević, Milan Dj. "Crtice za raniju sliku srpske prestonice." *Godišnjica Nikole Čupića*, knj. 22, Beograd, 1903, pp. 5-56.

__________. "Škole u Srbiji." *Glasnik* SUD, No. 24, Beograd, 1868, pp. 1-135.

Milivojev, Ivana and Djordje Vuković. "Od Liceja do Velike škole." *Student* (March 26), Beograd, 1963.

Miljković, Branislav. "Društvo srpske slovesnosti od 1841-1864.god." *Članci i prilozi o srpskoj književnosti prve polovine XIX veka*, Knjiga Matice srpske, No. 46, Novi Sad, 1914, pp. 18-81.

Milovanović, Radivoje T. "Prosveta u Srbiji krajem XVIII i početkom XIX veka." *Nastava i vaspitanje*, Nos. 2-3, Beograd, 1952, pp. 180-184.

__________. "Prosveta u Srbiji za vlade ustavobranitelja (1842-1858). *Savremena škola*, Nos. 5-6, Beograd, 1959, pp. 246-260.

Miodragović, Jov. "M.Dj. Milićević (nekrolog)." *Godišnjica Nikole Čupića*, knj. XXVIII, Beograd, 1909, pp. 295-303.

__________. "Narodno prosvećivanje u Srbiji u prošlom veku." *Godišnjica Nikole Čupića*, knj. 30, Beograd, 1911, pp. 235-258.

Mišić, Smilja. "Iz istorije Beogradskog liceja." *Srpski književni glasnik*, No. LIII, Beograd, 1938, pp. 443-450.

Mladenović, Živomir. "Napadi na Vuka u 'Srpskom ulaku'." *Kovčežić*, No. 3, Beograd, 1960, pp. 44-63.

Mosely, P.E. "Pan-slavist Memorandum of Ljudevit Gaj in 1838." *American Historical Review*, No. XL (July, 1935), pp. 704-716.

Mosely, P.E. "The Peasant Family: The *Zadruga* or Communial Joint-Family in the Balkans and Its Recent Evolution." In C.F. Ware, ed. *The Cultural Approach to History*. New York, 1940, pp. 95-108.

Mučalica, Olga. "Daničićevo službovanje u Beogradu." *Književnost i jezik*, Nos. 8-9, Beograd, 1956, pp. 425-433.

__________. "O arhivskom fondu Liceja." *Arhivski almanah*, Nos. 2-3, Beograd, 1960, pp. 53-70.

__________. "Od liceja do univerziteta u Beogradu (1838-1920)." *Nastava i vaspitanje*, Nos. 9-10, Beograd, 1963, pp. 455-463.

__________. "Osnivanje katedre istorije i književnosti i njen prvi profesor u liceju." *Arhivski almanah*, No. 1, Beograd, 1958, pp. 177-190.

__________. "Sterija u Srbiji." *Književnost i jezik u školi*, No. 1, Beograd, 1956, pp. 7-17.

Nedić, Ljubomir. "Nastavlenije mladićima, koji su u strane Države izučenija radi različni polezni znanija pošilju." *Nastavnik*, knj. 3, No. 6, Beograd, 1892, pp. 676-678.

"Nekrolog Djuri Daničiću." *Otadžbina*, knj. 11, Beograd, 1882, pp. 614-628.

"Nekrolog Koste Brankovića." *Glasnik* SUD, knj. 2, No. 19, Beograd, 1866, pp. 346-349.

Nikić, Ljubomir. "Autobiografija Anastasa Jovanovića." *Godišnjak Muzeja grada Beograda*, Beograd,1956, pp. 389-416.

Nikolajević, Svetomir. "Kraljevska srpska Velika škola za 50 njenih godina." *Godišnjica Nikole Čupića*, knj. 12, Beograd, 1891, pp. 202-223.

Nikolić, Milen M. "Licej." *Iz prošlosti Kragujevca*, Subotica, 1926.

__________. "Prvi prosvetni i kulturni centar obnovljene Srbije." *Šumadija u prošlosti i sadašnjosti*, Subotica, 1932, pp. 159-175.

Novakov, Dragoljub. "Prilog istoriji Kragujevačkog liceja 1840.godine." *Naučni zbornik Matice srpske*, knj. 8, Novi Sad, 1954.

Novaković, Stojan. "Dr. Janko Šafarik." *Rad JAZU*, No. XLI, Zagreb, 1877, pp. 190-226.

Novitković, Jerotije. "Trgovačka nastava i trgovačke škole u Srbiji." *Glasnik Jugoslovenskog profesorskog društva*, knj. 20, Nos. 11-2, Beograd, 1940, pp. 894-903.

Nušić, Branislav Dj. "Is poluprošlosti." *Sabrana dela*, Vol. 2, Beograd, 1935.

__________. "'Oda Sultanu' - jedno sećanje iz prošlosti," *Srpski književni glasnik*, knj. XXVI, No. 4, Beograd, 1911, pp. 257-263.

Obradović, Olga. "Osnivanje prvih ženskih škola u Beogradu." *Izveštaj V ženske gimnazije u Beogradu za 1939/40*, Beograd, 1940, pp. 38-45.

Papahristu, Anastasija. "Grčke škole u Beogradu u XIX veku." *Nastava i vaspitanje*, No. 3, Beograd, 1970, pp. 354-375.

Parunovac, Miodrag. "Podizanje prvih školskih i bolničkih zgrada u Beogradu i zanatski esnafi." *Zanatski glasnik* (May 15), Beograd, 1955, p. 6.

Perović, Radoslav. "Beograd za vreme Vučićeve bune." *Godišnjak Muzeja grada Beograda*, knj. 2, Beograd, 1955, pp. 181-204.

__________. "Oko 'Načertanija' iz 1844.godine." *Istorijski glasnik*, No. 1, Beograd, 1963, pp. 71-94.

Pijuković, Nikola. "Sto dvadeset i pet godina od osnivanja državne štamparije u Beogradu." *Godišnjak Muzeja grada Beograda*, knj. IV, Beograd, 1957, pp. 381-414.

Popović, D.S. "Povodom stogodišnjice Čačanske gimnazije." *Glasnik Jugoslovenskog društva*, knj. 18, No. 2, Beograd, 1937, pp. 89-96.

Popović, Jovan S. "Razlozi o nazivoslovnim rečima." *Glasnik*, DSS, No. 1, Beograd, 1847, pp. 9-16.

Popović, Mihailo. "Konstantin Branković, profesor filozofije i pisac prvog
udžbanika logike na beogradskoj Velikoj školi." *Zbornik Filozofskog
fakulteta*, No. 3, Beograd, 1955, pp. 591-598.

__________. "Prva srpska istorija filozofije - Matićeva adaptacija Sveglerove
istorije Filozofije." *Naučni prilozi studenata Filozofskog fakulteta*,
Beograd, 1949, pp. 65-74.

Popović, Miodrag. "Jakov Ignjatović u četrdesetosmoj." *Prilozi za
književnost, jezik, istoriju i folklor*, knj. XXI, Nos. 1-2, Beograd,
1955, pp. 47-72.

__________. "Kosta Popović (1842-1864)." *Prilozi za književnost, jezik,
istoriju i folklor*, knj. XXIII, Nos. 1-2, Beograd, 1957, pp. 58-66.

__________. "Načertanije i srpski pisci oko četrdesetosme." *Savremenik*, No.
6, Beograd, 1958, pp. 693-715.

__________. "Nenadovićeva 'Šumadinka'." *Istorijski glasnik*, Beograd, 1954,
No. 4, pp. 91-126.

Popović, Olga. "Biblioteka Serbskog Liceuma." *Bibliotekar*, Nos. 1-2,
Beograd, 1951, pp. 1-12.

__________. "Opšta bibiloteka Velike škole." *Bibliotekar*, Nos. 3-4, Beograd,
1951, pp. 97-107.

Popović, S.D. "Povodom stogodišnjice Čačanske gimnazije." *Glasnik
Jugoslovenskog profesorskog društva*, knj. XVIII, No. 2, Beograd,
1937, pp. 89-96.

Popović, Slobodan. "Jovan St. Popović i nastave živih jezika." *Srpski
književni glasnik*, knj. LI, Beograd, 1937, pp. 562-563.

Popović, Vasilj. "Djački putopis mitropolita Mihaila." *Prilozi za
književnost, jezik i folklor*, knj. XVIII, Nos. 1-2, Beograd, 1938, pp.
445-449.

__________. "Meternihovi pogledi o promeni u Srbiji 1842.i 1843." *Prilozi
za istoriju, književnost, jezik i folklor*, Nos. 1-2, Beograd, 1927, pp.
123-129.

"Prilog za povestnicu raznih zavedenija u Srbii, naročito artiljeriskog, od vremena vlade Aleksandra Karadjordjevića, u ono vreme od jednog očevidca spisan." *Ogledalo srbsko*, knj. 1, Novi Sad, 1864, pp. 101-112.

Prokić, Bogoljub. "Razvoj školske inspekcije u Srbiji." *Nastava i vaspitanje*, No. 6, Beograd, 1955, pp. 367-371.

Pržić, Ilija. "Osnivanje Pravnog fakulteta u Srbiji." *Arhiv za pravne i društvene nauke*, Nos. 1-2, knj. 58, Beograd, 1940, pp. 1-17.

Radenić, Andrija. "Prve novine u Srbiji." *Počeci štampe Jugoslovenskih naroda*, Beograd, 1969, pp. 59-120.

Radević, Milorad. "'Kratki životopis' Konstantina Brankovića." *Istorijski časopis*, knj. XVIII, Beograd, 1971, pp. 383-391.

__________. "O prvom kursu ruskog jezika pri Velikoj školi u Beogradu." *Istorijski glasnik*, Nos. 2-3, Beograd, 1964, pp. 149-156.

__________. "Počeci nastave ruskog jezika u Beogradu." *Nastava i vaspitanje*, No. 4, Beograd, 1971, pp. 493-505.

__________. "Prvi Rusi profesori u Beogradu." *Istorijski glasnik*, No. 1, Beograd, 1965, pp. 85-93.

__________. "Velikoškolci i suspendovanje Društva srbske slovesnosti (1864)." *Istorijski časopis*, knj. XVI-XVII, Beograd, 1970, pp. 133-141.

Radojćić, Nikola. "Uvodjenje Srbije u svetsku nauku." *Letopis Matice srpske*, knj. 323, No. 1, Novi Sad, 1930, pp. 29-43.

Ruzovska, Višnja. "Josif Pančić.Život i rad." *Riječka revija*, No. 12, Rijeka, 1964, pp. 907-928.

Savićević, Miroslav and Ljubomir Durković-Jakšić. "Fragmenti iz Dnevnika Dimitrija Matića." *Danas*, Nos. 3, 5, 8, Beograd, 1961.

Seton-Watson, R.W. "Pan-slavism." *Contemporary Review*, No. CX (1916), pp. 419-429.

Simić, Nenad. "Obaveze srpskih državnih pitomaca u inostranstvu sredinom prošlog stoleća." *Zbornik za historiju školstva i prosvete*, No. 6, Zagreb, 1971, pp. 147-154.

Simović, Božidar. "Osnivanje Vojne akademije u Srbiji." *Vojnoistroijski glasnik*, No. 5, Beograd, 1965, pp. 67-90.

Sindik, Dušan. "O jevrejskim školama u Beogradu u XIX veku." *Jevrejski almanah*, Beograd, 1961/62, pp. 98-105.

Skerlić, Jovan. "Družina mladeži srpske." *Srpski književni glasnik*, No. 15, Beograd, 1905, pp. 427-442.

__________. "Pisma iz Pariza Ljubomira Nenadovića." *Srpski književni glasnik*, No. 15, Beograd, 1905, pp. 859-864.

Slankamenac, Prvoš. "Osnivanje i karakter Beogradskog liceja." *Savremena škola*, Nos. 3-4, Beograd, 1952, pp. 9-22.

Spasić, Milovan. "Državopisni podatci školski zavedenija u knaž, srbskom od 1856/57. do 1860/61.god.školske." *Glasnik*, DSS, knj. 14, Beograd, 1862, pp. 282-304.

__________. "Neki podaci o osnovnim školama u Srbiji od 1845. do 1861.godine." *Glasnik* SUD, knj. 73, Beograd, 1892, pp. 187-227.

__________. "Štatistični podatci školski zavedenija." *Glasnik*, DSS, knj. 9, Beograd, 1857, pp. 162-188.

Stavrianos, L.S. "The Balkan Federation Movement: A Neglected Aspect." *American Historical Review* (October, 1942), pp. 30-51.

Stoianovich, Traian. "The Pattern of Serbian Intellectual Evolution, 1830-1880." *Comparative Studies in Society and History*, Vol. 1, The Hague, 1958-59, pp. 242-272.

Stojančević, Vladimir. "Jedna Obrenovićevska zavera protiv ustavobraniteljskog režima 1846.godine." *Istorijski časopis*, knj. XIV-XV, Beograd, 1965, pp. 111-131.

Stojković, Andrija. "Društveno-politički i sociološki pogledi Vuka Karadžića u odnosu prema Dositejovim." *Jugoslovenski istorijski časopis*, No. 1, Beograd, 1965, pp. 27-39.

__________. "Filozofski pogledi Vuka Karadžića u odnosu prema Dositejovim." *Zbornik Filozofskog fakulteta*, knj. IX-2, Beograd, 1967, pp. 139-186.

__________. "Misaoni razvitak Vuka Karadžića u odnosu prema Dositejovim." *Filozofija*, No. 4, Beograd, 1965, pp. 493-502.

Stojković, Borivoje S. "Pozorište-od prvih početaka do 1914." *Enciklopedija Jugoslavije*, Vol. 7, Zagreb, 1968, pp. 565-570.

Stokić, Petar. "O postanku bogoslovije u Srbiji." *Vesnik srpske crkve*, Beograd, 1903, pp. 9-16.

Stranjaković, Dragoslav. "Kako je postalo Garašaninovo 'Načertanije'." *Spomenik*, No. 91, Beograd, 1939, pp. 65-102.

__________. "Načertanije Ilije Garašanina." *Glasnik istorijskog društva*, knj. 4, No. 3, Novi Sad-Sremski Karlovci, 1931, pp. 392-418.

__________. "Politička propaganda Srbije u jugoslovenskim pokrajinama 1844-1858." *Glasnik istorijskog društva*, knj. IX, Nos. 2-3, Novi Sad, 1936, pp. 155-179; 301-315.

__________. "Srbija, privlačno središte Jugoslovena." *Srpski književni glasnik*, knj. LXI, No. 7, Beograd, 1940, pp. 508-524.

__________. "Svetozar Miletić i Jevrem Grujić 1848.godine." *Zbornik za društvene nauke Matice srpske*, knj. XIII-XIV, pp. 141-147.

__________. "Ukidanje 'Družine mladeži srbske'." *Srpski književni glasnik*, knj. XLIX, No. 6, Beograd, 1936, pp. 443-449.

Švabić, Pavle. "O postanku Beogradske bogoslovije." *Glasnik pravoslavne crkve*, Beograd, 1903, pp. 37-53.

Tešić, Vladeta M. "Prvi srpski blagodejanci u Beču i starateljski rad Vuka Stefanovića Karadžića." *Nastava i vaspitanje*, Nos. 5-6, Beograd, 1964, pp. 244-251.

Tomić, Stevan. "Sterijina delatnost na zaštiti spomenika kulture." *Naučni zbornik Matice srpske*, No. 3, Novi Sad, 1952, pp. 85-89.

__________. "Zaštita spomenika kulture u Srbiji 1828-1853." *Zbornik zaštite spomenika kulture*, knj. VIII, Beograd, 1957, pp. 1-19.

Valentić, Mirko. "Koncepcija Garašaninova 'Načertanija' (1844)." *Historijski pregled*, No. 2, Zagreb, 1961, pp. 128-137.

Vasić, Pavle. "Vojvodjanski slikari u Srbiji (1817-1850)." *Naučni zbornik Matice srpske*, No. 1, Novi Sad, 1950, pp. 93-109.

Vojvodić, Vaso. "O jednom pokušaju zabrane rasturanja dela u Srbiji 1841." *Godišnjak Filozofskog fakulteta u Novom Sadu*, knj. VIII, Novi Sad, 1964/65, pp. 71-79.

__________. "Rad Srbije na političkoj propagandi u Bosni i Hercegovini (1868-1873)." *Istorijski glasnik*, Nos. 1-2; 3-4, Beograd, 1960, pp. 3-50; 3-52.

Vrzalová, V. "Jihoslovanský státni a národní program Ilya Garašanin." *Prěhled*, No. XIV (1932), pp. 134-143.

Vučković, Vojislav J. "Knez Miloš i osnovna politčka misao sadržana u Garašaninovom 'Načertaniju'." *Jugoslovenska revija za medjunarodno pravo*, No. 1, Beograd, 1957, pp. 35-44.

__________. "Prilog proučavanja postanka 'Načertanija' (1844) i 'Osnovnih misli' (1847)." *Jugoslovenska revija za medjunarodno pravo*, No. 1, Beograd, 1961, pp. 49-79.

__________. "Učešće Hrvata u pripremi Garašaninovog 'Načertanija'." *Jugoslovenska revija za medjunarodno pravo*, No. 3, Beograd, 1954, pp. 44-58.

Vujačić, Milan. "Omladina iz Crne Gore i susednih oblasti pod Turskom na školovanju u Srbiji 1850-1878.godine i pomoć koju je Srbija pružila tim oblastima." *Arhivski almanah*, Nos. 2-3, Beograd, 1960, pp. 239-258.

Vukičević, Milenko M. "Osnovne škole u Srbiji prve polovine ovog veka." *Prosvetni glasnik*, Nos. 3, 4, 6, 8, 9, Beograd, 1899, pp. 146-149; 198-203; 318-321; 450-454; 508-515.

__________. "Program spoljne politike I. Garašanina na koncu 1844.god." *Delo*, knj. 38, Beograd, 1906, pp. 321-336.

__________. "Sudovi i njihovo uredjenje." *Policiski glasnik*, No. I, Beograd, 1905, pp. 276-278; 290-291; 298-299; 306-307; 315-316; 324-326; 339-340; 346-347; 362-363; 372-373; 378-381.

Vuković, Svetozar E. "Srpski pitomci na Halci u XIX i XX veku." *Glasnik*, službeni list Srpske Pravoslavne Patrijaršije, Beograd, 1954, pp. 200-204.

Wendel, H. "Marxism and the Southern Question." *Slavonic Review*, No. 2 (December, 1923), pp. 289-307.

Zazi, Mano Djordje. "Narodni muzej u Beogradu." *Godišnjak Muzeja grada Beograda*, knj. I, Beograd, 1954, pp. 307-316.

Živaljević, D.A. "Vuk Stef. Karadžić i zakonodavstvo o porezu u Srbiji 1861-64." *Godišnjica Nikole Čupića*, knj. XXVIII, Beograd, 1909, pp. 240-270.

Žuljević, Šefkija. "Pančićev pogled na svet." *Filozofski pregled*, No. 3, Beograd, 1954, pp. 54-62.

INDEX